CHAPTER ONE

THE RECTORY AND WINDMILL

"**A** wanton world! Yes, it's a wanton, shambolic affair, and no mistake! 'A mad world, my masters!' as the dramatist has aptly said. Yes, no mistake about it!" So Sir Terence Treadboards was often wont to exclaim at his current country-based residence, *Wanton Windmill*. The latter was a picturesque dwelling-place addition, located in the grounds of the *Rectory* at *Lower Wanton End*. The converted windmill with many recent internal modernisations was externally of a tower style, but now flattened out at its top (by a neat layer of bricks), instead of being capped. Possibly as an attempted compensation for such a 'beheading', a rather weathered Saint George flag had been fixed to a short pole, the latter being clamped to the flattened top's eastern side. The windmill also suffered from being deprived of its arms, (or in windmill terms, it's sails). To Sir Terence's trained classical mind, the sadly amputated windmill metaphorically reminded him of an Achilles without his armour. Why the windmill had wantonly been deprived of its cap and sails, we have not now the leisure or time to investigate. But behind the windmill, north-westwards across the fields and embellishing the horizon could be glimpsed a line of lately installed wind farms. Treadboards upon viewing these modernistic incarnations of windmills with their giant yet sleek working arms, would evince a grim kind of Quixotic, compensated satisfaction.

As to the adjective "wanton", which seemed so frequently upon the lips of Sir Terence, this can be explained by a crisis of debilitating depression which was still to some degree affecting this sixty-nine year old thespian. The crisis had been triggered two years ago by his much younger and beautiful wife suddenly taking off with a suitably younger man – a current TV celebrity. Apart from the note left on the dining room table of their expensive apartment in Kensington, there was no real explanation and Sir Terence had never seen her again. This sudden betrayal had had the effect of catapulting Sir Terence into the above mentioned state of severe depressive disorder.

Regarding offspring, the estimable thespian and his wife Marianne, had but one daughter, who took up nurse training, but being extremely headstrong, had gone off world trekking aged twenty-one against the protracted and severe injunctions of her father. This anti-filial event had occurred some fifteen years ago. The daughter, called Juniper had never come back home, having apparently hitched herself up with a young admiring male in Australia. Apart from the odd post card, letter and 'phone call, there was little communication between the respective antipodes. Matters were not helped by Sir Terence determinedly viewing his daughter as a renegade to all the love and expectations which formerly he had centred upon her. Mrs Treadboards had taken a more indulgent, philosophical attitude to her daughter's defiant rebellion and this had resulted in strained relations between husband and wife. It should be said here that Mrs

WANTON
WINDMILL

M.H. DAVIS

Matador
9 Priory Business Park,
Wistow Road, Kibworth Beauchamp,
Leicestershire. LE8 0RX
Tel: 0116 279 2299
Email: books@troubador.co.uk
Web: www.troubador.co.uk/matador
Twitter: @matadorbooks

ISBN 978 1785892 172

British Library Cataloguing in Publication Data.
A catalogue record for this book is available from the British Library.

Printed and bound by CPI Group (UK) Ltd, Croydon, CR0 4YY
Typeset in 11pt Minion Pro by Troubador Publishing Ltd, Leicester, UK

Matador is an imprint of Troubador Publishing Ltd

MIX
Paper from
responsible sources
FSC® C013604

To my wife, Ann

&

my mother

Treadboards, herself was endowed with a copious supply of headstrong and wilful genes which she had accordingly generously passed onto her daughter at birth. The worst of it all now was that the treacherous genes had rolled a double six again; *deja vu* – it was all happening again; first, Goneril then Regan betraying the all too indulgently fond king, but Sir Treadboards, unlike Lear had no third woman, no faithful Cordelia to love and respect her father, making up for the feckless ingratitude of the other two females.

Sir Terence, apart from being a curious mixture of aesthetic socialist and aesthetic, pre-Thatcherite Tory, was a successful and respected actor, having starred in a number of acclaimed films of the more serious variety. However, "treading the boards", particularly in classical productions, was what was nearest his heart. In fact, when it came down to it: Shakespeare. This, as far as Sir Terence was concerned pushed all film work into total eclipse; being nightly on the boards constituted for him the true time-honoured noble art of acting. And so Sir Terence had never allowed his facility with iambic pentameter to grow rusty on his tongue, making sure to always keep his hand in with Shakespearean repertoire. He had appeared in the West End and well regarded provincial theatres, managing during his acting years to play many of the leading Shakespearean roles, such as Hamlet, Macbeth, Othello, Shylock, Richard III, Antony, etc. But his one abiding regret was that he had never played King Lear. The opportunity had simply never arisen. And Sir Terence would often climb up the modernised connecting stairway to the top "Dust" floor of *Wanton Windmill* – now semi-converted to a kind of study-bedroom attic. He would then go out of a little side trap-door onto a safety-railed platform just below the windmill's bricked top and its flag. This reasonably wide platform ran round the windmill's circumference and had been built for observation purposes by a previous Rectory owner some years back. Sir Terence would up here or alternatively from the garden environs below, recite various speeches of King Lear, This was a kind of compensation on Sir Terence's part for his lack of opportunity to spout forth as the old king on a West End stage in front of packed stalls and circle. If it was fairly clement, windless weather, the thespian would invariably go up the windmill tower and outside on the platform to deliver various speeches of the king. However, on very windy days, Sir Terence's cousin and the latter's housekeeper insisted that going outside on the windmill top was not to be thought of in such conditions. Then Sir Terence had to be content going about in the garden, hovering round a flowerbed bordered by geraniums, gesturing wildly and declaiming the celebrated lines:

"Blow, winds, and crack your cheeks! Rage! Blow!" (etc & etc).

However, at such times, his only audience – and albeit a decidedly uninterested one at that – constituted of a few piebald cows munching the herb in a field directly backing onto the western side of *Wanton Windmill*.

Sir Terence had received his knighthood for services to the British stage and film industry and his established Shakespearean reputation and box-office successes made him a reasonably comfortably-off man. But it must be added that as far as "Shakespearean reputation" went, it did not reach the heights of being anything in comparison to an Olivier, Gielgud or Richardson. Sir Terence, despite his life-long commitment to Shakespeare, was on a rather lower ledge of theatrical glory. At twenty-five he had believed himself to be a modernised re-incarnation of one of his historical thespian heroes, such as Kean, Macready or Irving. But no it was not to be. And though Sir Terence's Buckingham in *Richard* III had been thought highly of, when it came to his Richard, the result was deemed too histrionic. The critics also viewed Sir Terence's Hamlet as being *too* boisterously decisive and not vague enough by half. Again, though his Banquo performance had been acclaimed, when it came to the great part of Macbeth, itself, the reviews were less favourable; the critical consensus hovered between Treadboards being either too bombastic or less than convincing. Again, Sir Terence made an excellent Malvolio in *Twelfth Night*, but when he took the leading male part in *Antony and Cleopatra*, critics felt that he portrayed insufficient sex-drive and warrior panache. (It is true that at the time of this performance Sir Terence was already sixty and having some physiotherapy for his knee-joints). The fact was that while Sir Terence was excellent in the secondary, roles, he never could scale the Olympian heights necessary to really bring alive the major Shakespearian tragic heroes. The rub was that he could never fully digest this galling truth. However, whenever the consciousness of it did arise, such inner distress ensued that Sir Terence in bitter comfort regaled himself with words from his most favourite Shakespearean hero, Antony. Thus his bellowing of the exasperated Roman's complaint: "The shirt of Nessus is upon me". What exactly such words meant, one cannot be too sure, but the Bard's phrase most probably arose from Treadboard's extrapolation that cruel nature had put a poisoned Elizabethan doublet upon him, curtailing his ability to succeed in the great leading roles. This, our estimable thespian found the cause of much secret bitterness which now along with his wife's departure (a modern variation of Elizabethan cuckolding, he maliciously assured himself), increasingly deflected him from the company of others. For what did all his film and theatrical successes amount to if he had failed in Shakespeare to gain the starry heights? It was anathema to be *merely* regarded as an excellent, dependable *secondary* actor in the Bard's great dramas.

Sir Terence was five foot ten inches tall, lean, with a mop of greying hair and piercing blue eyes which could disconcertingly open at times as wide as giant marbles. His recent breakdown had no doubt accentuated his leanness into a gauntness, admirably qualifying him for Cervantes' esteemed knight *De La Mancha*. *Wanton Windmill* would have embellished and sustained this happy association even further apart from the glaring disadvantage of the said building (as we have already noted) being wingless, armless or more plainly, devoid of sails. Sir Terence was in the main a charming, genial man, but now increasingly prone to abrupt mood swings – the latter being his black dog pessimistic streak – and had hitherto, until the absconding of his wife, always relied on a supply of self-confidence which flowed out of his intense, theatrical personality. But the geniality and confidence had taken something of a nose-dive after the betrayal of his erstwhile wife. And this event had also regenerated all his hardly suppressed upset over the apparently lost daughter. The result of all this was a severe onset of debilitating depression.

Alarmingly, Sir Terence descended into a haunted Hamlet-like mode. To his thespian colleagues he was a shadow of his former buoyant self. His maverick wit, incisiveness, sense of conviviality and indeed interest appeared to be migrating. He had now really lost the heart and nerve to carry on. But worse, Sir Terence was increasingly sardonic, critical and cantankerous towards those theatrical friends, both thespians and theatre managers who had counted him as an esteemed wag and drinking companion. Thus he blatantly upset several actresses, even his long standing leading actress friend, Dame Cynthia Plumb. (His killing remark regarding the latter's recent Lady Macbeth at the National, was that it was merely sleep-walking all the way through the performance). Sir Terence also highly upset his up-till-then good friend, the well-respected director Ivor Tossup, by inferring that the latter's latest West End Ibsen: *The Wild Duck*, was a dead duck in every sense.

Even worse still, was the result of a special Shakespearean fancy-dress party which the Knight was specially invited to in the feverish hope of re-awakening his old convivial self. It badly back-fired. Sir Terence came dressed in tights as an elderly version of Hamlet and proceeded to make cutting remarks to all and sundry. In the end, upon leaving, he regally declared that he sincerely "apologised to any one present" whom he had "neglected to insult". And so the malcontent thespian Knight alienated most of his erstwhile stage friends. Alarmed at his alienating behaviour some other non-thespian friends including his GP friend, Timothy Tadpole (who still commanded some respect from Sir Terence), strongly advised the Knight to take a kind of acting sabbatical break. Moreover, they also strongly encouraged him to seriously consider therapeutic consultation at Dr. Microbe's highly esteemed Chelsea-based, psychotherapy clinic. This, after some concerted persuasion, our much out-of-sorts Shakespearian hero agreed to with both reluctance and fatalism. And so it was that Sir Terence booked his first appointment for Dr. Microbe's acclaimed, mind recuperation methodology.

Although Sir Terence had no siblings, it so happened that he did have a gregarious cousin whom he had always kept on very good terms with since childhood. This cousin was a recently retired cleric, Percival Evergreen, formerly Bishop of Boffosbury, in the West Midlands. The Bishop was usually known affectionately by his colleagues, friends and erstwhile congregations as *Boffo*. The latter appeared by nature to be politically correct, of eager liberal persuasion as well as being an ardent universalist. His engagingly enthusiastic personality was connected to a tallish, long-limbed figure; his bright-eyed, banana-shaped face with its ready smile was ornamented by a neatly cut and long-tapered greying black beard. Now it was only about a year before Sir Terence's wife's sudden departure that our dear Bishop's wife also suddenly subtracted her presence from the Diocese. Thus it came about that Bishop Boffo's retirement (in his early sixties) had been somewhat accelerated by the rather controversial circumstances of his wife's taking off with the principal flower arranger of St. Whippet's Parish Church, where the aforesaid cleric often used to officiate. This had undoubtedly been rather a shock that Boffo's matronly wife, Prudence, of several years standing, should have suddenly left him high and dry as it were.

Although, it was rather ironic that the joyous ecclesiastic's largess of permissive tolerance had been all too well imbibed by his secretly bored wife. For the latter, along with the flower-arranger, Geraldine Simpkins, had taken to an extremely practical application of antinomianism. But given Bishop Boffo's vast liberal resources of tolerance and forgiveness, this shock leave-taking and same-sex liaison of his refractory wife had not had the same devastating effect produced on Sir Terence by his own recalcitrant wife's desertion. "Yes, we must suffer awhile through such human thoughtlessness, but the Lord bless them. Yes! Bless them, bless them all, bless all and everyone, politicians, bankers, dustbin men, hairdressers, traffic wardens – bless one and all"! the erstwhile Bishop would exclaim, his tearful face managing to somehow brighten to cherubic radiance. And much to the dismay and puzzlement of conservative or even liberal clerical friends, Boffo would always stand by his view of Judgement Day being akin to a great cosmic washing machine, transforming even the most stained garments whiter than white. Thus the new heavenly Jerusalem would, metaphorically speaking, most likely be characterised by an infinite washing line of gloriously shining and radiant renewed human souls.

But ecclesiastical and social judgement were not necessarily that sympathetic. The evangelical and middle-of-the-road elements in the Diocese regarded Boffo as an ineffective love-them-all idealist and many of the liberals found even the Bishop's exuberant universalism somewhat of an embarrassment to their cause. As for the incumbents, some also found him rather ridiculous in his liberal largesse views. Not only that, but it had been common knowledge in the choir of Boffosbury Cathedral that something unfortunate was going on between Prudence and Geraldine. So it proved prudent in the end for Boffo to retire early from a deteriorating situation of personal credibility. "The Lord has kindly spoken to me through this domestic chastisement. I must humbly accept that all is for the best; to pastures new I will go", our worthy ecclesiastic super-rationalised to himself. Because he had studied for his theological exams at Cambridge, Boffo was still very much an Oxbridge man at heart and so decided to live in vicinity of that famous Fenland university city. Therefore he decided upon moving to East Anglia, into the Cambridgeshire countryside, which was within reasonable striking distance of that aforesaid city. Having no great knowledge of the outlying Cambridgeshire area, only wishing to live in a reasonably secluded habitat, the ex-Bishop, shutting his eyes, with a fervent arrow-prayer, put a pin into a local map and it alighted on the quaintly named village of *Lower Wanton End.*

And there our retired-Bishop made his choice. "*Lower Wanton End* – or in nearby vicinity – then it shall be, by the grace of God"! our worthy cleric declared with resolution. The next thing was to see if any houses were currently for sale in this small hamlet. What Boffo had in mind was a goodly sized period residence with enough rooms to accommodate the many various friends and acquaintances he expected would be staying in social get-togethers of which our dear retired Bishop had always been so previously partial of by way of his genial and expansively adaptable nature. *Lower Wanton End* was a small village comprised of a Norman parish church, some largish and some smaller cottages, plus a few 1950's council houses. It chanced that there was one large sized property for sale, *Lower Wanton End Rectory.* The latter was in some respects, such as decoration and mod-cons, somewhat dilapidated, or as the local Muggets estate agents, euphemistically put it: in need of some upgrading. The Rectory, a yellow-grey bricked, late Victorian edifice, was of a modestly pleasing appearance. It was sufficiently large enough to entertain several guests with ample rooms to put up such visitors for the night. To Boffo, the fact of it being an ex-Rectory, seemed in itself an eminently appropriate sign to an ex-Bishop, looking for a suitable abode as a potential gathering place for his great variety of acquaintances from ecclesiastical and other walks of life. As might be expected, the Rectory's ground floor comprised generously sized drawing, dining and study rooms, as well as an imposing hall and ample-portioned kitchen. Upstairs, on the first floor, there were six adequate bedrooms and on the second floor, attic level, were a further six rooms – though these latter not only needed re-decorating but a vigorous campaign of cob-web clearing. Slightly separated from the right-hand frontage of the Rectory was another two-floor annexe building (formerly a stable), which housed another four spare rooms.

Wanton End Rectory was set in over an acre of land, the latter for which the greater part was to the property's rear. To the immediate rear of the house ran a narrow rose flowerbed. Behind that and running parallel with it was a small (in depth) lawned garden with a well-spread-out copper beech adjacent to the annexe building. This lawn, screened from behind by box hedges, led out through a gap past some big sheds to a sizeable field which enclosed within it a very large pond of about forty feet lengthways and ten feet wide. This pond which was rather reedy, requiring a good clean-out, was replete with weeping willows fringing its water's edges.

However, there were two other noteworthy objects to exceedingly arouse the retired cleric's enthusiastic interest.

The first (and most obvious) object was located in the smaller front grounds, where standing southwards to the left of the old Rectory, and close (perhaps too close), to a beautiful fully grown pink horse chestnut tree, was *Wanton Windmill*. As previously mentioned, it no longer had its sails or cap, but was otherwise renovated to ensure what remained was safe and sound in structure. The machinery apparatus inside the windmill had long since been dismantled, either scrapped or given to any interested agricultural bygone organisations or individual enthusiasts. Conversion steps had already been taken by the current owner, including the fitting of modern double-glazed windows to all floors and a proper stair-casing (rather than ladders) to access the levels. The five levels (ground to fourth floor), had also been wired up to facilitate lighting and heating appliances. But as yet there was no plumbing installed in the windmill.

The second object of interest, Boffo noted just as eagerly while the present owner showed him round the amply sized pond in the large back garden's field area. For running round the edge of the willow trees, which draped their boughs and leaves into the pond, was a narrow-gauge railway track. The track ran out of a sidings shed, which was just beyond the lawned garden and about a hundred yards from the eastern edge of the pond. The present owner, a septuagenarian, Mr. Siding, was himself an avid fan of trains and railways and as he was moving to a smaller residence, was quite happy that his narrow-gauge line and miniature train would be secure in the willing and enthusiastic hands of a man who instantly declared his like-minded interest. After these two gentlemen with equal fervour had examined the narrow-gauge track's condition and general layout, the host hastened to show our good cleric a siding shed where the track started and thence returned to. Here, lovingly was kept the miniature train (named *The Royal Robin*), along with its five open carriages of which comprised rudimentary wooden benches for passenger seating. Our retired Bishop's mind was made up. His several tastes encompassed the arts (including some of its more bizarre modern offerings); however, it was well known to many of Boffo's friends and acquaintances that top of his interests came a Quixotic attraction to windmills and an equal fascination with railways. Besides frequently visiting windmills up and down the country, Boffo visited various privately run steam, diesel and electric miniature railways. He also loved to visit the full-scale steam locomotives which still operated on special routes for the delectation of avid enthusiasts such as himself. Thus to acquire a property which included both a windmill (despite its lack of full parts) and its own small-gauge railway track, train and carriages, led the ex-Bishop into such rapturous delight that there was no hesitation in plumping to buy *Lower Wanton End Rectory*.

The addition of the windmill and its possibilities for further renovation enhancements, including the uses it might be able to encompass in the future challenged and excited Boffo's mind. Immediately he had various plans for upgrading the fairly rudimentary rooms within the windmill's five floors. Updating the Rectory seemed of lesser urgency. Boffo had many friends from the *arts* strata of society and it seemed that his windmill could provide at least two extra guest rooms among other things. The upshot was that our retired clergyman was successful in purchasing *Lower Wanton End Rectory* and was soon established there as the new owner. Boffo successfully persuaded his long standing faithful and resourceful church secretary from Boffosbury, Miss Muriel Muffin, to come and look after the domestic requirements of the new abode. Bit by bit, with gentle but insistent persuasion from Miss Muffin, Boffo was induced to get a few much needed basic repairs and minor decorating done to the Rectory, making the latter conform a little more closely to the domestic requirements of a human abode. But our retired Bishop concentrated more time and thought on his sail-less and cap-less windmill. The third and fourth levels (formerly the Millstone and Bin floors), were decoratively improved; beds and bedside furniture were added to make them reasonably inhabitable as overflow guest accommodation. But lack of further funds precluded as yet the addition of *en suite* facilities to the said rooms.

Some months later after Boffo's arrival at his new residence, there was a financial windfall arising from the Will of his recently departed, wealthy brother-in-law, Dr. Clarence Clipper. By way of necessary background, Boffo had two sisters, an older and younger one. The older one, Lucinda aged fifty-nine, was married to Reverend Halo, who commanded a strict, Calvinistic, Baptist church. But more of the theologically severe Reverend anon. Some thirteen years ago, Dr. Clipper, a retired surgeon and confirmed bachelor, had at sixty-five years of age married Boffo's younger sister Jasmine. The said sister, a reasonably paid hospital administrator, had met Dr. Clipper at his retirement leaving party. Jasmine, a most attractive middle-age woman, was twenty-three years younger than the just retired surgeon. She was divorced and no doubt sought solace in an older and accomplished man, a not uncommon psychological reversion device in the aftermath of a failed marriage. Dr.

Clipper, apart from his operating room skills, was an ardent amateur horticulturalist. His unexpected liberation from a prevailing reticence, was due to being passionately charmed by Jasmine's delicate flowering bloom. In short, his rather naive green head had been overruled by a suddenly aroused heart, resulting in the usual consequences of ill-matched conjugal relations. Jasmine was in fact a hardy annual who watered her own roots. This pro-active, financially ambitious young woman soon had enough of gardening, and was looking for a younger and wealthier liaison which she successfully found in a rich city banker by the name of Mr. Fatsnout. Consequently, twelve years later (the year Boffo took possession of the Rectory), Jasmine had bid a curt goodbye to the greenhouses, shrubberies, rockeries, herbaceous borders and lawns of Dr. Clipper.

After the canker and blight that had put paid to Dr. Clipper's marital situation, divorce proceedings soon followed. The green surgeon, now aged seventy-seven, had at first been understandably chagrined by the loss of Jasmine; a particularly most attractive flowering perennial, cruelly snatched out of his garden by some big-bonus, city vandal. However, being naturally of a phlegmatic nature he soon defaulted back to his old carry-on-as-usual attitude, tolerably contented with horticultural study books and greenhouse perambulations. The retired surgeon's sad demise had been precipitated a year later through an unintentional disembarking off a ladder while pruning a pear tree in his garden; being of a frail build and constitution he had never recovered from the fall and thereafter rapidly went downhill. It transpired that Dr. Clipper, who was childless, had left a surprisingly large amount of money to be shared between his brother-in-law, Boffo and his sister-in-law, Lucinda Halo. Nothing was left to the other renegade sister, for Dr. Clipper had made a new revised Will in the wake of Jasmine's departure for Mr. Fatsnout. This unlooked for sum of money was a welcome help in facilitating the ex-Bishop's cherished ongoing improvements to *Wanton Windmill.* Plumbing was therefore soon installed to provide the two designated windmill guest floors with *en suite* facilities. Dr. Clipper, who had in his time conceived many plant watering and drainage strategies, thus now posthumously, through his generous legacy, helped facilitate the means for bodily ablution necessities within the windmill.

* * *

The windmill's Dust floor, the fifth floor (which would have been below the cap, if the latter had still existed), had been left in a fairly rudimentary state by the previous owner, Mr. Siding as a study cum observation room. On the outside of this top level, the previous owner had added an encircling wooden platform (with safety rail) which was accessed by a little trap door from the rather cell-like study room. Later on, when Sir Terence was induced by Boffo to stay indefinitely with him at *Lower Wanton End*, a bed and tiny shower room were somehow squeezed into this small top floor. This was done as Sir Terence had strongly indicated his preference to use this room as his retreat and sleeping quarters. But this is to run ahead somewhat in my narrative.

Compared to the windmill's other three levels, it was the ground and first floors (levels one and two) for which our good cleric entertained his most ardent plans. Boffo had grandiose ideas about these levels being respectively translated into an art exhibition room and library floor. Doubtless, there was much needed to be done including minor internal repairs, decorating and installation of appropriate furnishing for the aforesaid rooms. And so it was the retired Bishop's enhancements went on apace to his headless, sail-less and sadly, technically speaking at any rate, un-Quixotic windmill. Although it must be again said, particularly in support of Miss Muffin's house-keeping point of view, that the Rectory's anciently picturesque shabby rooms, could also have benefited from a concerted program of repair and redecoration.

It was some further months later that Boffo first heard reports concerning his dear cousin and the absconding wife. Treadboards was by now embarked upon a series of appointments at Dr. Microbe's swish, Chelsea-based psychotherapy clinic, joining the ranks of other cracked-up media personalities. With charitable alacrity Boffo soon arrived at Kensington and thence regularly visited his cousin, who was now under Dr. Microbe's special new therapeutic counselling program entitled: *Microbe's Advanced Dynamic, Amalgamative, Individuation, Restoration Process.* This constituted a cunning synthesis of Freudian, Jungian, Adlerian therapies, judiciously garnished by bits from Carl Rogers, plus a sprinkling of cognitive behavioural therapy.

At first there was some difficulty in making communication with Sir Terence, who since his depressive breakdown had continued in a deep Hamlet-type reverie. For much of the time he was as incommunicado as a tortoise retreating into its shell. However, by and by Sir Terence started to be a little more communicative due to his cousin's sympathetic persistence. In fact, as the thespian started to recover, his main daily problem revolved round deciding whether the relation between his ego, superego and Id was in dynamic harmony; whether he was on friendly terms with his archetypes; what was the state of his various social complexes; whether he was in a liberated state of congruence and whether he was properly manipulating his behaviour to counteract adverse social re-enforcing factors. It was all somewhat incomprehensible to Sir Terence. But after he had tried a bit of psychoanalytic pondering, one positive result was that he could easily drop off into a peaceful sleep without having to resort to counting sheep or sleeping tablets. Sir Terence had great confidence in the undeniable reputation of Dr. Microbe, even though the former understood little of the latter's curative system and could not point to any tangible benefits which arose from it. Yet patient and Psychotherapist strangely warmed to each other, although there was no direct rational explanation for this. It may have been that both men unconsciously appreciated a kindred fellowship in "over egging the pudding" in their respective professional fields.

However, Sir Terence, although still rather subdued and withdrawn in terms of his former ebullient self, was after three months of several probing therapeutic sessions deemed by Dr. Microbe to have made satisfactorily improvement in his mental state. How much this improvement was due to the esteemed Psychotherapist's talking treatment or due to the warm sympathetic support of Boffo and other friends must be left in doubt. At any rate, Dr. Microbe now advised Sir Terence that it would be sensible to book some follow-up sessions at spaced intervals in order to check the latter's mental condition was still improving rather than relapsing.

* * *

Meanwhile, Boffo, along with other (still as yet un-alienated) non-thespian friends, were increasingly concerned that it was not conducive to Sir Terence's mental recovery for him to live alone at his Kensington apartment. Moreover, the presently un-deployed theatrical Knight often declared to Boffo that he had had enough of London and wished to retreat into the country. Our retired Bishop now therefore determined that his cousin should come and live with him at *Lower Wanton End Rectory*. This seemed an eminently sensible idea. Boffo could then keep a watchful eye on his cousin, also helping in his humble Christian way to further the rehabilitation program of Sir Terence's poor, unhappy mind. Also, as neither of them were getting any younger, it would be good for them both in their newly imposed bachelor states to keep company together. By the by, Boffo – as he himself conceived it – would invite his and his cousin's friends down to the Rectory in the added hope that seeing old and new faces would further rally Sir Terence's spirits. Clearly, these measures might go some way to help the Knight banish the flattened and disengaged behavioural symptoms which he was still prone to exhibiting. Everyone including Sir Terence was agreed with Boffo's scheme of action. And so it was that the two cousins one reasonably pleasant day in late April left Kensington for the charming desolated flatlands of Cambridgeshire. And the upshot was that our recuperating thespian once arrived at idyllic *Lower*

Wanton End, took an immediate shine to the windmill (if nothing much else). Thus, although he took his meals at the Rectory and sometimes in the drawing room ruefully played his baby Bluthner grand (which had been transported from the Kensington apartment), he insisted upon having his study and bedroom located on the windmill's highest floor and spent much of the day and sometimes night darkly meditating and declaiming Elizabethan or Jacobean verse.

There had always been certain Quixotic, not to say Shandy-like characteristics that now increasingly manifested themselves in Sir Terence's personality, seeming to come more to the fore in the recuperative aftermath of his depressive breakdown. Certainly, next to his beloved Shakespeare, plus other Elizabethans such as Marlowe, Dekker and Massinger, Sir Terence seemed to evince a morbid fascination for the darkly pessimistic Jacobean works of Middleton, Webster and Marston. And such works as *The Changeling*, *The Duchess of Malfi* and particularly *The Malcontent*, continuously seemed to feed into the dramatic landscape of his ruffled and melancholic personality. One might well wonder if Sir Terence would not have been happier treading the boards in that golden era when English drama richly unfolded and developed with such alacrity. Often, our ageing thespian would enter into arguments with Boffo's wide-ranging love of the British dramatic arts. Sir Terence, unlike Boffo, had little sympathy for Shaw (particularly not being very amused by the latter's sardonic diatribes at the great Bard), and certainly even less sympathy for anything from the 1950's new wave of dramatists, comprising the likes of Osborne, Arden, Wesker and Pinter. Boffo soon learnt to be conversationally discreet in theatrical matters where Sir Terence was concerned.

However, both these retired cousins, respectively of the cloth and boards, were strangely at one in their absorbing attraction to *Wanton Windmill*, whether it was Boffo's rolling programme of interior improvements or Sir Terence's seeing the defeated giant as now translated into a Quixotic chapel in which he could ruminate and guard his dented armour. Sir Terence thus ensconced himself in relative solitude on the windmill's top floor, excepting for meals, brief conversations with his cousin and Miss Muffin, plus occasionally tinkering on the Bluthner and going for walks. Boffo, while reluctantly accepting Sir Terence's insistent wishes for this existence of neo-monastic privacy, could only hope and pray that his thespian cousin's fragmented mind would somehow continue at its own pace to re-assemble itself. In the meantime our retired cleric and Miss Muffin were determined to keep a watchful eye on the erratically recovering Knight and stipulated that at least he must have all his meals and evening cocoa at the Rectory.

CHAPTER TWO

BIRTHDAY BREAKFAST

Some months after his establishment within the windmill at *Wanton End Rectory,* Sir Terence Treadboards was one fine Friday, early August morning taking breakfast with former Bishop Boffo, Miss Muffin, along with Boffo's sister Lucinda and her husband, the Reverend George Halo. The latter two who hailed from a Suffolk village near Bury St. Edmunds, were staying for a few days as guests with Boffo. George Halo, just below medium height, was strongly built with a rather grizzled face, the latter being topped with a prodigious greying mass of frizzled hair. His rather daunting (at first), warrior-like visage was belied by a fundamentally kindly nature within him. A physically and spiritually rigorous man in his early sixties, the Reverend Halo commanded a strict Baptist church which was defined by a no-quibbling, reformed theology approach. Boffo's liberalistic theology and Halo's brand of 'high' Calvinism were clearly not ideal stable mates for a convivial talk and the big-hearted ex-cleric tried to avoid inadvertently stumbling into this potential theological minefield.

Even with such a theologically recalcitrant person as his clerical brother-in-law, Boffo would always find the necessary strength in his seemingly infinite resources of love-them-all liberalism. "Yes, we are hardly to be called two peas in a pod with our differing approaches. Yes, hell-fire, damnation and endless talk of unpleasant things like wrath, depravity and demons is not acceptable – not acceptable in our enlightened world. Yes, we must at best humour people who entertain such medieval views. But we must love them – love them all, for *all*, even the most wicked will be saved at the end. None will be barred from entering the great gates which are always beckoning. Gates in fact, open all hours, for Love will never close them". So rationalised our good Boffo, always beaming a glow of supreme spiritual indulgence at the phrase, "love them all".

Moreover, Boffo knew that his sister and brother-in-law had also their particular cross to bear in terms of a daughter who had recently greatly spiritually strayed. The Halo's only child, Esther, whom they had begot quite late on in their marriage, had been brought up in strict love and had been exemplary in the local Girl's Brigade. Everything had been going to plan; a model God-fearing daughter, living up to the name of Queen Esther in her diligence and resourcefulness of faith. But only a mere year ago the devil had put his ugly spoke in. Living away from home and having just successfully completed her post-graduate law course at Gridlington University (in the East Midlands), and despite being in the Christian Union, Esther had absconded from the 'fold'. The only information to be gleaned by a communication from Esther was that she had found a "dream man". What this meant in mundane reality was that Esther had got mixed up with a rock guitarist and was now somewhere 'out on the road' as lead singer with a group picturesquely known as: *The Shrieking Friars*. This of course was a shocking and massive blow to the Halos, particularly the Reverend as he had set his daughter upon such a high spiritual pedestal – a pedestal too high as sadly proved by this errant act of filial rebellion. "Yes, we must pass through many upsets, even heartbreaks", Boffo commiserated in his mind, "but we must love them all, even the misfortunately named *Shrieking Friars,* twanging no doubt their annoyingly loud electric guitars and thoughtlessly misleading a well brought up young Christian woman. Yet, we must be tolerant – yes, tolerance, that is the indispensable word of our enlightened times – and bless them all, forgive them all". However, it was no doubt a bad business for the former Bishop's relations. What else could be done except to wait patiently for the prodigal daughter's change of heart and the heavenly Father's gracious restoration of all parties concerned. "Yes"! Boffo said to himself, "we must hope for a happy outcome this side rather than the other side of eternity".

For his part, the Reverend Halo tended to bite his tongue when Boffo tendered any religious observations during a conversation. The main thing that tended to hold the Reverend back from launching into a full-blooded revivalist panegyric was the pathetically pleading look in his rather cowed wife's eyes. However, Lucinda Halo, though despite embarrassed by the thought of her husband's impending strong viewpoints, always strove to back him up as a timid but faithful echo when he did make utterance. It was then that she would volunteer her catchphrase: "Listen to George". Apart from this rather irritating phrase, it was not usually known for Lucinda Halo to express herself with any greater depth or variety of speech.

"Please do cheer up Sir Terence. It's your birthday today

and look, I've made you a special cooked breakfast with your favourite, smoked kippers! Well, very many happy returns to you", announced the sprightly Miss Muriel Muffin, bringing in the breakfast tray. Boffo, sister and brother-in-law warmly endorsed their good wishes for Sir Terence's attainment of the proverbial three score and ten years. "Seventy indeed!" replied our tragedian, morosely. "Here I am, my mind shaken because of this wanton world! Seventy, indeed! What is there beyond smoked kippers for me? Is my future no more than kippers! Seventy indeed, kippers and a shaken mind! Is this 70 not prelude to the final stage, as our great bard has it:

"Last scene of all, That ends this strange eventful history, Is second childishness and mere oblivion, Sans teeth, sans eyes, sans taste, sans everything".

"Therefore, I say to you, one and all, goodnight nurse!"

"Now come now, dear Terence!" said Boffo, " Seventy is nothing nowadays. There is much to look forward to. The best is yet to come, as they say. You have your physical health and the prospect of re-meeting your friends and some interesting acquaintances of mine over this week-end. This will be such a tonic to your jaded spirits!" "Bah!" replied Sir Terence. "No doubt there will be plenty of clever, bluestocking but fundamentally wanton women among the guests. Well, I have learnt something conclusive and irrefutable out of all my recent distress through this delinquent world with its Jezebel women who betray you for some moronic pipsqueak of a boy! And what I have learnt is this: "All is vanity, all is vanity"; does it not exactly say so in your good black book?" "I wholeheartedly agree, Sir Terence", Reverend Halo briskly replied. "Yes, you have hit the bulls-eye by your designation of this world as wanton. For those that come to the bleeding lamb of life, there will be something more, infinitely more than smoked kippers; there you will have an unparalleled feast of non-perishable spiritual food; there in the gleaming city without sun nor moon; there where the river flows in fullness from the Godhead and is not polluted by human vanity and…" "Yes, of course, dear George" interjected Boffo, sensing that the dear Halo was himself going into full flow.

Sir Terence: Unfaithfulness. Yes, I know something about that my good people. As you know I am an established agnostic, but I submit that all our problems in society stem from adultery. Yes, my good Boffo and Halo, adultery! And it is – I am sorry to say this in front of good honest women like yourselves, Mrs Halo and Miss Muffin – yes it is women nine times out of ten who are the culprits – the Jezebels – not the men! Look at the experience of myself and the men present! We have the examples of my faithless wife and daughter, your faithless wife, Prudence, my dear Boffo, as well as your faithless sister Jasmine, who as you say, shamelessly left the poor, recently departed and no doubt broken-hearted Dr. Clipper. And you, my poor dear Halo – your sadly ungrateful daughter taking up with a load of head-banging, noise-pollution delinquents! Yes, I rest my case. The shirt of Nessus has come upon all us men! And I maintain it is the old Cleopatra syndrome transmuted into a modern formulation which is a thousand times worse in its sheer, unadulterated brazenness. We husbands and fathers here have trustingly tried our best but something diabolical has corrupted the women of today. All it needs is a little crumb of temptation and bingo! Is this all so-called feminism has achieved – merely making it easier for women to say yes to deceit and fornication?

Reverend Halo: Let all the tempters go the devil – they are foredoomed to do so as surely as night follows day. The way is either up or down and most certainly down to hell in their case. Yea, these are the only two directions, up among the blessed faithful or down into the sizzling frying pan! But let not Satan's tempters take our dear wives and daughters with them. Indeed, there are enough Jezebels about and feminism has been their minds' devilish incubator. But let the blood of the sinless lamb redeem our precious ones from the smouldering saucepan, just as Mary Magdalene was delivered from the seven devils…

And here, Boffo seeing that his brother-in-law's ears were starting to steam as he gathered momentum, resolved to intercept but was beaten to it by his faithful housekeeper.

Miss Muffin: "Well, I do not know about any ups and downs apart from the sort you get from awkward men! Now, Sir Terence, you must not be morbid on your birthday. There *is* so much for you to look forward to still. Surely, being away from the hurly-burly of city life and being in this tranquil countryside, is already refreshing your hurt and tired spirit?"

Sir Terence Treadboards: Countryside, bah! You call this countryside? There is more countryside down Kensington high street than in this desolate wasteland! Yes, *Lower Wanton End* is as good as any name for this area. Countryside, hah! Look at it: Devastated or non-existent hedgerows, trees no bigger than matchsticks and hardly any livestock or even birds to be seen or heard; nothing but over-farmed fields, polluted and choked with chemicals. So much for the pastoral therapy!

Bishop Boffo: Oh come now, Terence! You take a rather jaundiced view of this pleasantly unassuming East Anglia countryside. If you went out walking more, I'm sure you would discover the calm and reticent charms of this area.

Sir Treadboards: My dear Boffo, the place is a wasteland! There is more fauna and bird-life in Kensington Gardens or Holland Park than around here! There has been wanton destruction afoot here, mark me. I attempted going for a so-called refreshing country walk around here in Spring. Did I hear the Cuckoo? No I did not. Did I hear any other soothing nature sounds? No I did not. But I did hear the booming of those infernal bird-scarer devices, which seem to be in every field and go off every other minute. Boom, boom! It would have been quieter on an army firing range. No doubt our dear farmers here are not satisfied having pulled up all the hedges to make prairie, dust-bowl fields; not satisfied with chemically poisoning all the trees till they start falling apart branch by branch; no, they finish off the bird and other wild life populations by either scaring them to death, potting or poisoning them! So much for the environment, so much for East Anglia's contribution to conserving our good planet!

Reverend Halo: Yes, there is more devilry afoot and above, as you say. Satan and his minions will pour forth their noise, poison and destruction. It is their depraved nature to do so. They cannot help themselves".

Lucinda Halo: Oh yes, listen to George. He knows all about the devil, he's an expert when it comes to that subject.

Bishop Boffo: Yes, no doubt. However Terence, I feel you are being a little hard on farmers – bless them all, they have a lot to contend with, what with droughts and all the other problems which continually assail them. I'm sure it's not their intention to destroy nature. They are, after all, like us all, merely trying to make a living.

Sir Treadboards: Don't be naïve, man! Surely your little black book tells you somewhere in it that greed corrupts the heart, just as infatuation corrupted the heart of my Jezebel wife for some pimply schoolboy!

Reverend Halo: Corruption, ah, you have scored bulls-eye again! Does not the evangelist warn us all that the whole world is under the Evil One? Does not my favourite Biblical prophet, second only to the Baptist – does not Jeremiah say that the human heart is corrupt, depraved beyond all limits? Yes, the worm of sin and death finds an easy entrance there. Satan is at work – he is at work continually – never asleep like our complacent liberal bishops in their fine, fancy palaces!

Lucinda Halo: Yes, listen to George, he knows all about Satan and complacent liberal bishops in their palaces.

Bishop Boffo: No doubt, but I must defend our good bishops from Reverend George's accusation of their being morally asleep. On the contrary, they work very hard to make our society a more kindly, tolerant place, They never stop working for the cause of tolerance – and why? Why, because our God is a liberal God of tolerance. What is God's holiness but tolerance? Without tolerance we would be going back to being barbarians – pre-Christians.

Sir Terence: I personally think, my dear Boffo, your God has slipped up a bit since he moved into *The New Testament.* For it is precisely this tolerance you are always championing, which has allowed, even condoned the wantonness – the wretched betrayals – of these present day modern Jezebels! From the bits I have read in the Bible, part one – *The Old Testament* – God didn't fiddle about. Look what finally happened to Jezebel, herself! Thrown straight out of the window and that was it. There was none of your PC God tolerance there. He was always telling the good kings and leaders of those ancient times to get rid of all those who were wanton and mischievous blighters – whether men or women. And if his representatives didn't do it to the letter, he went bananas! There was none of your namby-pamby tolerance there. Get rid of the lot of them and then start with a clean sheet. Was not that the thinking behind your *Old Testament* God when he sent the flood in Noah's time? It was quite straightforward then. If they've all gone wanton, like a load of infected apples, get rid of them (or at any rate most of them) and start again. At least, whatever its obvious, ancient, uncivilised barbarity, you are left in no doubt about what the score is. But it's your Bible part two – what you call *The New Testament* – which is the problem; you know, the part where God specially visited earth and allowed these disciple fellows of his to know him informally by names such as Son or Jesus. That was a big mistake, I think. Surely, if you're God, you don't change your name, even if it is to curry a bit more favour, trying to make yourself a bit more approachable. Anyway, taking that tack obviously didn't work. Look what happened to him! And things have never been the same since. You can't have a God coming down to earth. It's not on. Either he stays up there in his heavens or he loses his credibility mixing with a load of wanton scruff bags down here! Yes, where was the punishment for those who did him in? The God of the first Bible part – which I increasingly now have some sympathy with – wouldn't have stood for that outrage to himself without immediately sending down fire and brimstone. Yet this mark-two God version – which I'm greatly suspicious of – keeps forgiving them, even when they are in the process of doing him in!

Reverend Halo: Despite your lack of reformed theological understanding, I must make an Amen to much of what you say, for I can see you are intrinsically a man after my own heart, although necessarily we are at opposite poles in terms of being unregenerate and regenerate creatures. Yet despite the crippling weakness of fallen nature you seek righteousness. This is most commendable. Hallelujah! Like myself, you hate evil and believe in its unequivocal and ordained punishment. That is indeed good, Amen! And it can only show that prevenient grace has already in the divine scheme of things been allotted to you. But at this still unsaved, old Adam stage, you very naturally misconstrue our Great Maker. He has not changed. You can be assured that the wrathful fire He sent down on Sodom and Gomorrah and (figuratively speaking) also upon His dear Son at Calvary is the same wrathful fire which will come to all divinely designated reprobates on Judgement Day.

Sir Terence: Be that as it may, I still maintain either God took a wrong turning in the part-two Bible or more probably those who wrote about him got the information down drastically wrong. Tolerance and forgiveness, too much of it in that part! Everyone gets away with it nowadays because of this tolerance – situation ethics is I believe the glorified PC name for it. No, tell your dear God that he had got it right in the first bit, *The Old Testament* part. He obviously knew what he was doing *then,* about dealing with wanton delinquency. But ever since the other Testament bit, with all this forgiveness lark he must have lost the plot. And reading too much of this second Bible bit merely encourages you, Boffo and all your Anglican pals to turn an indulgent eye towards our wanton culture.

Bishop Boffo: I can assure you both there is nothing indulgent about our liberal Anglicanism. The way to deal with wanton delinquency is precisely to deal with it by love and that means by being tolerant and that in turn means forgiveness. God has always been love. Dear Terence, if you are really searching for salvation, please at least eschew the old two Gods, Marcion heresy – one bad tempered and the other kind – for that I'm afraid is a disastrous model. There is only one God and he is not George's unkind, hell-fire version, but rather the version I espouse, that of infinite, unconditional loving-kindness, who will not let any person perish.

Reverend Halo: Well, for my part, Sir Terence, despite our good friend's last, vastly over-optimistic remarks, I believe you are not far from the Kingdom. Turn to the right, yea, repent and carry straight on; these are the only directions; yea, repent, be washed in the lamb's blood and head on upwards. For I feel the good yet wrathful Lord is even now opening a page for you in the Book of Life. A page prepared for you before the dawn of time. Yea, let then the tolerant remain blinded, even innocently and virtuously good as they may be in your case, Boffo – but God will not be mocked. He has already blocked out all the confirmed, hopeless sinners from His book of life. The wrath of God is upon our nation! For he is a God of wrath not a clap-happy, liberal Creator, tolerating human depravity.

Lucinda Halo: Oh listen to George, he's an expert on wrath and depravity!

By now, Boffo could see that not only had the potential theological minefield he so dreaded been stepped into, but also it had fully detonated, and therefore a change in the direction of discourse was urgently required in order to make some salvage of the devastated situation. Thus his rejoinder to Lucinda Halo was of both the conciliatory and curt variety. "No doubt, Lucinda, your dear George, makes up for my ignorance about God's wrath, although in turn, I think I make up for your husband's lack of perception in the matter of tolerance. Now, however, can we please talk of happier things?" And then focusing his sweet, benign look on Sir Terence, said: "Dear cousin, please try to brighten up for this special occasion. Let us try to get on to a different subject which can effect more sanguine thoughts and emotions on your part". And Miss Muffin helpfully chimed in with, "Yes, Sir Terence, think of all the invited guests who will brighten us all up shortly, this weekend! It's obviously a great shame that most of your theatrical friends could not come for one reason or other. *(She added diplomatically):* Perhaps some of them were on a special Broadway tour or had some other prior engagement. Anyway, Sir Terence, there are plenty of others to fill their places! Dear Boffo has invited all sorts of your and his old acquaintances; amongst others, an M.P., a professor, doctor, concert pianist, media columnists, an artist, poet and a literary arts critic. But I believe, after all, there is a guest who is a very well known TV and film star, Giles Truebore!"

At these last words of Miss Muffin, there was an audible groan, or perhaps more of a disapproving growl from Sir Terence. For in his days attending Dr. Microbe's clinic and his subsequent time of lonely meditations in Wanton Windmill, the ageing thespian had come to an ineluctable conclusion that the acting profession was now, like everything else, riddled with wantonness and consequently he was thankfully well out of it.

Boffo: Yes, Muriel. My dear Terence, surely you remember or have come across Giles Truebore, who has made such a notable movie career in celebrated box office successes – so I have been reliably informed – such as *Desperate Oblivion*, *The Serial Maniac* and *The Last Bus to Bethnal Green.*

Sir Terence: Bah! So it may be the case if you like that sort of wanton stuff. But the real test, my good fellow, is when you tread the boards, utterly exposed to several hundred pairs of eyes. That sorts out the boys from the men. That shows up those who can only act from the neck upwards!

Bishop Boffo: Are you not being a little harsh on the poor fellow. Think of the good example he is setting to his many friends and fans with championing environmental causes. Besides, he has not had the benefit of your vast Shakespearean acting experience. But this will come with time. Mr. Truebore is currently due to act the title role of *Hamlet* in what is billed as an exciting modern-dress production at the *Old Vic*. It's expected to be a sell-out.

Sir Terence: Bah! Only a couple of years ago I saw him act at the *National* in the Olivier theatre. Truebore took the title role in *Richard II* and I was sitting right in the front row stalls. What an anaemic performance! He was gorgeously attired in regal costume but couldn't do a thing with the part. Not a thing. He could just about spout out the words, twirl about a bit, but his voice, man, it was so weak, so feeble! You need to shape and mould the words, express yourself with your body and particularly your eyes otherwise it's just a Sunday jaunt in the park! Yes, if your eyes don't glint and your voice doesn't thunder, it's a waste of time for all concerned and a mockery of the great Bard. I even heard some fellow cry out from the back of the auditorium: "Speak up, will you, we can't hear you, we missed that last bit!" Well, if you can't carry your voice to the back rows you might as well give up. Good luck, I say, to Truebore having the folly to have a go at *Hamlet*. He will find enough to keep his mouth occupied with there! Hah! If he cannot do anything with *Richard II*, he will have an extremely ticklish job doing something with the great Dane! Yes, I would come to watch it as a farce and that's all. And the best bit will be when Laerte's poisoned-tip blade finishes him off and puts all the audience out of its colossal, not to say expensive misery!

"Shame on you, Sir Terence! That is rather uncharitable of you towards the poor fellow", piped up Miss Muffin in the latter's defence. But here we must leave Sir Terence, now getting into his critical and most likely, unstoppable Shakespearean stride. The genial Boffo we must also leave, feeling some sorrow for his discomfort. He had after all tried his best but in the event had only moved from one minefield to another and in each case unwittingly effected successful detonation. It would seem in Sir Terence's current state of displaced humour, there is not much hope of any particular conversational topic placating him. So we may both logically and appropriately move on to the very one and same person who was just now the subject and target of Sir Terence's scathing and no doubt, secretly enjoyable thespian vitriol.

CHAPTER THREE

TRAVELLING DELIGHTS (ONE)

That same fine, Friday August morning a sleek, high-turbined and extremely greedy, gas-guzzling state-of-the-art sporty saloon car was having some difficulty in making any quantifiable progress, being relegated to a crab-crawling pace between Egham and Heathrow Airport on the M25. Comfortably and irritably trapped within this gorgeous beast of super-locomotion (or at least in theory locomotion when now and again there happened to be a traffic-jam free road) were three persons optimistically heading for *Lower Wanton End*, weekend invitees to the birthday celebrations of Sir Terence Treadboards. The driver of this metallic purring panther (rather a sulky panther and driver because neither could at present get beyond second gear) was a Mr. Giles Truebore, a well known, handsomely greying, middle-aged film and TV actor. Truebore had recently generated much media attention by a dramatic article in *The Daily Twitter* announcing his environmental concern for the planet. He had, as a further result of this great concern, deservedly attracted much publicity through the great sacrifice of selling three of his five sports cars and also (with great humility) deciding to travel by private jet only once instead of three times a week. Mr. Truebore's two passengers included a thirty-something, smartly-dressed, lady friend (on the driver's near-side) by the name of Melissa Puff-Up, a well-known literary and arts critic. A cursory, yet discerning observation of this lady would possibly conclude that Miss Puff-Up's pretty face was adversely ornamented by a fixed, arched and pertly clever expression. The other passenger sitting backseat was the rather highly-strung, young Mr. Edmund Edgy. The latter, who was almost painfully tall and thin, with unfortunately large projecting ears, had (many thought) otherwise the features for a pleasingly mild face, if only it wasn't for his habitual look of a startled rabbit. Mr. Edgy, an aspiring poet and playwright, had as yet failed to scent the sweet smelling aroma of any notable success. Moreover, highly awkward and gauche with the opposite sex, he housed an incipient inferiority complex within himself and entertained somewhat smouldering, ambivalent feelings towards his two self-assured travelling companions. We might also mention that Mr. Edgy, despite being severely pessimistic of contemporary life and future prospects, was unaccountably enthusiastic about the supposed paradisal virtues of England during the years 400 to 1066.

Truebore: What are things coming to? Why on earth don't they build more lanes or better still another motorway to take traffic pressure off the M25? There would also then be less pollution in this area. It's traffic queuing like this which makes for bad air quality and a high wastage of oil resources.

Puff-up: Exactly. All this spoils our potentially excellent road transport system. There's something quirkily beautiful, so hauntingly humorous and intangibly poetical about motorways, cars, juggernauts and service stations with their "happy eater" and shopping complexes. When properly flowing, this is the crowning glory of all *Futurism's* dreams of perpetual movement. Artistically, the motorway is the logical offshoot of technological civilisation's inevitable progress. Governments have a duty to build and maintain motorways and keep our country on the move. Forget Wordsworth and his daffodils. That type of thing is too picturesquely static and artistically unproductive in terms of our post-modern age. We've now moved on into a new exciting time of continuous motion. It of course naturally follows that what any art worth its salt does is to reflect and celebrate human mobility.

Edgy: But I don't see why we should forget Wordsworth just because he liked daffodils. If I were building motorways I would plant daffodils all along the road sides. At least that would destroy something of the monotony and boredom when one gets stuck in wretched traffic-jams.

Truebore: I take your point. However, environmentalism and progress are a balance. We can easily have both up to a certain reasonable point. We can in fact have a sustainable economy and environment. Though naturally sacrifices have to be made. Omelettes are only made by cracking eggs. Something always has to go. There's simply not enough room for all existing countryside, extended or bigger roads and new building opportunities. Daffodils and such-like may be often part of the sacrifice. The problem is if we stand still we go backwards. There's unfortunately no middle position; we cannot unravel technology and become feudal barbarians again. But we can make a little less smoke and fumes, so accordingly lessen the ratio of green-house gases and thus sleep with clean environmental consciences.

Puff-Up: Of course and as you imply, Giles, we are fully in the scientific age now. Everything, including the arts need to adjust to our technological milieu. Poetic language, for instance, is no longer the frivolously outmoded *la-de-da* language of hills, vales, woods, primroses, birds and bees. We must pursue the concrete and non-elitist chatty language patterns which people today use and understand.

Edgy: And what exactly are those?

Puff-Up: What else, dear Edmund, but the language which people – the majority – understand: money, social status, self-interest, wellbeing and the body beautiful. This is today's reality. Only the eccentric minority *continually* want Mozart, Beethoven and Shakespeare; the latter great as they are, should only be had discreetly in small dosages. We must all be scientists, economists and entrepreneurs now in our handling of truth. The health of our minds and bodies is clearly connected with our being in touch with the scientific and economic movements of our age. Look at the enhancements science has brought to us through its products: hospital diagnostic and scanning machines, computers and the internet, to name a few. If we try to artistically opt out of a world which brings such obvious benefits, we become ostriches, burying our heads in the sand.

Truebore: Yes, we must go with the flow or be swept aside. Though we must adjust appropriately here and there when it comes to the planet's health. But I believe such adjustments can be made and are now being made. Every time we thoughtfully turn off a light switch we are helping to save the planet and no doubt doing something positive to stop the polar ice-cap melting.

Edgy: I wish it were as simple as that. Anyone who has connected with my plays or poetry will be aware we are heading for ecological Armageddon. We are all being swept along like lava to annihilation. The planet has already had it. Look at all the constant natural disasters. Soon the rain forests will be all gone; the Artic ice-less and despoiled by oil drilling, losing its beautiful polar bears and bowhead whales. No doubt everyone in Britain will in a few years be sweltering and ill with malaria if they haven't already been drowned by tropical-style rain storms. Or it may be that drought finishes us all off. The fools at the *National Theatre* refused my latest – and best play: *Despair, Misery and Final Doom* just as they did my previous work: *Return to the Primeval Sludge*. And for why? They say I am being too negative and pessimistic. I, alone in the arts, shine as a warning light to disaster and yet they all refuse to listen! It is only the greatness of art, whether poetry, drama, literature, music or such-like which will save the world!

Truebore: Forgive me my dear fellow but you are at times somewhat fanatical in the way you talk. In answer to your tirade of doom and gloom, let me make my own position clear. You see, while I have made what I feel is an important and significant step in publicly declaring my concern for our global environment, I am not one of these global warming extremists like yourself. There is too much alarmism in this new religion of global warming. Too much scare-mongering which merely results in weak-minded sections of the public becoming hysterical. These minority alarmist scientists and pressure groups responsible for such alarmism lack amongst other things a sense of historical perspective. For instance, in terms of good old Britain, overly warm periods have been common fare from time immemorial and ice skating and fairs on the Thames and other great rivers were hardly unusual in medieval times. And all this blame-throwing! The global fundamentalists always like to blame someone or other. It is in my view unhelpful to always consider everything that's environmentally wrong as being humanly caused. After all, there are many natural forces bigger than those of so-called human pollution. Take volcanoes and earthquakes for example! Good old earth has been doing its own thing from the big bang onwards. It will continue to do so whatever the global warming brigade say or do. After all what sane person would blame a yet non-existent humanity for the ice-age and all the incredible geological shifts in the earth and seas which happened millions and billions of year ago!

Edgy (visibly upset and punctured): What about Chernobel, Fukushima and catastrophic oil spills like the BP Gulf of Mexico one? They didn't just happen by bad luck! These disasters were due to human errors such as negligent safety procedures – and in Fukushima's case, it being crazily sited within an earthquake zone. We all live in the wake of these calamities which are nothing other than massive pointers to our impending destruction. The pollution and degradation of all these type of disasters will live with us forever and drag us down with them.

Truebore: Nonsense, pure nonsense. You are talking in biblical hyperbole. All these oil spills, for instance are cleaned up usually in about six months. Yes, of course I don't deny human error in these instances. It is much regrettable. But all this talk of such pollution lasting for a couple of million years is poppycock. In most of these places it's now business as usual. Old planet earth has, like the human body in many ways, a tried and tested means of self-recovery. It cleans itself up. Of course the green

41

extremists would find it inconvenient to talk of such a blindingly obvious notion.

Puff-Up: Admit it, Edmund, you're defeated! Giles has taken the wind out of your sails. You're never happy unless you are contemplating and finding the apocalypse in every little disaster that crops up. Admit it, such temporary disasters are the flip side of the risks human progress has to take to get anywhere at all. In the scale of things they are a small price to pay. Stop being a Jeremiah!

Mr. Edgy, whose conversation expended a lot of nervous energy was now feeling extremely deflated and at an hostile impasse. Rather than attempting to argue further he momentarily paused, muttering dolefully: "small price to pay". Then rather sulkily addressing Miss Puff-Up, Mr. Edgy changed the present subject: "Anyway, Melissa, going back to your previous viewpoint, the last thing I want to be is a scientist, economist or businessman. What has any of that got to do with art of any sort?

Puff-Up: Really, Edmund, wake up to reality! Business, science and economy have *everything* to do with art. They spell success and that surely, is it not, what *you* want, success as a playwright and poet? For you won't get anywhere nowadays without a business, economic and scientific sense, I can assure you. Publishers don't have any room for people with flowery mindsets like Keats, Shelley or Wordsworth any more. They look for people with the right media know-how and connections, which means artistic entrepreneurs who think scientifically and economically. Art will hardly save the world by itself, as you seem to think. But art working in conjunction with the experts – that is the scientists, economists and business brains, that is the way forward.

The Arts have got to pool their resources with those who understand the mechanics of the world as it operates financially and environmentally. And as for the planet's health and future, you take far too dim a view of it. Look at how things have been getting rapidly better since the Second World War. Yes, still poverty and environmental destruction, I grant you, but look at the great strides of improvement for millions and millions of people health and lifestyles across the globe. The world today is a more democratic place and people are actually more civilised and middle classed – on the whole than ever before…

Edgy: Not necessarily. It depends where you are. What about many areas in of the Middle-East, Latin America and Africa? Even a so-called democratic uprising in these places can soon turn sour and…

At this moment Edmund Edgy was interrupted as the snarled up traffic at Chorley Wood was un-snarling itself and at last Giles Truebore, along with all the other thousands of fuming, deadlocked drivers, could elatedly put his frustrated beast up into its higher gears. In a crystalline moment the sleek panther was purring along un-ecologically and indeed, illegally at ninety-five miles an hour with the result of Edward Edgy becoming even more nervously uncomfortable than usual. But Giles Truebore, on the contrary was feeling happier as he delightedly shoved his foot down on the accelerator pedal. He did not notice his back-seat passenger cringing with apprehension as the panther swept across the middle carriageway into the fast lane, contemptuously passing two juggernauts and five other vehicles.

Truebore: You must take a more sanguine view of things, Edmund. The world isn't going to end tomorrow. There have been doleful Cassandras from time immemorial going around spreading prophecies of doom. And has there ever been a time in human history when every place on our dear globe has been perfectly at peace? Of course not and you can't unless you are a quack or utopian expect such an unreal state of affairs. Human life can never be the garden of Eden. It simply doesn't fit the scientific, economic or sociological framework. But just for instance think of our own country. Look on the plus side of things which Melissa has just reminded us of. Where is the old poverty, for instance, which characterised Dickens' Victorian England? That, my good fellow, has all thankfully gone for ever. New towns in the 1950's onwards cleared out the old slums for good. Improved road and motorway networks meant that working class people could get to the sea-side and really improve their health and life-styles. Everyone is entitled to use the NHS and now many people are living contentedly into their nineties.

Puff-Up: Yes, we don't know how lucky we all are. And it's all thanks to science and technology, which far from ruining the planet have made, on the whole, our living conditions today inconceivably more easy and pleasant than those of our forebears a few generations back. Nearly everyone is healthier and living longer. What can be possibly wrong with that?

Edgy (recovering somewhat): You've indeed hit upon exactly what *is* the problem: population. There you have it, living longer. Too many of us human beings for the planet to properly sustain. World population is going bonkers and it's swamping the planet with everyone fighting for scarce natural resources. Just look at our own poor bulging England, packed to capacity with human beings. We shall soon run out of farming land because of the constant house building demand. And that means surviving by imports, but the other nations will need their foodstuffs for themselves. And where will it all lead? Vegetable famine and food riots – riots for potatoes and greens which we always take for granted. What good will your motorways and computers be then? Oh, that we were back in the glorious agrarian age of our Anglo-Saxon heritage! Particularly, the eighth century – the age of Alcuin of York, who not only was a great learned teacher but also a poet. In those halcyon days our ancestors most likely did not exceed a million and a half and were self-subsistent. What breathing space and virtually everyone a farmer! They were probably the most ecological people our land has ever known! Today, compared to that period, there are over six times more people living in London, alone. The result is that we are all now in the process of being mentally or literally squashed to death by one another. We are like cars – perhaps highly sophisticated and sleek cars – but without enough road space to travel on in comfort or safety. Yes, just like potential high-performance cars stuck nose-to-nose on this wretched M25! But think of the Anglo-Saxon era; a purely agrarian people who we can thank for virtually inventing organised husbandry and its fundamental techniques. Yes wild, unspoilt landscapes and an ecologically-sized population! Think of all the virgin space to roam around in; the peace and quiet; no noisy power tools – indeed, no machines whatsoever; no artificial lights, just natural mother nature! Think of the simple, natural lifestyles such people led. We may scoff and say it was merely a time of ignorance and uncouth savagery, yet I say that it was a period of order and pure creativity; there were proper codes of law, skilful craftsmen, unpretentious little churches and ecologically sized dwelling places; close-knit communities, proper family bonding – even then women had some rights – and it was this very organically compact and well organised era which apportioned our land into the beautiful shires still with us today. Yes, small was definitely beautiful and could take a justified pride in being so. How I loathe *The Doomsday Book*; that interfering, taxation inventory compiled on behalf of a vicious, psychopathic Normandy thug who ruined, plundered and corrupted our beautiful and largely un-desecrated country. A price tag on everything from a bale of straw to a pig! That of course was the beginning of the end for the only innocent and organic England there has ever been. Given time and critical encouragement, I have it in me to write a haunting play or epic poem lamenting the passing forever of such our once idyllic English paradise!

Puff-Up: Idyllic, I doubt it. Either you ended up as a snack for wild beasts such as wolves, or you caught an infection and died of some plague about five minutes later; or some passing delinquent, who wasn't aware of the word "law" decided to knock your brains out just for the fun of it. And don't forget the friendly men from the North who started their visits even in your dear Alcuin's time. In any case, in those days your average life expectancy was probably less than thirty or so years. Of course, if you happened to be a slave or hard-up churl, even those short years were nothing but a time of abject misery. And concerning your wonderfully small Anglo-Saxon population, I remember my school history books telling me that it was precisely lack of people – moreover, people fit to fight – that defeated Harold at Hastings. He sorted out the

Norwegians at Stamford Bridge, but as the historians tell us, he lost a lot of men in doing so and those remaining were a tired and spent force. With such a small Saxon population, where were the replenishments to come from? So you can see, Edmund, it would have been better for Harold and your dear Anglo-Saxons if there *had* been a larger population. But small, closed-up, insular populations never survive for long. They can't. Progress, whether some of us like you resent it, must come and follow its course. It's survival of the biggest and fittest, but the biggest and fittest in terms of being able to endow a country and its inhabitants with vital wealth creation and thus material living improvements. Even if the Norman Conquest was only just another preliminary stepping stone to such things, without it we would undoubtedly not be where we are now. Who wants to live, shivering forever in a wattle hut without proper amenities?

Truebore: Exactly! Well, Edmund, you don't really want to shiver in a smelly, overcrowded and smoky thatched hut, do you? And worse, time-travelling back to those "halcyon" days, you would also find that nearly everyone was illiterate! For it was an illiterate age – apart from Bede and a smattering of other learned people no one was able to read or write. And that's why we know next to nothing about the mind-sets of these people – and let's face it, un-reflecting people who merely lived just to subsist if they could. But why choose the Anglo-Saxon age? At least if you must return to a less populated past, go for the mid or late nineteenth century, when improved living standards, medicine and sanitation would on the whole give you a better life-expectancy.

Edgy: Oh no, the age of Victorian progress with its ugly industrialisation, filthy fumes and relentless house-building programs – that was the era responsible for accelerating the wholesale ruination of our green and pleasant land! It was *that* age of heartless mechanisation which led directly to this mindless technocratic age we live in today. No, Victorianism is merely Norman vandalism *par excellence*!

Truebore: It's all relative, all in the eye of the beholder. The golden age of the past doesn't exist except in some rosy, nostalgic compartment in people's minds. There are always those who yearn wistfully for the past. But this is going against the grain of progress and it's folly to go against the law of progress. On the whole, human life *is* getting better and better. All we need to do is a few fine adjustments to cut down carbon emissions, and that's exactly what I've done with my new state-of-the-art car exhaust system.

Edgy: But what will happen if oil runs out. We shall have to think again and go back to nature, but it'll be too late. And what good will be….

But just then Truebore put his foot right down again and the purring panther torpedoed itself past another ten vehicles. While Melissa Puff-up was smiling appreciatively at Truebore, the voice from the backseat was mumbling something about: "I feel rather faint, I wish I'd taken the train…"

* * *

Meanwhile, coming from another direction on the M25, a golden coloured, regal metallic beast was languishing in a severe traffic hold-up at the Dartford Tunnel. The four occupants in this impressive, stately saloon car were also invitees for the weekend birthday celebrations at *Lower*

Wanton End and therefore aiming like the other already mentioned car to somehow eventually get off the M25 onto the M11 and hence onto the respective A and B roads which terminated in their destination. This second, more sedate gas guzzler was being driven by the well-known, arts-loving MP., Mr. Geoffrey Havealot. The latter was a sixty-something with imposing, yet relaxed bearing, suggesting, particularly through a distinguished greying moustache, all the confidence and conveniences of an assured, privileged upbringing. In the front passenger seat was Mr. Ashley Dunce, a youngish looking, fluffy haired forty-something man, though prematurely portly in build, who was political founder of the newly formed: *Consensus Diversity Party.* (Known as, *CDP*, for short). Backseat, the two female passengers (both around their mid-fifties, but still retaining traces of physical good looks), comprised the right wing, monarchist, pro-privatisation, anti-welfare state, journalist, Clara Clouthard, leading opinion columnist of the *Daily Hobbyhorse* and Prunella Makepiece, the left-wing anti-monarchist, pro-nationalisation, Marxist journalist, who was leading opinion columnist of the *Clarion Echo.*

Havealot: All this annoying jam-up is ironically due to the very success of the car as the most efficient form of transportation ever devised. Of course, we do need to keep up momentum with road building. However, I think the real next great step forward on progress' agenda will be flying cars. They've already started in America producing a combined car and plane. Just think of it! What a terrific boost to the economy if such a thing takes off over here – excuse my pun by the way, ha hah! Think of it though, virtually a new industry, offering loads of skilled employment and all the good knock-on effects for allied industries. The skies will be the limit! Oh excuse me again, yet another pun, hah ha!

Dunce: Extremely witty, Geoffrey. Yes, I must agree with your point of view. There are no doubt other points of view to be considered, but I think your point is both extremely sound and interesting.

Makepiece: I am not so sanguine as you, Ashley. What about the insurance costs – I should imagine they will be pretty *sky-high*! And you'll need some strict form of air traffic control if there's hundreds or more planes zooming all over the place. And surely you can't just take off from your own drive. You must at least need some little run-way space to get off the ground, and where can you safely find that on our crowded roads? I would personally find it alarming, driving behind a vehicle which suddenly decides to take-off without even a signal! The whole business is a pipe dream. The so-called flying car will turn out to be as white an elephant as the old Zeppelin was.

Havealot: Oh, those concerns you mention can soon be sorted out. Progress always finds a way round obstacles. Inventors and entrepreneurs and governments have been finding ways round things since the wheel was invented. Oh gracious me, yet another pun! Ha, hah, how do I manage it!

Dunce: What a wit you are, Geoffrey! It must be a natural gift amongst your many other talents. On the one hand I have known a many great wits and yet on the other I find it a rare commodity in society.

Clouthard: Prunella, dear, you always put such a damper on everything, particularly anything that smacks of good entrepreneurial sense! It's our hard-working entrepreneurs, who make this country great. They're the ones who put themselves on the line, taking enormous risks, making great personal sacrifices for the benefit of the common good. These are the people who strive to make a better life for everyone including you, me and our families.

Makepiece: Common good! I suppose increased air pollution – more greenhouse gases – is good for us all. Your common good actually translates as quick prosperity for the few at the expense of the many.

Havealot: Surely you take a too negative view of the matter Prunella. New industries have always created problems and tensions, but the upshot has been ultimately the astounding creation of our present technological society. We must not therefore be Luddites in our attitudes. And Luddites are always losers anyway.

Dunce: I agree with you there. There are of course other differing views that could be considered, but I think your view on the whole a good and representative one. While one must sympathise to some or even a great extent today with the neo-Luddites' frustration, there is no doubt that they ought to tow the line when all things are considered.

Clouthard: Of course you are right, Geoffrey! *You* are always on the losing side Prunella. That's why the left – socialism and its evil bedfellow, Marxism, is now defunct, a dead cause. The left really represents nothing but envy and resentment. It doesn't like to see wealth-creation, free-market capitalism triumphantly glowing in its success. All you want is to continually bash the rich. Richness equals badness in your socialist slot-ruler mentality. You can't seem to grasp that even in a democratic society some people are more equal than others precisely because they have been endowed with more financially acute and hard-working brains. You astonishingly seem to think there is something intrinsically wrong with this. Do we all want to end up as road sweepers? Do we all want to be factory operatives? Of course not. Variety – difference – is good and if there were no wealthy or wealth-creating people society would be just a mass of indolence. We would all consequently end up as paupers clinging onto the welfare state. But instead, it is the virtuous wealth-creators: bankers, financial speculators, directors and all earners in the top ten per cent who work their guts out to make this country a successful and high quality nation.

Dunce: How well put, Clara. I feel the consensus must be with your view and yet there will be other views which may need equal consideration. We must be thankful for the top ten per cent. There may be inveterate tax-dodgers here and there, or even more than here and there, and we cannot overlook such instances entirely, but as you say, we must not bash the rich. That would not get us anywhere. We should, I propose, not go around with closed eyes, but neither should we be over-opening our eyes through being too critical.

Makepiece: Well, Clara, it's alright in your book to bash the poor and you, Ashley, make your casual reference to the parasites who habitually dodge taxes by either paying their monies into offshore banks or putting it into the names of their spouses or relatives. And of course, Clara, it's alright to defend the banking speculators who single-handedly caused our last massive recession. Don't bash the rich you say. But the inordinately wealthy are invariably greedy. What good have the rich ever done for anyone but their own ilk? Who benefits but them from their several big houses? What children but their own benefit from being sent to expensive private schools? Do they, in their large detached dwelling places, situated either in select leafy suburbs or secluded villages in the Shires, ever have to worry about rising damp, vandalism and noise from dysfunctional neighbours? Do they ever have to worry about paying the bills and having enough money to have a proper holiday with the kids?

Dunce: I must concede there is some merit in your view, Prunella, but there again may well be some merit in other views which should not, in my opinion be entirely omitted from due consideration.

Clouthard: What a miserable view of the world you take, Prunella. Does it not all stem from a wretchedly faulty view of human nature? Socialism is coloured with jealous resentment and rationalises this by seeing all success – particularly financial and business success – as stemming from an inherently fallen and perverted human nature. Of course lefties are themselves exempt from the depravity and selfish greed with which they conveniently tar everyone else with. The truth is, is it not, Prunella, that the people who whinge about the well-off, would in reality be quite happy to exchange places with those whom they so self-righteously criticise? But what your myopic socialist fails to realise is that you don't get to being better off – wealthier – without the dedicated hard graft and total sacrificial commitment that goes with it. And anyway, it's only a small percentage of the wealthy who can be genuinely said to be tax frauds or parasites. We are where we are today – as a front rank democratic and deeply caring nation – precisely because the rich *have* and *are* bearing the burden of the common good. It's their huge tax bills which greatly contribute to our country's continuing economic prosperity, health and international profile. And this doesn't come out of a vacuum; it results from painstakingly and creatively hard-earned capital. And those responsible for that are, whether you like it or not, necessarily from the wealthy strata. The poor and the envious scroungers don't make wealth. That's obvious truth. They are where they are, on the main, because of their own incompetence and their crass failure to take advantage of education opportunities.

Havealot: Of course. You give them the opportunities – schools and the whole welfare state caboodle and what do they do with it? They take all the benefits without bothering with the education bit and in consequence we end up with a bunch of delinquent illiterates who can't tell a Pinter from a Beckett play; a Bartok quartet from a Schoenberg, or the difference between contemporary, cutting-edge, *Tate Modern* installations and painting by numbers..

Dunce: Very piquantly and vibrantly put, I must say. Such viewpoints can in my opinion be hardly challenged, although no doubt they can be challenged and very probably will be. Yes, the poor may well be disadvantaged by living in cash-starved districts along with inadequate educational resources but that can be no excuse for their failing to distinguish the niceties of the modern arts (such as *Tate Modern*) and failing to contribute to wealth creation. Yes I, myself, am all for wealth creation and the common good, although there are pros and cons, for's and againsts, whichever way one looks at it. In fact, I always personally – and it is the policy of my party – look at a thing from all sides and from all angles, all viewpoints and all perspectives.

Havealot: Quite. Well, I agree with you most strongly Clara. Wealth creation is essential to any healthy, forward-looking society and that of course means capital accumulation. It's the private sector which everything hinges upon. Because that's where the more gifted intelligent people naturally gravitate to. And that's the only hope for putting the country back on its feet, undoing the damage of years of nationalisation. What can be done without capital? Without it we would all be barbarians, wearing loin cloths and living in wattle huts. Who supplies the capital? Who supplies the energy, drive and know-all to acquire it? Brains and commitment to the common interest don't just grow on normal trees. They have to grow out of specially privately planted trees – not those mass produced by the Forestry Commission which are only good for making matchsticks. Wealth creation is a job for the esoteric financial specialists, in short, a job for the specialised private sector, those who know best about capital accumulation.

Makepiece: What is privatisation? It isn't creating wealth at all, but rather swiping it from what already exists. No more than Robin Hood in reverse; make sure the rich have more and the poor have even less! Ashley, where do you and your *Consensus Diversity Party* stand on this matter?

Dunce: A good question, Prunella, and I may say that getting to the bottom of matters is all about asking interesting and apt questions which involve the issues of consensus and diversity. And it is precisely these issues which generally circumference and order the agenda of my party. We are all for consensus but also all for diversity, which means we are an all-inclusive party. Furthermore, that is why I have said on numerous occasions that we would form a coalition with any of the main parties – or indeed any of the minor parties – and work together, in happy unison. As Clara has mentioned the phrase, *Common Good*, so that is what we would work for in any coalition framework. For whether the policy is nationalisation, privatisation, free-market or closed-market, wealth creation or wealth reduction, we are quite happy to play our part. In fact one of our slogans is precisely: "Whatever is, we will accommodate; whatever isn't we will accommodate and whatever may be yet to come we will accommodate". Thus we will offend no-one by turning the other cheek. We will say: "Let us work together, whatever we are working together for, and if what we are working together must change into something else, be that as it may, we will not be discouraged, we will not give up, we will stick at it, whatever it is"…

And so Mr. Dunce continued as if some alarm clock had just suddenly unwound in his head urging him into verbal action. Even the two sharp-minded, sharp-tongued, sparring journalists were strangely agreed in a kind of mutual dumb, open-mouthed fascination at how Mr. Dunce could violate with his air vibrations the rules of verbal logic through such a fabulously fatuous, oratorical display. Mr. Havealot, however was not at all bothered. He had automatically switched off from his front-seat passenger's eloquent, mini-epic discourse as the traffic was now starting to move from out of the Dartford Tunnel's lighted catacomb. The golden, two-litre, regal beast was on the move once more and that liberating fact, for the Right Honourable Mr. Havelot, consigned the burbling discourse of Mr. Dunce into the abyss of utter insignificance.

* * *

And even though the respective metallic beasts of Mr. Truebore and the Honourable Mr. Havelot were now at last allowed to be unleashed from the confines of traffic hold-ups, for another driver and her passenger, also making for *Lower Wanton End*, there had been no such problems on the M25 at all. Dare-take-all, forty-something, Alison Acrylic, the newly nationally esteemed artist of vast, vibrantly crayoned coloured, wall-sized paintings fame, was joyously driving her two-wheeled 1000cc motorbike past all the queues, like a knife cutting through butter. Riding pillion and firmly holding onto her, and also experiencing exhilarated contentment, was her thirty-something partner, with copious, golden hair streaming out from under her crash helmet.

CHAPTER FOUR

TRAVELLING DELIGHTS (TWO)

A t about the same time as our previously mentioned two separate journeying cars had been imprisoned at different points on the renowned M25, the fifteen minutes past ten, fast train from Kings Cross to Cambridge was also held up somewhere between Hitchin and Stevenage due to a signals failure. Inside a First Class compartment, Dr. Gustaf Microbe, that same well-known psychotherapist, who had treated Sir Terence and who still kept up a precautionary correspondence with the latter, was travelling with a companion by the name of Julian Morbid. Dr. Microbe, of Austrian extraction, in his early sixties, with a balding head, looked like a kind of human-sized, learned mole who had somehow fantastically burrowed his way up the evolutionary scale from creature to man. This apparent synthesis between mole and human biped was rather confirmed by his finely cut, small-featured face with its intent, roving eyes, the latter shielded by small, round-lensed glasses. Dr. Microbe's manner was relaxed, yet running parallel with this seemingly urbane ease was an acute, ongoing observation of his companion. Mr. Julian Morbid was an on-and-off private patient of the esteemed psychotherapist, who was just now sitting beside him. The First Class carriage was empty apart from four other talkative but not unruly men at the other end of the compartment. As it happened, the foursome group was also travelling to Cambridge and on to *Lower Wanton End*, being invitees to Sir Terence's weekend birthday celebrations. But we will hear more of them anon.

Julian Morbid's trademark harried look was to a significant extent due to his flitting and ferret-like eyes encased behind thick-rimmed glasses. To a cursory but educated guess, Mr. Morbid could be seen to be a person bordering on the circumference of probable neurosis. However, the reality was that he was at times veering more towards a psychosis, although fortunately through therapy and the compensations of classical music and his own musical abilities thereof, Mr. Morbid so far had avoided such a dark mental abyss. His whole manner was suggestive of unease and incipient agitation. In turn, nervousness, hesitancy, suspiciousness and repeated concern that he had forgotten or omitted to do certain domestic or other tasks, unmasked to any intelligent observer – and particularly, Dr. Microbe – the dominating pattern of his state of mind. Middle-aged and with black-greying hair, Julian Morbid had thick eye-brows, a dominant nose and a wide square-jawed face. Mr. Morbid's facial features flitted about in a kind of negative mobility, while his large hands, and finely tapered fingers fluttered and flapped around in obvious unease. A confirmed bachelor, he was a concert pianist, not perhaps of the first-rank of consummate artistry but nevertheless considered by many a very capable, reliable exponent of the classical and romantic periods. Mr. Morbid particularly liked to specialise in plumbing the depths of such harrowing opus pieces as Liszt's B minor sonata, Schubert's last joy and agonised tinged sonatas, Chopin's B minor and Beethoven's final sonatas.

Sir Terence, a devotee of classical music and also a passable amateur pianist, had been to several of Julian's recitals and admired his playing. The Knight, after an appointment at Microbe's clinic, had bumped into Mr. Morbid on one of the latter's visits for therapeutic counselling. Sir Terence, although sorry to see the pianist reduced to needing such consultation, was nevertheless delighted to meet him and lavishly showered his praises upon Mr. Morbid's superior ability to interpret the great classical and romantic works. In return, Mr. Morbid said he had greatly admired once seeing Sir Terence's rendition of Antony in the Bard's great Roman tragedy. Morbid, as was his wont, only enjoyed tragedies if he ever patronised the theatre. "Happy ever after" endings in theatre and literature were not to his taste as he considered these "unreal" and "chimerical" in terms of reality. Sir Terence concurred; he admitted to having now, through the wanton betrayals of women, come to the same conclusion. Julian Morbid opined that having always believed the female sex was extremely dangerous and therefore to be resolutely avoided in terms of intimate relationships, he had fortunately not had the misfortune of being exposed to the dangers of a wife and daughter. As a result of this happy chance meeting at the clinic, both men exchanged their business address cards with Julian Morbid feeling unusually flattered by both Sir Terence's adulation and the fact that he had found someone who happily seemed to share his tragic view of life. And even more unusually for this reticent, self-doubting pianist, was his offer of being very happy to play one day privately for Sir Terence and talk further with him on music and other subjects relating to high and irredeemably tragic art.

When Boffo had raised the idea with Sir Terence about a special weekend comprising invited guests to celebrate the latter's seventieth birthday, there were initially grunts of dissatisfaction. However, Sir Terence, seeing Boffo's determination that the birthday must be enjoyed in the context of a great socialite weekend celebration, resignedly commented that in that case an invitation should be extended to Julian Morbid, also inviting the latter to give a recital on the Saturday evening. Thus, the invitation had gone out to Mr. Morbid. But Sir Terence had not forgotten Dr. Microbe's theoretically pivotal part in his recovery process, so the great psychotherapist amalgamator was also invited. At this particular time of the impending birthday celebration weekend, Julian Morbid, who lived in outer London, was currently having some further consultations after warning signs concerning his mental stability. It therefore seemed sensible to Dr. Microbe, as Mr. Morbid was set on fulfilling his recital invitation, that they should both travel together from Kings Cross station to *Lower Wanton End.* The good psychotherapist felt that this trip into the outside world with Mr. Morbid would serve at least two useful purposes. Firstly, it would be useful to observe how Julian Morbid coped (or failed to cope) within a social gathering situation. Secondly, Dr. Microbe would be on hand to give moral and psychological support in case, his patient started to relapse or lose his courage in the face of such a high-flying assembly and assortment of cultural intelligentsia.

Microbe: I feel this journey together gives us a further chance – and in fact a unique chance – away from a clinical environment to develop our relationship in a more natural, relaxed form. There is nobody else apart from those four men debating together in a reasonably intelligent fashion at the back of our carriage. Thus, we are both free of the usual invidious inhibitions which inevitably arise from the consulting room. Although we may be technically in a public place, I think we can talk here without the worry of being eavesdropped upon.

Julian Morbid's ears pricked up at the phrase "being eavesdropped upon", but otherwise Dr. Microbe's words seemed to run through and past him. Ever since embarking upon the train at Kings Cross Julian had been rummaging through a thin attache case to check that he had remembered to bring some music manuscripts pertinent to his impending recital at Wanton Rectory. Now with the delay due to signal failure, Mr. Morbid's lack of ease was further in evidence. Thus he now replied with a *non-sequitur*.

Morbid: I hope there has nothing serious happened on the line. With all this privatisation, one never knows what level of competence upholds the safety of our public utilities nowadays. Everything is contracted out to unskilled labour, untrained supervisors and uninformed managers who know nothing about proper safety procedures. In consequence, we, the general public are more at risk than ever. Who can even trust these railway company announcements? They may well be bogus red-herring, information A bridge may have semi-collapsed ahead of us. The line may be damaged, the signal system totally up the creek. Who knows? There may be some poor fellow who ended it all on the line – but we shall never know. We are totally at the mercy of these privatised companies – these idiots who think only of profit while jeopardising their passengers. Travelling is the most dangerous aspect of life today. You are not safe whichever form you take, car, train, plane or boat. If only one could fly like a bird or wave a magic wand in order to travel where we want to.

Dr. Microbe: Wish-fulfilment Julian! Of course we would all like reality to be as it is not. Life, my dear fellow is an open Pandora Box of various risks. When we enter this world we do not come with a written guarantee attached to us! The kettle may blow up in our faces; the cat or dog – if we have one – may trip us up; even going outside our own front door a roof tile may fall upon us. Who knows? We do not have access to crystal balls – no! not even I, both a trained psychoanalyst and psychotherapist, who has observed, studied life and human beings for all my professional life. What I am saying therefore, is that we must at least to a sensible extent *go with the risk* – we must as in popular parlance *go with the flow*. Otherwise what happens? We stay at home, probably vegetating. We become mentally if not physically agoraphobic. And that is no good, no good for you, nor for anyone, my dear Julian. We must take the daily risk. We must take it because it is only a relative risk. It is part of the necessary patterning of daily, healthy functioning. So what if the train derails, the car steering goes dangerously awry, the plane's propeller drops off or the boat develops a leak? What can we do in the face of risk suddenly materialising? But in the nature of normal occurrences none of these things are that likely. In our modern western world we have far higher and more stringent levels of safety checking – privatisation or no privatisation – than that of our forbears. This is your problem Julian, you think of risk as probability. Risk is risk precisely because it is only possibility. If it became probability it would not be risk – it would instead be present reality. Do you not see therefore, my good friend, your problem is that you are always, as they say, *jumping the gun?* And if you could stop *jumping the gun* you could arrest this incipient growing snowball of worry that is spoiling life for you. You could relax and take in more the interesting and varied details of life. You see, even though we are held up for the moment, I still maintain *my* equilibrium. I look out of the window and take things in. Life goes on. And we should not let minor hindrances put us out of kilter. Why should there be dark shadows on the horizon? Why, because we mentally put them there. Inside our minds we construct our own problems. Yet, in life, Julian, one finds, as long as one has a reasonable smattering of intelligence and self-awareness, that things generally work their way out. Thus we must always strive to trust life more as well as build-up our self-resources. By this combination of both dependence and self-resourcefulness, we can achieve resilience in our personality structures. However, my dear friend, remember there is more order and organisation in our world than you think.

Morbid (somewhat exasperated): I cannot share your optimism. Life as I see it is a chaotic mess. It is only by the most careful diligence and by taking constant precautions that we can, in my opinion, avoid all the countless traps, deceptions and con-people who constantly confront us trying to cast us into all sorts of miserable pits! Yes, life is risk alright! Smooth-talking salespeople, politicians etc., and etc., this is an ugly and false world to be an adult in. I am not made for combat in this type of set-up. No wonder I was happiest when a child. Adulthood is a punishment on the whole for people like me.

Dr. Microbe: That should not be so, dear Julian! It is true the world of interacting human beings must at many points be problematical, but that is how life *is*. The only answer is self-strength through a proper integration of the various positive values of personality. Today, it is true, our contemporary society is unhealthily obsessed with self-esteem, however, you could most definitely do with elevating your sense of self-worth! You say you were happier as a child, but perhaps that happiness had a dominant and regressive element of escapism in it; a fearful clinging on to what should only be a mere stage in one's necessary development to adolescence and then to adulthood. Of course, childhood still remains with us all if only because we have necessarily emerged from it; it has come and gone and yet its luggage is still and will be forever with us. However, for some, like yourself, childhood looms large, perhaps too large. As I have always said to you, my dear Julian, our problems go back to when the life-pattern development goes askew at childhood. And this is the root causality responsible for de-railing us in later life . Ah! Forgive me, I see you wince at my last unwise metaphor!

Morbid: Yes, what with this unexplained, mysterious hold up, the general danger of travelling on privatised, badly-serviced, re-cycled trains, we can expect anything! Just thinking of it makes me feel that one of my funny turns is about to come on!

Dr. Microbe: Don't think of it! Hesitancy, self-doubt, nervousness and excessive fears of small, insignificant things going wrong – all these things are due to your wrong life-movement. Remember my maxim: psychological salvation lies in knowledge that there is a problem due to a misdirected life-movement! When all goes reasonably well in the human psyche there is nothing much to notice for people in my profession; the life-movement is integrated congruently with sociality. But as psychological physicians – such as myself – it is our sad but needful business of probing the problems of distraught human psyches. It is like perhaps being on an archaeological dig, except, dear Julian, the remains in this case are those of childhood development, which are psychologically speaking, very much alive and kicking!

Morbid (somewhat darkly and petulantly): I admit I have problems. I suppose that is why I come to you for consultation and advice. Yet my very nature is not to be sanguine. We are all different. I suppose if I were of your observant and balanced clinical temperament I would also be a psychotherapist. But I am, for all my faults an *artistic* person. Life, for me, is tragic, unsafe and uncertain.

Dr. Microbe: But why so, my dear fellow?

Morbid: Because it just is and always will be for me. If it were not so, I would have changed my personality. I admit that you do greatly help me and I thank you heartily for it, but I cannot see myself changing my leopard spots. I enjoy the beauty of life at its highest levels, but those levels, particularly in the great works of musical composition, are saturated in tragedy as well as glory. Life is not a cup of tea. We are here to suffer if we want to achieve anything worthwhile. And you may laugh, but I have on several occasions heard the voices of Beethoven, Brahms and Liszt in my head. They have all confirmed that it's beauty coupled with punishment down in this place called *Planet Earth*. We are not here to enjoy ourselves. Beauty and its real enjoyment entails a high price. You, of necessity cannot believe that, because to some extent your job is to teach us poor patients that equilibrium is to have your cake and manage to eat at least a good proportion of it.

Dr. Microbe: Tell me more, Julian about your conversations with the voices of Beethoven and Brahms. Interestingly, two master composers who were also considerable pianists. Believe me I am not laughing or wishing to mock you. I am genuinely interested. Do these voices come to you in dreams or in your waking hours? Are these voices helpful to you in your understanding of life and in your playing? Or are they making life harder for you? Do these great musical men criticise you or place very high demands upon you, especially when you are playing their works?

Morbid: (Uneasily, tentatively): You will probably laugh if I tell you of my conversations, which in fact are fairly brief and not always as distinct as I would like them to be. But I have to say, apart from you, these people – or phantoms if you wish to call them so – are my only real friends. It is true I am only a musical insect compared to such giants. But yes, even the glorious Beethoven deigns to speak with me. The voices usually speak to me when I am at the piano. I suddenly seem to also have an inner vision of them in their studios, or wherever they were when they usually composed.

Dr. Microbe: What are the types of things they usually say to you?

Morbid: Well, Beethoven told me firmly but with surprising politeness where I was going wrong in my conception and dynamics in the *Hammerklavier sonata*. In fact I greatly appreciated this advice afterwards, although it was a bit galling at the time. Beethoven is certainly a stickler for performing works to exactly the way he conceives they should be played. In fact I didn't agree with everything he said, but naturally I acquiesced out of sheer reverence for the great man. Brahms, I found quite congenial, talkative and not necessarily like he is commonly portrayed as an impossible mood-swinging bear of a man. He admired my hands and said they were of a good size, similar in fact to his own. And I remember him actually showing me his hands and then proceeding to honour me with playing the opening theme of the sublime *Handel Variations*. After that I distinctly remember him saying: "It's no use trying to play this with tiny woman-like hands. It would be the same as trying to sail down the Danube in a bath tub!" But the best thing of all was when Brahms told me I had exactly the right disposition to be able to play his music effectively. Can you believe that!"

Dr. Microbe: "Right disposition? What exactly do you mean – or what did your visitor, Herr Brahms mean by that?

Morbid: Yes, Brahms told me it's no good at all being of a cheerful disposition attempting to play his music. One must be decidedly melancholic and indeed he went so far as to tell me that it is a great advantage to be living on the verge of constant acute depression. He actually praised me on this account. I remember very distinctly his words to me: "Julian, my boy, you have exactly the melancholic outlook necessary to play my music with the subtle inner accuracy it demands. Well done, my boy! And for goodness sake don't let anyone cure you of your fine and healthy melancholy and depressive tendencies. That would be fatal for interpreting my works." I remember on another occasion when Brahms said much the same thing. Now what was it he said? Ah, yes, he said something like: "Life is far more interesting and agreeable being unhappy. Contrary to the belief of the world, it is being sociable which is too much of a strain. No great lasting work comes out of sociability. Mark me! Melancholy is the healing way of survival. Always remember that my dear boy, beauty doesn't arise out of conviviality!"

Dr. Microbe: That is most interesting. Herr Brahms even instructed you not to seek a remedy for your inner problems. This apparition of Brahms believed like yourself that beauty – musical excellence – comes out of suffering. That is an interesting co-incidence of thought! So do you then become or in a sense – re-embody – these great composers like Brahms when you play their piano compositions?

Morbid: Yes, it is true I play like a Beethoven or Brahms at times but sadly it is only in some sections of their music that I am able to do so and sometimes when my interpretation and inspiration are off-target or my execution is off-par, everything goes to pot. That is the whole trouble, my problem, that perfection evades me. If I do reach it, it is only momentarily.

Dr. Microbe: You are a perfectionist of course. You conceive in your mind the ideal result, the perfect product of sound and expression and it hurts and torments you that you can at best only attain this perfection momentarily. I understand, that as a very fine musician you want to attain perfection in your art. But the problem in your case, Julian is that this desire for perfection has invaded your whole life movement.

Morbid: I can't be other than I am. The pieces of music I play are like life-tasks to be solved. My best and only constant friend is the piano. But because of my imperfections it often becomes the vehicle of my defeat. I have to overcome myself and my limitations or else the battle is lost.

Dr. Microbe: But Julian it is precisely this pressure you constantly exert on yourself which rules your life movement. Are there not many paths in life? Are there not also differing ways of interpreting a sonata of Beethoven, for instance? Life is such that we must not expect to hit the bulls-eye as a matter of course. Many of the highest, the most sublime geniuses did not manage to stay at the mountain's apex for more than a fractional percentage of their lives. You have of course heard the expression: "Homer nodded". Well, most of us lesser mortals are like constantly nodding dogs! But you should be pleased that as a result of admirable and committed musical abilities your percentage of nodding is fairly negligible. If you saw life more as a constant yet positive learning-curve instead of as a battle you could relax that much more. Let us be honest, Julian, you see everything in struggle – combat – terms. You tell me you have no close friends – that the only woman in your life was your mother… Now with your great pianistic gifts, surely you could have met not only understanding and intelligent friends but probably also a sympathetic and attractive woman? We are not islands as the poet said; we need each other for support and encouragement. Why be such a loner, cutting yourself off from others in this desperate striving always for perfection? Is not your detachment – your avoidance of close ties with other people – also bound up with seeing them also as imperfect musical performances, albeit imperfect life performances? But my dear Julian, it is our nature to be imperfect! We are what we are! We can modify to some extent – improve in some degrees, but no more than that. Just as you make too high demands of yourself, you make too high demands of your fellow human travellers.

Morbid, (rather darkly, after this onslaught): If it wasn't for the real world outside – real to most people and you, but not to me – I would probably be fine! You see I have been born on the wrong planet – or born in an epoch where I am condemned to be apart from others. Hence, I suppose that is why I get on better with my great voices from the past. You may laugh, I know, but I have, apart from when I play the piano, nothing in common with other human beings. Most people – apart from you – cannot be trusted. People are generally like those four empty-headed chatterboxes behind us. They could be from the media spying on us. You simply can't trust anyone. And as for women, yes it's true I've never met one who matched the standards of my mother.

Dr. Microbe (mischievously and changing the subject): Going back to your composers' voices, have you ever heard from Franz Liszt? Might not at least, the young Liszt have pointed out to you that your recent profoundly moving Royal Festival Hall concert renditions of his *Dante Sonata* and *Vallee d'Obermann*, have probably left some lovely, discriminating woman with a great crush on you? You fail to appreciate that you *do* convey your personality and its gifts outwards to others. Is it not the case, Julian, that all your repressed, locked-up desires for human love and companionship are teeming their way out in the concert hall. Music-making is your release of libido…

Morbid (quickly): Oh, no, no, not at all. That is the wrong end of the stick, I assure you. I play as my only means of survival. That is all I have. But women! I don't trust or understand them, I never could fathom them – they're too dangerous! No, better off without them. No, I don't as a rule like to get involved in that direction.

71

Dr. Microbe, (ironical and shaking his head): And yet you had such a close relationship with your late mother! Again, we are back to the bugbear of perfectionism, Julian! How many of your significant dreams which you have related to me have involved beautiful, intelligent women – in short, perfect women. And the situations follow a common pattern. These dream women, all I suggest, have facets of your very remarkable – but let me say it – dominating mother. And what happens in these dreams? Just as you seem to make some sort of contact with these perfect women figures – they vanish, they elude you. Is not all this a regressive wish for the return of your mother? Perfection for you in terms of human relationships is nothing more than a return into the womb of motherhood; it is the great escape which in fact never happens, nor never can happen. But how many men seek it in their desire to reincarnate their mothers and how many women seek it in their desire to reincarnate their fathers! However, what is happening, Julian, is merely projection, projection, as I have said to you many times! Alas, we cannot project our parents – esteemed by us as they may be – onto a reality which is composed of different individual people. It is not fair, not right and moreover demands the impossible from people who are *not* our esteemed parents. And therefore what is the end result? Just as the so-called perfect mother-type women of your dream disappear, because you can never bring back your mother again, so too do people – especially women – recede from you; you demand too much of them and therefore they can never come up to scratch, as it were. You build, do you not, a chasm between yourself and the opposite sex? You do not like them, but only because they do not fulfil an impossible criteria!

Moribid: You will go on about my dreams about women! What is wrong about having certain standards in life? Can I help it if I find women too problematic in reality because they are as a rule incapable of understanding the depths of a sublime Beethoven sonata? What good is a concern with fashion, soap-operas and all that kind of trivia when one must attend to the wound of life; that is, one must focus on what it is to suffer as a human being? Now, my mother understood something about that. Nor do I deny my mother was a marvellous pianist and overlooked composer. However, you forget that I also looked up to my father who was an excellent viola player. He may have been a weaker character than my mother, dying as a result of his breakdown while I was still a young boy. Yet I look up to him as much as my mother…So I am not the obsessed mother's boy you think I am.

Microbe: No it is, I agree, more complicated than just that. You also sometimes dream about perfect male friends. Yes, your dreams consist so often of the frustration of meeting a perfect person or persons – male or female – only to find that at that very felicitous moment of a significantly deep meeting point, the person or persons in question disappointingly disappears. The dream ends as utopia mischievously fades away. It fades away because it is a dream. But the dream itself points to the unreality – the fantasy basis of your expectations from other people. My dear Julian, with regard to other people you are like a chess player who will perhaps play his Pawns and even begrudgingly play a Knight, but never bring his more important pieces into action such as Rooks, Bishops and Queen. Only in the heights and depths of your music do you experience freedom; there you play all your key chess pieces – and even then it is often a driven sort of freedom. But think what you could do in your life – in the world of human relationships – if, without any great fear you started putting into action all your chess pieces! Remember, my friend, what the great Bard said: "Ripeness is all".

After this last apparent metaphorical summation of our virtuoso pianist, Julian Morbid was for the moment left dazed and like a child who has no more toys to throw out of his pram. But now we must leave our dear Dr. Microbe and his recalcitrant, yet somehow endearing patient, Julian Morbid, to spend some time with the four earnestly engaged men seated at the rear of the First Class compartment.

FURTHER IDEAS IN MOTION

Seated on that same train from King's Cross bound to Cambridge were the previously mentioned four men, who also aspired thereafter to arrive at *Lower Wanton End*. They were located at the other end of the First Class carriage and engaged intently and intellectually with great issues which appeared to engross each of their fervent attentions. As we now move into their focus range, the man first encountered is a square jawed fellow of medium height with an imposing wide forehead, lightly decorated by some receding, distinguished grey hair. He also is equipped with a sharp, determined nose, firm mouth and steely grey yet animated eyes. Our gentleman is Dr. Timothy Tadpole, a G.P., a generally affable urbane man and a convinced humanist in his late fifties, who is also a keen amateur astronomer. He is mild and controlled enough apart from when he is aroused by his pet subject of science and especially neo-Darwinian evolution; then it is that Dr. Tadpole's personality traits chemically undergo a kind of osmosis. This results in a waspish, argumentative, fully-armoured, exclamation marked version of that aforesaid, reasonable and committed medical practitioner. At the moment Dr. Tadpole's attention is wholly focused on Canon Donald Hollow, who is sitting directly opposite him in the group of four. Canon Hollow, a neo-Lamarckian evolutionist, sports a venerable Darwinian-type beard which engulfs his lower face. He has just been enthusing about the afore mentioned (either infamous or famous) French naturalist. The Canon is a good friend of Dr. Tadpole and both of them are also good friends of our dear friend, ex-Bishop Boffo. Donald Hollow, in his early sixties, exhibits a tallish, languidly stooping figure and speaks with at times an irritatingly over articulated velvet-voice. For a reason known only in his own nebulous depths, he is much given to using the grammatical varieties of the adjective: *particular.* As a Canon, our ecclesiastical gentleman is quite happy to espouse a subjectively orientated Christianity, somewhat shorn of its classical doctrines which he believes are not helpful for the post-modern age. One might add here that to some of his acquaintances such as Dr. Tadpole, the Canon has acquired the mischievous nickname of "Giraffe", which refers both to his height and neo-Lamarckian views. We catch the Doctor and Canon in mid-debate.

Dr. Tadpole: My dear Donald, don't please recite those too well known giraffe, elephant or wading bird illustrations yet again! We all know that according to Monsieur Lamarck, want fulfilment – or perhaps better – Freudian wish fulfilment is the key to it all! I want to reach the leaves, fruit or whatever is out of my reach. Simple, if I happen to be a giraffe I stretch out my neck and my forelegs. Hey presto, evolution in a jiffy!

Canon Hollow: Oh, come now, Timothy, that is a rather unfair travesty of Lamarck. Do at least apply some particularisation to your comments!

Dr. Tadpole: But my dear fellow, where would Lamarckian supporters be without their famous giraffes? Let's face it, the man was in terms of evolution a primitive weather-forecaster! Lamarck and his invisible, nervous fluids; it's all in the vital fluids, my boy! Who on earth today would want to plough through *The Philosophie Zoologique* to find out about such discredited, laughable theories? But of course you are not deterred, are you, my good Canon? Now take *The Origin of Species*, that is where you have your readable best seller!

Here a young man called Guy St. Bland interjected: "But uncle Timothy, you are straying away as usual from the relevant issue, ha, ha, ha!" The young man in question, nephew to Dr. Tadpole, was a precocious, sceptically-minded, ex-philosophy and sociology student in his late twenties, now turned to free-lance writing and editor of his own recently created intellectual forum magazine: *Social Sophist Today*. Guy St. Bland, was of short build, displaying a high forehead with blondish tangle of hair. This young maverick also in suitable Shelleyian mode emblazoned the air waves with a rather high-pitched voice, which could at times veer towards an incipient shriek. Another endearing trademark was a tendency to both punctuate and close his conversation with something akin to a naughty six-form schoolboy laugh, particularly so after thinking he had said something apposite.

Dr. Tadpole (undeterred, now moving up a few gears): How can you answer disproved nonsense? Lamarck knew nothing of natural selection. That insurmountable fact speaks for itself. Without natural selection all you get is this wishy-washy "acquired characteristics". So what? I don't discount adaptation. Nor did Darwin. However, Lamarck's theory, if you can call it that, is too casual a view in terms of real evolutionary theory. Desire, wants, a bit of muscular stretching and that's all there is to it! Far too easy because life is not a gentle utopia of pass-the-parcel acquired family and communal traits! It's a tough struggle which stretches over generations; we all know that. Evolutionary progress is characterised by competition which in terms of survival means outsmarting rivals and predators. Lamarck, with his nice straight line of progression is far too tidy and simplistic. In terms of logic, mutation is messy, random – and tending to a more branching type of development. It's life and life develops through survival – where it can and when it can. Good gracious, my dear fellow, look around you! Look at your own delightfully kept garden, which as you say, is hard work maintaining. Where do the strongest weeds come from? Why does your favourite fragile plant – if you do not take very careful precautions – get eaten up or choked out of life's race by some nasty little or not so little slug or weed? Why, because the nasty slug or weed is stronger and knows how to survive! So what if slugs and weeds are just nasty, random survival results; they have nevertheless been rubber stamped for continued existence by natural selection. The battle for survival is raging in every nook and cranny of creation. Weeds, who planted them? Natural design? Well, you, the gardener certainly did not plant them like you carefully plant your Gladiolus and other hardy perennials. No, these pests come themselves, unbidden, uninvited! Natural selection, that's what gives them their licence to exist and their passport to come and compete in the arena of life. If the mutation is strong enough it's a case of successful self-design even if you're a mere slug! And now these avowed foes of yours, dear Canon, in terms of maintaining their mandate for self-survival – they need to invade and utilise a conducive environment such as your prized garden! And these garden enemies know in their simple, blind instinctual way that they have the strength to make a big fight of it. In fact, without your assiduous weeding or weed killers, they would win!

St. Bland: Aha, I knew it! We are all in reality either flowers or weeds! Now which ones of us are the roses and which are of the thistle variety? Let's candidly all own up!

Canon Holloway: (irritated, yet with cool composure): Your attacks, Timothy, centre on a failure to particularise fairly. The first thing to say in reply is that Lamarck is *the* founder of evolution – not Darwin. And this is the particularised truth of the matter. Everything is already there in Lamarck, fifty years before Darwin got out of bed! For a start, apart from the ground-breaking idea of acquired characteristics with its inherent prefiguring of genetics, we can also credit Lamarck with fossil record awareness – the new radical understanding of a massive time-scale going far beyond the accepted biblical creation theory of six thousand years. And in this respect Lamarck is also well in advance of Charles Lyell's geological based ideas. But furthermore, let us remember Lamarck's new particularistic understanding of development in terms of from simple to the complex; in others words, a dramatic shift from the static view of life to the idea of mobility – progress, in a word! Moreover, let us also give him credit for already possessing a good understanding of such things as survival struggle, the importance of growth or its opposite, atrophy; the importance too of such things as changes of habits and favourable or unfavourable geographical circumstances. And I could go on! But the point is, dear Timothy, that Lamarck's evolution – if taken up – would make us more human, rather than your neo-Darwinian law of the fittest, which makes us all like competitive breeding rabbits! Lamarck offers us a *directed evolution*; purpose coupled with co-operation rather than competition. That is, the species strives ideally *as a whole* to make itself fit, rather than sink down to a random survival of the fittest ones within it. In fact, we would not be sitting here today in a civilised technological world except for the significant, particularistic development of co-operation occurring through the history of *homo sapiens*. Leave it to Darwinian theory and humankind would only be a total pawn to random mutations, and where would that get us? Precisely nowhere. Moreover, natural selection is nothing but a theory of purposeless and indeed, destructive warfare! Surely any civilised person wants to move away from *that*. Darwin's so-called great discovery amounts to nothing more than Thomas Hobbes' depressing view of the aggressive individual transcribed into terms of biological aggrandisement. We need instead Lamarck's evolutionary basis, which is purpose driven, and is indeed sensitive, less arbitrary, less cruel in its optimistic openness to co-operation of the species.

St. Bland: Bravo, bravo, excellent Canon! One in the eye for Hobbes as well! Darwin and Hobbes do make a miserable pair, don't they, with their respective, cheerful views about humanity and evolution! Well, what do you say to all that, uncle Timothy? Are you now not roundly defeated with your beloved natural selection a bleeding concept on its own field of battle, killed with Lamarck's evolutionary kindness, as it were? Ha, ha, ha!

Dr. Tadpole (ignoring this insolent interjection and blowing up a head of steam):

Alright, take yet another example. Look at today's great

supermarket chains. Look how they demonstrate natural selection. Remember once, years ago, your nice little family run shops: greengrocers, butchers, ironmongers, fishmongers, tailors, dressmakers, etc and etc. Now all of them regrettably no longer in existence. Wallop, the larger rapacious sharks have swallowed them all up! So how does all this rampant economic hegemony occur? It certainly has nothing to do with your supposed Lamarck's inherited species improvements. If it was all as utopian as merely passing on acquired characteristics for the good of all, we would have a nice level playing field. Well, of course that just isn't the case! Our dear little family grocer of several generations back, who just wants to make an honest, unspectacular living – what chance does he or she stand against the multi-billionaire food giant corporations, who plan their conquests with the painstaking precision of military commanders? This is reality, my dear man, the reality of what goes on in our world today of unashamed neo-liberalism. Read a book about it if you don't believe me! Of course it would be nice if this wasn't so, but fairness, decency and egalitarianism are just about as chimerical in a free-market world as the notion of evolution minus natural selection!

At this point, enter into the fray our remaining, hitherto silent member of the quartet of train-journeying friends. Silent so far, but nevertheless carefully following and attentively scrutinising the foregoing debate. Our patient and controlled man is Father Godfrey Goodbalance, a Jesuit Priest in his early seventies. He offers a small, rather closed up walnut-lined face, penetrated by a gently ironic and sagacious expression. His shrewd, somewhat squinting eyes hide behind glasses reminiscent of NHS spectacles from the nineteen-fifties.

Father Goodbalance: Are we not now changing our criterion from the scientific dimension to the moral-stroke religious dimension? Injustice as we all know belongs to the domain of human greed. Thus, Timothy, when you talk about planned calculation – premeditated selfishness – are you not in effect talking about a deliberate choosing, which issues in a misuse of human freedom; what I would call in my profession, and presumably in yours, Donald, human sinfulness? You see, when we move up the creation ladder past the merely instinctive species – beyond all those creatures lacking the faculty of self-consciousness, we reach human beings, some of them unfortunately ruled by massive self-interest, particularly those as you just now mentioned; those who own and organise the big food-chain corporations. My point is that natural selection is an inappropriate paradigm to use in explaining the actions of human beings who badly misuse their divinely-given freedom by violating the freedom of others. Natural selection, in the way you have just referred to it, suggests a world where everything, including human beings (that means us), is dominated by a blind, determinist force. And if that is the case, assuming we are not utter hedonists, but intelligent people, we might as well all become Roman stoics or French existentialists.

St. Bland: Ha, ha, ha! Another deadly salvo in your direction, uncle Timothy! Now we are not just dealing with merely human opposition – Jean-Baptiste de Lamarck – but rather with religion – the transcendent – and to be more precise, the three-in-one Holy Trinity! How will you now cope with such cosmic odds arrayed against you?

Dr. Tadpole: Natural selection means there is no point

in God. He or whatever he is simply doesn't come into it. Nature does everything on its own – self-design!

Canon Hollow: I greatly wonder how you can equate evolutionary progress with such a random, not to say capricious, haphazard method. Now Lamarckian evolution does concede the existence of an Ultimate Being and if that is so such a Being must have responsibility for the design aspect which confronts our gaze everywhere in the various particularities of Creation. In particular, how can you have self-design – design by accident, as it were – when you rule out any concept of a designer? Without a designer the word design can have no meaning whatsoever.

Dr. Tadpole: I don't see why not. You can have Creation without a Creator; that to me has certainly never been a problem. This is a do-it-yourself universe. It is merely a matter of giving things time – yes, millions, billions of years, I grant you – and when chance is magnified to such a colossal extent, then random self-design can occur. Of course, we can't think in such unimaginable time-blocks; it isn't natural for us to do so, yet that is nevertheless the way evolution works. That is the way life on planet earth has developed; over aeons and aeons developmental opportunities will arise. The cosmic roulette wheel, if it goes round long enough, will eventually come up with the number that makes possible a signal breakthrough in the progress of species. So what if it does take aeons and aeons? The real point is that it *does happen* and billions of years later we are here to tell the tale. Life on earth's huge, virtually mind-stunning time scale is precisely what is necessary for the evolution of species, including our own *homo sapiens*. This is the only way evolution can develop; everything can self-design itself, even a mollusc, given the required time. We are also self-designed animals, albeit the most advanced there is so far.

Canon Hollow: Do-it-yourself design, indeed! Adaptation, yes, as per Lamarck's important evolutionary insight that species change their characteristics in response to environmental changes. But adaptation is essentially co-operation as opposed to the ugly, Darwinian, "winner takes all" scenario. This Lamarckian basis surely suggests to us that evolution *is* purposeful, being a responsive, sensitive and working relationship between species and their surroundings. It is not – and this is a particularly important point – merely your Darwinian survivalist opportunism; it's collaboration, my dear Timothy! Nature works in a much more integrated way than it is given credit for. Lamarck understood that but Darwin didn't. Consequently your fictitious Darwinian highwaymen, those opportunist mutations, who supposedly plunder for their own advantage evolution's ponderous stagecoach, leave us with a law of the jungle which in turn leaves us with a less meaningful rather than more meaningful world.

St. Bland: Another direct hit, ha, ha! That is what you get uncle for being such an absolutist neo-Darwinian!

Dr. Tadpole (unruffled): Meaningful, in what sense? Design in the utopian, Godly sense, I suppose. Randomness, individual mutation, survival, all these things carry their own self-contained meaning. But don't look any further than that. Life on earth does not have a pre-planned communal meaning. The universe is not one big happy family system as God-idealists would love to think. The world is composed of parts, infinite parts. They don't come together nicely like some giant cosmic jigsaw puzzle. Creation is precisely a random evolving. This, as I have just said, involves chance over a stupendous framework of time. The formation of the first single cells and gradually the joining of billions upon billions of these, combining in ever-increasing complexity to make humans – but not through any fanciful supernatural designer! Evolution is all about the law of infinite probability over vast gulfs of time. Don't, my dear Father, look for any meaning beyond that. There is absolutely no warrant or evidence to build Eden-like visions, wrongly assuming evolution as the result of integrated design. Remember, even members of the same species have differing organisms. Your dim (compared to Darwin) Lamarck didn't notice or understand this now obvious fact: divergence. But it is precisely these random variations within the species which help the species as a whole to ultimately adapt, survive. Natural selection, my good Canon, that's the key to why we're here at all today! And it doesn't happen overnight! A whole species does not change just because one elephant decides to start stretching its trunk. All it means is that the lazy, dim elephants will probably die off, whereas the instinctually more astute ones will evolve survival techniques, live and produce more offspring. Natural selection in a nutshell! There is competition within each species and a good job too, else we would end up with a dead-end natural world and dead-end human world. In fact without competition, with its vital regulative and progressive roles, all species would invariably die out! It's a pity your dear Monsieur Lamarck was not around long enough to read Darwin's great masterpiece – then he would have realized this astoundingly crucial fact!

St. Bland: So if you are dumbo the elephant you don't get into the school cricket eleven, ha, ha, ha! Down with lazy elephants! Let's all be competitive; up the rat-race! Ha, ha!

Canon Hollow (regally ignoring St. Bland's interjection): Of course, nature does not integrate in a *consciously volitional sense*, but it is nevertheless pre-planned to evolve, advance by integration. After all, what are families and larger communities for? Lamarck respected the fact that there *are* regulative laws or principles of nature. And if you have laws, then it follows there must be some sort of base, some foundations and consequently a higher meaning and purpose to life.

Father Good balance (briskly joining in): From the admission that there are laws, principles of nature, it would seem quite logical to then enquire how they happen to be there. Science and certainly evolution are incapable of answering the question why these laws or principles exist. Why should there be gravity, proportion in living matter, structure, extension, space, weight, light, darkness, warmth and cold, etc and etc.? I personally believe all this is due to a Father Creator God who is a designer. However, He designs by processes subject often to massive time scales, and these processes work according to laws of nature. And what are laws of nature but laws of God's Creation – laws of divine ordained necessity – which allow both for regularity and modulations of development within those regularities. In other words, our good Creator doesn't design directly, but rather cumulatively – in the evolutionary sense – through His laws of nature. The laws of nature are nothing other than a design blueprint. Evolution without design is merely cosmic anarchy!

Dr. Tadpole: The world works by itself! The supposed

laws, principles of nature are merely what has resulted from a very, very old world (at least in terms of our human conceiving of time). Any regularity, any semblance of order has therefore evolved out of a process of massive time-scale proportions. If there is anything remotely like a system, the only one I know of is natural selection's filtering mechanism which enables survival and progress.

Canon Hollow: Yes, natural selection is really nothing other than an evolutionary super-market check-out point for certain successful adaptations. But these checked- out "products" have *already* been produced by adaptive necessity and co-operation, not by random mutation and blind survival. That is to say, natural selection is not an efficient cause in itself, but unfortunately, this is precisely the abiding illusion of neo-Darwinism. The truth, my dear Timothy, which you continually refuse to swallow, is that Lamarck discovered the primary factors of evolution and Darwin discovered the secondary factors which include your beloved and highly overrated natural selection. What actually is natural selection able to tell us about the origin of species? All it gives us are the results of evolutionary modifications, but it cannot show us how such changes originated. Lamarck's greatness lies in that he was the first to find the real laws of change and thus of origin.

St. Bland: Oh, sacrilege, from you of all people, Canon Hollow! To enter the holies of holies and utter such desecrating words! You have been floored now, uncle Timothy. What hope is left when Darwin's very inner evolutionary altar has been defiled!

Dr. Tadpole (impatiently but unperturbed): Rubbish! Darwin's landmark discovery of natural selection is the main reason for Lamarck's oblivion today. And it also puts the Judaic-Christian God out of employment! You can forget Lamarck, your great primeval scientist who was dumb enough to believe in spontaneous generation. You can also forget a God who spontaneously produces fully developed species, from out of his magic hat!

Father Goodbalance: Of course God didn't create nature in a perfect static, immutable sense. God's Creation has its laws of development but within these laws there is scope for freedom. Thus, Timothy, it is no good arguing for instance that the Panda's acquired thumb – through evolution – means that God was a very poor original designer! Rather it merely means that God allows a freedom of evolutionary progression to develop. Just as our good Creator never intended to create perfect human puppets, neither did He intend to create in just one go, as it were, a perfect, un-problematical nature and animal kingdom. Even nature – particularly the higher animals – has been given a certain freedom to develop as it goes along. What I am thus saying is that natural selection does not rule out God. The former is merely an associated part of the mechanism of freedom the Creator has given to all living things, including us.

Dr. Tadpole: Very clever, my dear Godfrey, but it still needs explaining where we human beings have come from. I thought in Christian terms we were supposed to have come from God's very image. How is that idea to be squared with our freedom of evolutionary development? For if we were supposedly created in God's own likeness, we must of necessity be separately created species, thus overleaping the process of evolution and with it natural selection. We just pop out of a cosmic magician's hat! Now what is rational about a divine conjuring trick, when all the evidence points to the cumulative, long-drawn out evolution from swampy, murky amoeba onwards!

St. Bland: It is one thing us developing and adapting through mutations and natural selection, but I personally draw the line at having originally, billions of years ago mutated from primeval sludge. From sludge to Einstein, that's quite an evolution, ha, ha, ha!

Canon Hollow: I must second that reaction in terms of the badly particularised terms of your reference, Timothy.

Father Goodbalance: I agree. The infinitely rich and noble concept of humanity deserves something better than primeval sludge as its starting point. Self-consciousness is the proper marking-off point for *homo sapiens*. Self-consciousness is a huge qualitative difference of kind which Darwinists or any other evolutionists have never been able to account for. It is obviously a significant branching off from the evolutionary series trajectory up to that point. The reason for this may well be that this was the point where our Creator had decided that *we* – or rather our first true human ancestors – should enter into the picture!

Dr. Tadpole (undaunted): God the magician again! The Adam and Eve special dispensation! What's wrong with amoeba out of a primeval stew? Everything has to have its elementary starting point. Look at your helpless baby which wets itself and can't even utter a single comprehensible sentence! All of us have been at that rudimentary stage, but now we are adults able to engage in debate, utilising the full capacities of our developed brains. Therefore in the evolutionary scale what does it matter where the start point is as long as there is development? The fact of progress, that there is evolution – that we have arisen from its processes – is what is important! Scientific study of the evolutionary series clearly evidences a progression after billions of years to a prototype human conclusion with the first hominids. However, according to the *Genesis* biblical account, human beings in the shape of Adam and Eve arrive fully developed, cutting out all the evolutionary middle-men, so to speak! Our first theological ancestors don't even have to come out of an embryo – how convenient! So, my dear Father, even if you try and go along with evolution, as God's supposed way of doing things, you still have a big problem when you come to human beings!

St. Bland: Yes, certainly, when we come to good old Adam and Eve! You will now no doubt tell us, Father Godfrey, that Plan A was the Garden of Eden, which our naughty first ancestors messed up through being conned by a crafty snake salesman offering them high-powered, knowledge inducing apples. The result was that A & E got kicked out of the garden and demoted into the evolutionary series! God was highly inconvenienced and thus had to scrap Plan A and resort to Plan B!

Father Goodbalance: But I don't take a literal view of Adam and Eve and nor necessarily did the ancient writer or writers responsible for the *Genesis* Creation and Fall accounts. Adam and Eve, as I see it, rather represent the whole of the human race, at all times throughout human history. Having said that, they must also represent some kind of divine 'jump' within creation. Figuratively as well as in reality, they represent an unprecedented species development resulting from unfathomable grace; an incredible divinely-directed evolutionary step-forward whereby we have human creatures made in the Creator's image. An image, by the way, which has (before the fall), an extraordinary privilege of being able to reflect God through the mirror of self-consciousness.

St. Bland: Perhaps a rather double-edged gift, Father Godfrey. I, for instance, have always been self-conscious of my lack of height! Just think of a world without self-consciousness. No hang-ups, no terrible soul-searching, We could all get on happily with the life business without feeling guilty and continually measuring ourselves against one another! Ha, ha, ha!

Father Good balance (somewhat darkly): And what of morality?

Canon Hollow: My dear Father Godfrey, I so far agree with you. However, in terms of the so-called fall in *Genesis,* I sincerely trust you do not align yourself with Saint Augustine's now dated and appalling Original Sin extrapolation.

Father Goodbalance: Original Sin is of course, as you say, an extrapolation from *Genesis,* therefore it is in itself not a Biblical ordinance. The possibility of sin comes in with the freedom engendered through a special being created with self-consciousness. We and all human beings, unless we are seriously mentally deficient, fall into that category. Consciousness, the fall and sin are inter-related terms. The fall begins when consciousness begins. The history of consciousness is the ongoing history of the fall which is perpetuated in every single human being. The first conscious human beings fell into sin and the pattern was set thereafter in a flawed human condition. It does not greatly matter who were the first 'original human parents'. The fact of a fall and an ongoing fall is what alone matters. It happens every day and throughout human history because the human race is fundamentally flawed and therefore disobedient to God. Sin, itself, is simply the result of using our free-will to make a bad choice which will hurt our Maker and our fellow beings. Sin is therefore the tough price we humans pay for this most precious gift of freedom. As our renowned Palaeontologist Jesuit, Teilhard De Chardin has suggested, in his provocatively original writings, the human fall is concomitant with Creation. For the very idea of Creation obviously implies progress – something existing from nothing – and where you have progress, in terms of living things, freedom must be predicated. However, we humans, created in God's image – endowed with the extraordinary gift of self-consciousness – must above all the rest of Creation, bear the responsibility for freedom and its all too prevalent misuse.

Cannon Hollow: As far as I can see, there is not much else but confusion in Teilhard De Chardin. He seems to think the whole human race will end up being a Christianised version of Nietzsche's superman. All very nice, but in today's dysfunctional international and domestic world, the facts simply don't bear out such a pleasant pipe-dream.

Father Goodbalance: He admittedly tends to rather naively view sin as something which can be ultimately ironed out if evolution is directed properly. This of course would tend to a universalist notion of human salvation. And I must agree that that sort of optimism is hardly warranted when we face the facts of human reality.

St. Bland (suddenly, excitedly): Well, that is our noble Jesuit Palaeontologist sorted out! Why don't we now move to a far more relevant philosophical figure, Jean Paul Sartre, who posed the only really interesting question there is: Why is there anything at all? Why something rather than nothing?

And from this stem other questions: If there is a God, why should he make supposedly two perfect human beings, who in one unguarded moment let themselves be tricked and consequently ruin everything for themselves and for everyone else, including us? Or, looking at the scientific, evolutionary view, why should there be such a laborious process with its colossal wastefulness and consequent ongoing misery along the way, for animals and humans alike? What is the point of all the struggle, us being here and then dying? Why do we need to be here at all?

Dr. Tadpole (now rattled): For goodness sake, Guy, I would have thought my Darwinist account should have made those type of questions irrelevant! The "whys" aren't important – the fact that there *is* something and it's developed into us is the only thing that matters. Let's not enter now into the delusive questions of metaphysics! Try reading a book – *The Origin of Species* would be ideal. That would hopefully keep you quiet for a bit!

Just then the environs of Cambridge swung into the four travellers' view and with that Timothy Tadpole breathed an extreme sigh of relief. Even he, who when debate required it, possessed such a gusto of energy, had no wish to plough the ontological depths of Guy St. Bland's sudden, reckless questions. And so perhaps we, the unseen onlookers should also for the moment breath a sigh of relief.

CHAPTER SIX

AN AFTERNOON WALK

Seventy years ago, when describing a rural scene in East Anglia, the would-be writer might have still had some justification for extolling, by re-animating to the best of his or her abilities, the green and soothing pastoral delights of Shakespeare's dear old Albion. Unfortunately, in the cold, mercenary and bulldozed reality of the twenty-first century, our contemporary writer would be hard put to do much else than strain to resuscitate a desecrated and dying corpse with the dead machinery of possibly charming but wholly inapplicable poetry.

If one is going to have a rural idyll, it follows there must be certain ingredients present. A principal ingredient would be the unwavering, good shepherd, that commendable bucolic figure, so deeply committed to his woolly flock. However, in our present glorious technocratic age, that once bulwark of Arcadia would not be so readily apparent, if apparent at all. In fact, in many areas, neither would his woolly flock be readily apparent. Where too would one now find abundant cattle, healthy, luxuriant hedges, meadows and trees in their full resplendent prime of life – such as oaks, elms, sycamores, beeches and horse chestnuts?

Arcadian idylls are, as we all know, only a non-existent

shepherd's pipe dream. Admittedly, they have tended to make pleasing, even beautiful poetry, ever since particularly the time of Virgil's eclogues. And who cannot feel a little more connected to this strange, mysterious and forbidding universe we inhabit, while having a peaceful afternoon stroll amidst pleasant vistas, lush woodland, meadows and fertile fields – if they indeed still existed? So it is we find the possibly unlikely connection of Reverend Halo and Sir Terence Treadboards engaged upon a short early afternoon stroll while Percival "Boffo" Evergreen, Muriel Muffin and Lucinda Halo are busy with last minute hospitality arrangements for the soon expected weekend guests – who will be staying either at the Rectory or in the overflow bed chambers within *Wanton Windmill.*

Our two friends, who do not really have that much in common, nevertheless do share a generalised gloomy pessimism, lamenting in their respective agnostic and theological contexts the wanton wickedness of contemporary life. They are found walking down the little side lane at *Lower Wanton End*, which leads off at one end from *Wanton End Rectory* and its Windmill.

Halo: I agree, Sir Terence, that as countryside goes, this is rather desolate, showing signs of savage depravity from those who have not heeded the good Lord's command to be responsible stewards. However, this land still is blessed with quietness through the great Creator's unique stamp of benevolence and abundance. It is at least better than the iniquity of those towers of Babel – I mean, the cities, where all sorts of temptations can worm their defiling way into even the pure and innocent. Ah, such was once, my dear daughter, Esther! Now, alack, what should have crowned my last ripe years with parental joy, has turned to bitter wormwood and ashes – that she should have been plucked from me in this way! Yes, to go off with some devil's apprentice – to sell her innocence to such depraved, damned souls. It does not bear thinking about! Lost, lost, lost, snatched out of the Kingdom! Ah, yes, she should never have gone to Gridlington – never to a city, where wickedness abounds. Yea, these are the dens of iniquity, where faith falters, resolution fails, for in the corrupt cities the devil and his minions are afoot with boundless mischief!

Treadboards: I must disagree with you there. Cities are surely no more worse than anywhere else for vice. Yes, there is more corruption in cities, but only relatively so in terms of their greater population. But that is merely increased probability of wantonness purely because of larger numbers. I read once in your little black book that some prophet – Jeremiah, I think – called the human heart deceitful beyond all things. Well, I now fully see he obviously had a point there – although he could have added it was women who were mainly the ones with deceitful hearts! The heart can be deceitful wherever it happens to be – city or village. No, my dear Halo, the city with its theatres, concert halls, opera houses, art galleries and museums, offers aesthetic cultivation – the chance for meaningful grandness and intelligent discrimination. What is there here in this wasteland, this pathetic so-called rural location – savaged by intensive farming – which can lift up the human spirit? Nothing, nothing, I tell you. And this lamentable desolation naturally reminds me of poor King Lear's sad words (who as you know was much abused by his wanton daughters): "nothing can come from nothing". As you know, I too lost a dear but headstrong daughter – as well as a wife, but what difference does it make whether their wanton betrayal of my love and trust took place in a city or a rural location? It could have happened anywhere – the heart of a woman is indeed wanton beyond all hope!

The two men walked on, now feeling equally crestfallen by the renewed remembrances of their past domestic woes. Along the dusty, late summer lane, they both noticed a straggle of wild flowers here and there: ragwort, yarrow, mallow and Sir Terence remarked grimly, "Is this all the so-called rural pastoral can offer us! I boasted a better selection of flowers in my window-box at Kensington!" All his companion could do was to proffer a scowl of commiseration. A little further on by their left, slightly screened by a medium height hedge, behind a little ditch, was a farm with a couple of black silage barns and a cattle pen barn. From the pen's open entrance there could be heard what sounded like the distraught lowing of cows. A burly man was verbally driving a few cows from some other area into the pen's entrance. Sir Terence stopped, peered above the hedge on the ditch's edge and could see some dappled cows herded together in the pen's stalls.

Sir Terence: Poor devils! Penned in their dark prison! Welcome to country ways! And welcome to our compassionate farmers! Look, my dear Halo, there are several empty grazing fields behind that dismal barn where our poor dumb friends are condemned to live this sunny August day! But our fat-head farmer is too lazy to allow his cows the luxury of enjoying their few brief days grazing in the open under a blue sky. The more I see of this poisoned agro-business, country idyll, I wish I were back in London – back in civilisation!

They continued their increasingly miserable perambulation with the Reverend Halo desperately wishing he could redeem this soured pastoral by pointing out at last something positive in the landscape. Then, after having left the barns behind and just past a small cottage on their right, appeared a little field containing cows and calves.

Halo: Ah, but look! I see there are actually a few cows with their calves in the field to our right. Here at last is some evidence of the good Lord's provision of uncorrupted innocence. See how the little calves are basking in the field, enjoying this pleasant August day!

Treadboards: Ha! cows, calves, you say! Yes, indeed a pretty and touching sight for any who have a shred of the Bard's compassion left within them! Six un-penned cows and two calves, we see before us – as much livestock freedom as one might hope to find in this land ruled by the greedy corporate locusts! Yes, here is your biblical innocence – if there be any at all. Let these cows and little calves enjoy washing themselves and basking in the sunshine. Let them enjoy it before they all too soon become sacrificial victims to wanton *homo sapiens!* Yes, let them enjoy their fill today, drink in the blue, glorious air before they are assailed by the deadly smell of the abattoir! Then it will all end up on the butcher's counter, or in the frozen section of some giant supermarket! And that is why, my dear Halo, I have now become a convinced vegetarian. I will not be party any longer to the wanton cruelty of our age.

While the Reverend Halo was thinking how to make a suitable (or any) follow-up remark after this unexpected reaction – or rather outburst – of Sir Terence, the pastoral vista opening up ahead (after a little bend in the lane), now included a few emaciated beeches just behind a ditch to the left-hand side of the two walkers. To their right, behind a skeletal hedge, recently savaged by a mad, remorseless hedge-cutting vehicle, they were presented with a much branch-lolloped and sorry remnant of what was once a reasonably intact horse chestnut tree. Sir Terence, who now seemed to have moved into one of his black mood-swings, looking towards the few scraggy beeches, opined: "One push and the whole poor lot will keel over like ninepins!" At this sardonic remark, George Halo could merely muster a muted, commiserating sigh, and begin to remark: "Well, my dear Sir Terence, one must console ourselves for all this neglect and vandalism of our land; the wrath will fall upon the devil and his minions on Judgement..."

But before the venerable Halo could complete his sentence, Judgement Day, suddenly indeed, appeared to be looming. For, like the proverbial bat out of hell in full fury of speed, bearing down upon the two unsuspecting walkers thundered a 1000cc motorbike driven by Alison Acrylic in an all black leather suit and golden helmet. The long golden hair of the latter's pillion passenger, flashed in the sunlight, streaming out from under a bright red helmet. As the roughly half mile long lane was mainly straight apart from the bend that our walkers were just emerging out of, Alison Acrylic was wantonly opening up the throttle of her metallic speed-monster. It was only at the last moment, seeing the two pedestrians, that the nation's esteemed woman artist managed to swerve slightly away to avoid a direct hit. Sir Terence, taking evasive action and with Hamlet-like aplomb, jumped across the ditch on his left and managed to grab hold of a strong-enough branch from a dilapidated beech. Not so fortunate, our dear Reverend Halo; he also jumped but sadly his trajectory was misconceived through a combination of poor athletics and evil fortune. As the poor fellow landed with a little splash in the ditch he was heard to cry: "It is here, the time of Armageddon has arrived!"

Alison Acrylic, seeing the havoc behind her, and being prodded by her golden-haired pillion passenger, stopped the bike like a decent citizen, turning her vehicle round and driving back to examine the disarray she had unwittingly created. Sir Terence had momentary forgotten his companion, who was now somewhat entangled and constricted in the ditch. Seeing the two helmeted leather-clad figures advancing and all the more incensed at seeing they had lithe, female figures, he, in no uncertain terms gave loud dramatic vent to his anger with Shakespearian interpolations: "Vanish, or I shall give thee thy deserving! But no, do not go, for I will give you thy wanton deserving! Yes – I will have such revenges on you both – you and your wanton friend. I will do such things…they shall be the terrors of the earth to you. Yes, King Lear, Shakespeare, which I don't suppose delinquents like you understand. Nor do you obviously understand speed limits, the highway code and common consideration to other venerable members of society. And if there were such a thing as a village policeman anymore, which unfortunately there isn't in this anarchist, liberal free-for-all country, I would run you both in for terrorism and attempted murder!" Then hearing a groan behind him, Sir Terence remembered his erstwhile companion, George Halo. "Ah, friend Halo, where are you?" "Down here, in this place of dark wrath!" came the answer.

But the golden-haired pillion passenger had already spotted Reverend Halo's plight and was helping to extricate him out of the ditch. Alison Acrylic, more used to being constantly lauded by friends, critics, public and alike, and not used to being berated in such a manner, took off her helmet and exclaimed somewhat petulantly: "Excuse me, there's no need to start being abusive! You both seemed to appear out of nowhere – out of this hidden bend. However, I must accept some blame for this mishap. But let me please check to see if you are alright? I've got St. John's training in first Aid and my companion here, used to be a paramedic, so don't worry!" Sir Terence, on seeing Alison Acrylic now unveiled from her helmet, beheld a round-faced, boyishly attractive late-forties woman. Her platinum dyed hair was cropped above her neck and fringed across her forehead. Although he was now theoretically, ideologically anti the female sex, yet in the physical presence of attractive women, Sir Terence found the old, archetypal chemical stimulations bringing out almost involuntarily his old debonair charm into play. Thus, regaining his graciousness, almost unawares, he replied: "My dear young lady, I am in fact alright – a bit jarred perhaps – but no harm done. Fortunately, despite advancing age, I gained a lot of dexterity in my acting profession – particularly in my days of treading the boards, playing such characters as Hamlet, Richard III, Antony and Romeo. Allow me to introduce myself: Sir Terence Treadboards, now at present retired from the theatre." "Oh, Sir Terence!" gasped Alison Acyrlic with a delighted smile, "goodness, we – my companion and I are invitees through dear Percival – Boffo, to your special birthday weekend. Oh dear, and to think we nearly ran you over!" "Never mind, never mind" replied Sir Terence, now recovered and almost with a beam in his eyes, "no harm done – but wait, how is my dear friend doing, and who is your companion?"

The other pillion rider had also taken off her helmet; however she had been facing away from Sir Terence solicitously tending to George Halo, now out of the ditch. The Reverend who was visibly shaken, seemed also slightly deranged; he was heard periodically to mutter to his young helper: "We are not safe brethren, I tell you, we are not safe, this side of eternity. Therefore take care!" Disregarding these after-the- event, prophetic words, the strong featured, strikingly attractive golden haired lady turned round and exclaimed with a definite semi-Australian twang in her voice: "Hello dad – long time no see! There's no need to worry about your friend, I'll look after him, it's just a little shock – surely you remember I was trained as a nurse – but afterwards I became a paramedic!" Sir Terence visibly rocked on his feet: "Good grief! My long lost wanton daughter, Juniper"! And with that he leapt across to the said young lady with alacrity to embrace her, even against all his apparently fixed determination of never to forgive a recklessly headstrong daughter. In so doing, Juniper, who was steadying Reverend Halo, nearly let go of the latter, almost to his imperilment of once again landing in the ditch. However, she quickly avoided such a repetitious calamity, re-grasping with admirably strong arms her peevish and somewhat bedraggled patient and the situation was saved.

And so we take leave of this pastoral tableau, where out of apparent impending disaster there is now happy recognition and we trust, incipient reconcilement between parent and child. It is indeed, Leontes and his long lost but now found Perdita! Let us then let them both get on with the necessary emotional re-connection process as they walk back together towards the Windmill and Rectory. But we might as well eves-drop on some of their conversation if only to get the most cursory outline concerning how it happened that Juniper was back in her home country.

Juniper: Yes, dad, although I have no regrets about Australia, I admit I was a wombat to get mixed up with that blockhead over there. Anyway, I ditched him late last year. I just got fed up of being knocked around verbally and physically by the bloke. In the end I decided I wasn't going to be his punch bag any more. I had already got a job as a paramedic, which meant I was pretty fit. I now took up classes in Judo and Karate. Then, one day when the donut went for me, I well and truly gave him what for. In fact, I didn't know my own strength by then! I even felt sorry for him when, writhing on the ground in agony, the big Mr. Macho cried like a baby. After that, when he managed to crawl away, I never saw anything more of the pathetic cissie.

Sir Treadboards: But how, my dear girl, did you come to know this Alison Acrylic? And why did you decide to come home?

Juniper: Oh, I'd had enough of macho men and then I happened to meet Alison at a private view of an exhibition she was doing in Sydney. We became really good friends immediately. Alison was seeking to branch out into crayon life-drawing and had been looking for ages to find the right person – someone like me – with a good figure and looks. I was bowled over by the honour. I really loved her type of bright and vivid, epic wall-sized masterpieces. How could I refuse her offer?

Sir Treadboards (with uncertainty): You like her... paintings, or whatever they are?

Juniper: Oh, yes dad, I love them! Don't be a square and

say they're just lurid, splashy works, like vulgar street-murals – as some unsophisticated, out-of-touch bores do! Anyway, I'm currently staying in Oxford with Alison and you should be very pleased to see again your beloved daughter of many talents, shouldn't you, now! Remember, dear dad, the old schoolmaster tactics will never work with me!

And with that straight down-the-line approach of Sir Terence's no-nonsense daughter (who in many ways was quite similar in tenacity to her dear dad), we will leave off eves-dropping, without waiting to see how the seventy-year old thespian will frame his response. And as for the other slightly older, platinum-fringed, artistic city shepherdess, after seeing that the aged country pastor, although now recovered somewhat, was still a bit unsteady for walking, drove him pillion on her motorbike back to the Rectory. This was, of course, after pleasant but necessarily strong persuasion. I leave it to you, the reader, to wonder at what depths of embarrassment the good Reverend must have experienced as, for a quarter of a mile, he held on tightly (as instructed) to his black leathered, two-wheeled chauffer.

CHAPTER SEVEN

ALL SAFELY GATHERED IN

ifty yards down the road from *Wanton Rectory*, the parish church clock of *Lower Wanton End* has just struck eight o clock. Never mind that the ancient clock is unpunctual, being six minutes slow; the chimes are at least an affirmation of the enduring if largely neglected presence of this honey-hued, square towered, stone and flint Norman edifice. "I am still here, I am still here" cry the plaintive yet strangely firm tones of this venerable, time-stained edifice, as this August evening begins to enwrap it in deepening twilight. In truth, it lives a twilight life hosting services once or twice a month. But all else is remarkably still in the Rectory environs. Thankfully, at this time of day there is an absence of harsh grating sounds; those sounds that usually emanate from ubiquitous power-tools which liquidate silence. Nor does the gentle late-summer breeze, wafting along from the nearest village of *West Wanton*, bring any fuss with it. This latter parish similarly boasts a square towered Norman church and also enjoys the infrequent privilege of hosting a service to a scanty congregation. Oblivious to such bare facts, the August evening continues to retain a pleasantly warm temperature helped by the affably mild wind.

Throughout the afternoon to early evening, guests were

arriving at the Rectory in dribs and drabs. In terms of the twenty plus invited guests, all who were able to accept the weekend invitation have been safely gathered in since about half-past six. The intrepid M25 voyagers, whom we have previously eavesdropped upon are arrived, their four-wheeled, gleaming, high performance beasts along with Alison Acrylic's thunderous two-wheeled, metallic mammal, are now docile, safely stabled for the night. So too, are the six King's Cross train travellers now relaxing in capacious arm chairs, fortified with biscuits, scones and beverages via Miss Muffin. Among those who could not come were the renowned sculptor Gordon Grimley, who sent apologies, explaining that currently he was busily involved setting up his latest *Tate Modern* installation of forty inflated sheep casts. The poetess laureate, Penny Trifle, also sent apologies, saying she was currently on tour, reading extracts from her latest poetic work, *Mincing Along Nicely,* to delightedly anaesthetised audiences in such places as Sidcup and Basildon. Also, Boffo's older sister, Jasmine and her younger banking husband, Fatsnout, had sent their apologies, being engaged on the arduous tasks of sunbathing and site-seeing connected with a Mediterranean cruise. However, there is one more invited guest, the renowned Professor Benjamin Babble, who has arrived late in a rather flustered state at around seven-thirty, coming by taxi from Cambridge. Professor Babble is another unique human item from Bishop Boffo's eclectic set of acquaintances. But more of our late guest anon.

Meanwhile the big horse chestnut tree to the left side of the windmill sways in a relatively relaxed tempo, gradually becoming more indistinct as it falls prey to the sly, enveloping darkness. The Saint George flag cresting the windmill's top makes a gallant little flutter, though the headless and sail-less windmill is unable to do anything further with the breeze. Perhaps the latter gently mocks the windmill for not needing its services anymore? The Rectory windows on the ground level already wink and glow in artificial tints of orange and yellow. The evening supper is about to be served and everyone is more than ready to partake of it.

The Dining Room is well and truly adequate in its dimensions to accommodate everyone. A massive, rectangular walnut table more or less fills the room's centre. This impressive fortress for the receiving of dinner and diners can accommodate up to fourteen people allowing for a slight squeeze along its flanks. However, tonight it is laid for two persons at each end and four people down each flank. To cater for the remaining diners, two moderately sized tables have been additionally joined together and laid. Courtesy of Muriel Muffin's management instructions, these conjugated tables have filled an accommodating space close to the front house windows, running more or less parallel to the main table. Due to Miss Muffin's judicious calculations, these augmentative seating arrangements still leave enough of a space-gap between the central and window-situated tables, and therefore none of the participant diners feels as if one of their elbows will collide with other elbows from the table parallel to them.

Muriel Muffin was and is an extremely competent cook, but on occasions such as this birthday celebration meal, she has excelled herself, pulling all the stops out. To achieve this not inconsiderable domestic feat of feeding twenty diners, Mrs Muffin had enlisted two worthy lady friends from *West*

Wanton and thereabouts to assist her in culinary matters and at table service. And now all was running like clockwork. The tables were laid with initial birthday celebratory champagne poured into glasses. Along the tables were also strategically placed bottles of a favourite red wine of Sir Terence's. For those, like the Halos and Julian Morbid who were teetotallers, non-alcoholic wine was provided. At five past eight the *hors d'oeuvre* (or more colloquially called, *Starters*), was being graciously deposited by Muriel and her team on the guests' placemats. This opening course comprised of home-made field mushroom soup, accompanied with tarragon cream and warm crusty bread. The initial arrival of a plate of piping hot food in front of a diner tends to signal a marvellous awed hush. For that particular moment there is the enveloping sense of impending replenishment; the age-old sense of meeting the needs of bodily appetite. Whether it is a meagre poverty meal of rice or the sumptuous repast of wealthy people, the core desire of feeding is the same despite on the one hand a placating of dire, absolute survival need and on the other hand, a placating of a mere relative (and often surplus) need to eat.

On the joined-together side tables by the front windows, Professor Benjamin Babble is rapidly and joyously engaging with his soup and bread. Professor Babble, a man in his mid-sixties, hails from Australia and is currently a visiting behavioural psychology lecturer at Cambridge University. He had just given an afternoon lecture at one of the colleges and only realised when it was about six o'clock that he was also booked by his old Oxford University friend, Boffo, for Sir Terence's birthday dinner and an overnight stay at *Lower Wanton End Rectory*. Hence the Professor had been in some haste to pack a small week-end suitcase which included essentials such as pyjamas and tooth-brush.

Benjamin Babble is sitting at the top end of the joined tables alongside the tall sash windows. This had been judiciously decided upon due to Boffo informing Muriel Muffins about the Professor's size and consequent space requirements at dinner. Benjamin Babble is of a medium height, rather over-weight, with a round genial face (and personality), adorned by glasses with very thick lenses. His eyesight is sadly poor, and he often cheerfully admits that people usually sight him before he sights them, or more often by way of collision. Our Professor also is often heard to say after finishing a lecture and attempting to leave the room: "There must be a door somewhere in this wall!" However, he has the great compensation that his appetite is extremely healthy. Accordingly, the Professor has finished his soup and bread with great relish and gusto. After the other diners have also finished their first course, there is a short lull before the arrival of the next, main culinary instalment.

The Professor's seven other companions comprise Dr. Tadpole, St. Bland, Dr. Microbe (along the window side); Boffo at the other table end, and on the other table side, Morbid opposite Microbe, Goodbalance opposite St. Bland and Canon Hollow opposite Dr. Tadpole. The latter personage is raring to initiate conversation with the esteemed Professor, whom he greatly respects, mainly because he believes the latter's behaviourist views are very conducive to his own world-view; that in short, Benjamin Babble is 'on his side'.

Professor Babble: Well, that was a very satisfying start to the culinary proceedings! It is amazing how we forget that all this is really thanks to evolution and the advanced organisation of environmental and social contingencies! Where would we be if merely left to our individual selves, without social behavioural patterning? Well, of course we would be running amok and starving, like poor Rousseau's hypothetical 'natural man'. If such people did and still do exist, it can only be in a meagre state of incompetence. And what good is that to anyone? Society is all. There is nothing coherent beyond that. But, as I keep telling my students, society – proper social, technological arrangement and planning is still held back and thus forced to remain in its infancy. We are still bedevilled by the old, old superstitious fantasy of free-will and autonomy! Once we can rid ourselves of that amongst other things our feeding arrangements will vastly improve. Not only will we always have better diners, but of course, more importantly we will be able to feed the whole world properly. The whole mess we are in at the moment – world-wide – is due to idealism, the idealism of the free agent: the individual. Get rid of that and we can start properly organising this planet on a corporate behavioural basis!

Dr. Tadpole: Of course! I heartily agree. All this useless liberal talk about freedom, individuality and autonomy is flying in the face of evolutionary facts! Where has all this metaphysical fantasy got us? All these thousands of years particularly of western philosophy, from the pre-Socratic era to scholasticism, German idealism, Marxism, existentialism and so on to goodness knows what! All this has filled heads with weird, wonderful, even dangerous ideas and concepts, but where has it got society, life as a whole? It is only science and the scientific approach to finding solutions for human needs and arrangements which has truly brought human life forward. Individualism alone cannot organise, it only ends up making a mess – anarchy. Of course, Darwin can in one sense be classed an individual but he was in fact working on the back of a big ongoing corporate enterprise. What I mean here is the perhaps at times virtually invisible work of likeminded scientifically imbibed people through the centuries, who have seen or at least sufficiently glimpsed the combined potential of science and evolution. And surely our ongoing task lies in the gradual correct understanding and proper exploiting of this combination – which will alone save and sustain the human race. That is why it's essential we jettison all these useless abstract philosophies along with superstitious religions.

St. Bland: Here we are again uncle Timothy! Out with religion, out with philosophy, out with all useless ideas. Let us enter the brave new world of scientific planning where we all become compliant robots! Ha, ha, ha!

Professor Babble: No young man, we are not talking about robots, automatons or puppets. We are seriously talking about solving *serious problems* such as population control, resources management, climate care and also responsible human behaviour control. These are problems, which you must admit, face us and the whole planet earth. Such problems have not been so far solved by philosophy or religion, but now that we have sufficiently advanced into the scientific age we have the technological possibilities to once and for all really organise our societies on sounder lines. This type of re-organisation, re-planning has never been tried before, largely because there wasn't the scientific, technological know-how to attempt it. But the time has arrived and it would be foolish when we at long last have the requisite resources, to let the opportunity slip by us.

At this point, further discussion was interrupted, almost adventitiously by the advent of Miss Muriel and her female worthies, bearing like ancient temple votaries various platters of which made up the main meal's components; namely, steamed wild sea bass, with buttered potatoes, leeks, mushrooms compounded with artichoke puree. For those, such as Dr. Tadpole (and Sir Terence on the main table), who were devout vegans, or those who had mentioned in advance an aversion to fish, another platter soon followed containing an enterprising pea and artichoke risotto. While Miss Muriel and her assistants were intently engaged in serving out the main meals along with the accompanying vegetables, there was a deterministic hush on the guests' part. Free-will, if indeed it existed, had appeared to have been at least momentarily suspended or eclipsed by environmental and cultural conditioning. However, after the initial engagement of forks and knifes with the delightful offering adorning each place mat, and with the great advantage that Benjamin Babble was too rigorously occupied with the business of species survival, Canon Hollow was first off the mark to respond to the former's remarks.

Canon Hollow: My dear Professor, it seems you are saying that we can solve – or attempt to solve – all our pressing world problems by ditching free-will, dispensing with particularity. However, one may ask, where would we be as human beings without particularity?

Professor *Babble:* Far better off! The mythology of some kind of inner man or woman dwelling within each of us has ultimately not done the human race any good. It is at best a red-herring, though I admit it produces some interesting, even noble literature, drama and poetry. What we think is free-will is in fact the result of past and ongoing evolutionary processes: natural selection and operant conditioning. And what exactly are these? Natural selection helps develop biological evolutionary processes that build up functioning mechanisms in both our bodies and minds. And operant conditioning, as a by-product of these biological processes, sustains and develops cultural habit-conditioning processes. What we choose today is a result of antecedent events, some of which of course are too far buried in the collective human past for us to unearth properly. We are in fact controlled by the un-intentionality of a vast repertoire of evolutional and cultural events beyond the locus of our minds. If, for instance, I am partial to rhubarb tart and custard, it may seem to you that that is a result of being able to choose as a free agent. However, there are undoubtedly biological, genetic and cultural reasons for such a choice. And when I answer my GP, after he advises me to lose weight, I say most truly: "I cannot help myself with respect to rhubarb tart and custard!" There is too much stacked against any attempt to fight genetic endowment and the cultural conditioning of generations of over-weight Babbles! Merely using my will-power to stop partaking of such delightful substances is not enough. For will-power is not free will but rather like taking the brain on a forced route march. But the route march is merely mental muscle strain; just an imposition. We are creatures determined by our biological and cultural past narratives! My dear dining friends, there is no freedom beyond what lies within those evolutionary and environmental narratives!

Dr. Microbe: So your poor Hamlet can no longer say: "To be, or not to be – that is the question. Whether 'tis nobler in the mind to suffer the slings and arrows of outrageous fortune, or to take arms against a sea of troubles..." For whatever poor Hamlet does, he is being forced by biological, social and psychological conditioning to do it! And I think your great Shakespeare is no better off either, for he is, according to you, Professor, only a environmental and cultural Elizabethan product, himself! So Hamlet and Shakespeare redundant – and I too, shall be out of a job! I cannot do my work if everything is cut and dried, as you say in your country!

Hollow: So shall I be redundant!

Morbid: So shall all interpreters of the master composers!

Goodbalance (dryly): So shall God!

Boffo: (amusedly): Well, I'm glad I retired, so at least I shan't be out of a job!

Dr. Tadpole: I'm not out of a job! I don't need free-will, not when I have the whole armoury of science to help me, thanks to the great march of intelligence which is now emancipating us from the superstitious errors of religion and outmoded metaphysical philosophy!

St. Bland: Oh uncle, there you go again! What will happen to your patients if they all disbelieve in free will and become determinists? Surely you will lose them either by their becoming hedonistic epicureans, miserable stoics or rabid scientific utopians like yourself! Dear me, what a choice! Yes, admittedly we have more than reached Comte's third positive stage – the scientific era; but entirely throwing out philosophy as well as religion! Even with religion it has its communal togetherness uses. But philosophy, where would we be without debate and dialectics? I feel you have pulled the carpet from under us all, Professor Babble. Ha, ha, ha!

Timothy Tadpole was about to make a severely profound reply to his irritating nephew when the dessert course made its welcome entrance amongst the diners; the second course having been finished and its mainly empty plates having been efficiently gathered and whisked away by Miss Muffin and her redoubtable assistants. Muriel Muffin was indeed masterful in her desserts and had endeavoured to offer the guests a choice of either a plum and spiced apple tart with custard or cream, or a raspberry crème brulee. Although Benjamin Babble may have been somewhat disappointed not to be confronted with his esteemed rhubarb tart and custard, he was nevertheless attacking what he considered the next best thing – the plum and spiced apple tart, supplemented lavishly with custard. Again, given that the Professor was so occupied with the digestive consequences of his gastronomic natural selectivity and operant conditioning principles, our ex-Bishop Boffo, decided to enter into the contentious debate which had been momentarily suspended.

Boffo: I have heard it claimed triumphantly by behavioural neuro-physiologists that the brain has already decided things several seconds before our human consciousness gets wind of it. However, I do not see that as a case against free-will. After all our brains are part of ourselves, a gift of God are they not? Of course I admire these learned specialists along with our distinguished guest here tonight with us. We must all learn from one another, respect and love one another. And even if our free-will is a trifle less than we previously realized, we will all safely enter into the kingdom of the good Lord in the end. We can all be finally given a heavenly clean-up even if there is the odd bit of purging to be done.

Professor Babble: (momentarily suspending his next sortie at the rapidly diminishing plum and spiced apple on his plate): But I say there is *no* free will. There is of course choice but that is largely determined by unseen factors beyond the control of our immediate consciousness.

Tadpole (triumphantly): And without free-will religion, including Christianity, doesn't work! It's just Freudian wish-fulfilment! My dear Boffo, wake up to the scientific age! Yes, it is a nice fantasy – this eternal life of yours! Well, of course science is doing her best and more people *are* living into their nineties and even hundreds – but the real issue is not the survival of me and you as individuals but rather the survival of the species, particularly those who come after us, namely our offspring and those who follow them.

St. Bland: Ha, ha, so that means I'm more important than you uncle Timothy, ha ha! I'm part of the next instalment after you – of species immortality, ha, ha!

Goodbalance: (who as usual has been following matters quietly, attentively with his scrutinizing eyes): You can of course have both redemption and eternal personality survival in Jesus Christ. But what good in fact is species immortality to anyone? It's not, you must admit, much of a consolation when you are very ill or on your death bed. All this species survival, Timothy, is just brave talk. Was it not Spinoza who enunciated so clearly as a principle, what we all feel deep down in our human condition, namely the desire to persist forever in our human identity? If there is no free-will our identity is virtually crippled. We have less identity than the worm or the blackbird which decides to make a meal out of the worm. Yet our brains are proof that we have been created in God's image and therefore that we are not merely just one set of relay-runners in the ongoing species Olympics!

Dr. Microbe: Yes, as you say, we are not worms or blackbirds. I treat those who find it difficult living, or more precisely, being human. The species are no interest to me. It is, as you say in your country, John, Jack, Jill, Tom, Sally and Gloria who interest me. The individual is what is important and that is why I attempt to help repair the breakdown or neurosis of deadlock in their minds. One cannot treat or cure species. That is too much too ask!

Canon Hollow (impatiently breaking in): Of course we cannot. We are dealing with particularized individuals! Only particularized individuals have self-consciousness which means awareness and deliberation. The species has to be treated one by one precisely because it is composed of *individuals.* 'Species' is nothing but a composite abstract entity useful for statistics and behaviourists. But life itself only carries on through individuals using their supreme God-given gift of self-consciousness!

Professor Babble: My dear Canon, awareness and deliberation are merely the hand-maidens to processes beyond our necessary human choosing. They are *necessary responses* not self-initiated by your supposed mythical free-will. We 'will' things, of course, but we are not in charge of the processes that are fundamental to cause us to 'will' such things. It is one thing to say that we 'will' certain things, but quite another to say *why* we choose to 'will' such things. I elected with my 'will' to choose the plum and spiced apple rather than the raspberry brulee. A free choice on the surface. But was it actually a free choice on my part? What about the evolutionary and genetic endowment which has gone into forming my digestive system? What about all the previous decisions I and my ancestors have made in terms of culinary consumption? My dear friends, is it not the truth that we are already wired up for the choices we now make today in our lives? You see, we are all full of mental baggage. How could we not be? No one can possibly live an autonomous life. We must be already equipped to do anything at all! You can't live on the spur of the moment, literally making life up as you go along! Impossible. Thus we do not just carry about with us in our brains the present moment but rather the whole matrix of our previous behavioural conditioning, as well as the behavioural development patterns which go back to the advent of this evolutionary adventure of planet earth!

Dr. Tadpole: Of course, of course! Bravo! We are evolutionary beings; the only significant freedom we have is to modify – to modify our evolution by channelling it into the right mental and physical behavioural patterns. And that is where the beauty of scientific progress comes in!

St. Bland: Yes, bravo, bravo, uncle Timothy! Bravo, brave new world!

Father Goodbalance (wryly): As far as I see it we are then trapped in a vicious circle of which the collective history of the human species has largely been party to its making. As you would say, dear Professor, we are determined both by evolution and our historical determination of it. But what if we are determined to play another game at the same time, namely, one which is linear rather than circular? What if this game – which is of course not a game but something urgently real, spiritual and vital – is able to bypass the circle and lift us into the sphere of a transcendental Designer? And suppose that this Designer can re-design our inner lives and re-orientate us in better ways which also help to benefit others in our human species as well as animal and vegetation species?

Professor Babble: But that is hypothetical, with all respect, Father. What you say concerns religious revelation and belief. And such things do not admit of being evidence-based. There have been thousands upon thousands of years in terms of religious systems on our planet. And I don't doubt some good men and women have been produced as a result of all this. However, we are in a serious mess as a human race and the faulty programming of Christianity and the other major religions has if anything been a large causative part of the problems we now face.

Dr. Tadpole: Here, here! It's time for religion to leave the field entirely!

Canon Hollow: I disagree! We must safeguard human particularity!

Dr. Microbe: In my opinion we must safeguard whatever helps Jack and Jill!

Morbid: Let Bach, Mozart, Beethoven, Schubert and Brahms be our programmes!

Boffo: Let us all to our own and one day find happiness together in heaven!

St. Bland: Let's have a bit of everything in a giant cocktail! Ha, ha!

Father Goodbalance: Let the good Lord save us by His wisdom!

Benjamin Babble was about to add his own apostrophic epilogue to the foregoing statements, but just then his attention became felicitously diverted by the arrival of coffee, tea and the ineluctable cheeseboard.

CHAPTER EIGHT

FURTHER TABLE TALK

Let us leave our animated diners on the joined-up side tables discussing (if they still feel like it), their freedom or non-freedom – whether or not they are the playthings of evolutional, genetic, environmental conditioning and social re-enforcing. However they are enjoying their apparent liberty to partake or non-partake of cheese, coffee and after-dinner mints. Perhaps human freedom is chimerical, but whatever our chains of duties, commitments, disadvantages and hang-ups, life at least seems to have a certain fluidity and undiminished knack for surprises which make me for one feel that there must be something left in the notion of free-will. Well, one would hope there is, at any rate. The idea of being a puppet is slightly galling to say the least and moreover raises a number of awkward perplexities such as: "Shall I in light of this new ontological situation, carry on as before? Will it dampen my outlook? Should I go and get some advice from the nearest neuroscientist or behaviourist expert? Do I need to use a diary planner any longer? Should I start looking for perpendicular strings coming out of my head, arms and legs? And what happens if you manage to cut these said strings? The questions would seem to be devastatingly mad and endless.

All in all I heartily resist the abolishment of human dignity by those who would consign free-will to their equally extremist theological or atheist outlooks. On the theological side, I would devoutly avoid becoming a non-blossoming TULIP doll of the ultra-Calvinist variety. And I am wary of Molina's half-blooming ROSES doll. On the atheist side, I certainly do not want to be a manikin jointly controlled by Darwinian and Skinnerian evolutionary and behavioural conditioning. If anything, whilst writing this book I can at least project this whole ticklish problem onto the puppets called up out of my mind. In this respect there are advantages to be had from being a puppeteer. It lets one personally off the hook for a bit. Well, just supposing free-will is a mirage, at least as a puppet master there is some consoling satisfaction in playing around with the (fictional) free-wills of others. Though here I am bound to add that any worthwhile puppet will have a good dollop of careful authorial perception within its fictionally sculpted brain. So at any rate, if my own puppeteer's strings are ordained to be pulled either by harsh reformed Protestant theology or harsh hyper-Darwinism, or harsh social conditioning, I gain some compensation by pulling as many strings as I am able to create (including even those of Reverend Halo, Dr. Tadpole and Professor Babble), without I trust, becoming a total bore or overweening tyrant.

But even as a self-articled puppet-master, I fear the strings seem to pull themselves, or at least give some wilful jerks, as if these puppets were mutineers, having somehow realised that they can deliberate, decide and if necessary cheerfully delude themselves without any real interference or manipulation from a mere plodding author. For instance, only the other day as I was attempting to write, Father

Godfrey Goodbalance suddenly sprang to life of his own accord out of the puppet box. There he was with his shrewd, quietly knowing eyes, peeping through his old-style glasses. "Oh", I said, "you gave me quite a shock. I hadn't called you up, you know". He coolly replied in his typically measured tones: "Well, dear sir, I took the great liberty of calling myself up". I then mustered some questions: "Are you here now through some dissatisfaction concerning your part in the script? Have you some special request of me?" "As a matter of fact I do have a request" replied my visiting puppet. "I would like at some point before you finish your authorial proceedings to have a quiet little chat with Canon Hollow. A dear fellow, but at times a trifle infuriating. He gets away with far too much, you know". I duly promised that I would do my best to find somewhere to fit in this extra little dialogue. Father Goodbalance seemed quite content after that assurance and was gone in a trice, back into his box. Perhaps I should have asserted my authority and sent him back to sleep. However, when confronted with the boldness of an endearingly wise puppet, un-inhibited in his free-will, I succumbed. For sure, there goes my authorial sovereignty a-tumbling!

Be that as it may, let us however turn now our attention to the more commodiously sized main table. Here, there is a more gender-egalitarian-friendly distribution of the sexes. Our dear Boffo had thought it more diplomatically expedient to put Benjamin Babble on an all-male table, as his esteemed friend liked to extol his creed mainly to those of the same gender; the Professor, being like Julian Morbid, a confirmed bachelor, was not greatly at home conversing in the company of females. Added to this, Boffo reasoned that the women present would quite probably be bored witless with behaviourism and free-will as the more than likely – or shall we say predestined? – main topic of conversation. And further to this, Boffo also reasoned that Sir Terence would, in his short-fused vestige of tolerance, find any such irritating ontological topic a signal for a high combustion outburst which cared nothing for its un-diplomatic consequences. Moreover, the ex-Bishop also deemed it advisable to keep the Reverend Halo away from such a provocative environment, otherwise the latter would be like an infuriated bull heckled by red flags. Hence, pacifism was the driving logic in seating arrangements.

At the head of the main table sits Sir Terence, distinctly more cheerful with his newly retrieved daughter next to him on his right. Along the table's left flank (parallel to the joined side tables), sits Edmund Edgy, Giles Truebore, Lucinda Halo and Clara Clouthard. On the right flank, sits Melissa Puff-Up opposite Edgy, Reverend Halo opposite Truebore, Ashley Dunce opposite Lucinda and Prunella Makepiece opposite Clouthard. The lower head of the table is graced by the Honourable Havealot and Alison Acrylic. Concerning our dear new alternative consensus political party leader, Mr. Dunce, he finds his mid-table position particularly convenient. For topographically, his seating position enables him to add his sensitive and finely-honed consensus weight to different conversations going on at both ends of the table. We might also perhaps slyly note here that Edmund Edgy is already mooning over Juniper with the long flowing golden locks, idealising her as a Saxon princess somehow translated by a happy accident of mysterious providence into the twenty-first century. However let that observation rest for the present, as one can but smile at pleasant but blind human misapprehension, as it is in Mr. Edgy's sad case. Let us instead, in order to continue with the pressing immediate purposes of this narrative, take further advantage of my omniscient zoom lens to find out what the semi or totally mutinous puppets are now up to. And first we hear Ashley Dunce's voice addressing Giles Truebore. "Well, Mr. Truebore what do you say to this year's April floods? Is this our human fault – global warming – or is it simply mother nature being capriciously malicious towards us poor human beings? Of course, either answer will be supported strongly by my party, the *CDP*. We are, by the way, if I may conveniently say so, a radically new party which refuses to be confrontational. Unite! Yes, that is our motto. The way forward in our opinion is to go onwards together forgetting contradiction and seeking to build whatever we all have into one big-top-tent consensus, as it were".

Truebore: I would say you have a point Mr. Dunce in diplomatically stating both sides of the argument. So-called conclusions on this matter one way or the other are not going to be that helpful. On the one hand, alarmism is too often the weapon of many environmentalists. On the other hand, we clearly cannot sit back and do nothing. Whether some of the fault does lie with us for being a bit cavalier with our treatment of the planet's resources, or whether in fact most of the fault – as you suggest as the other alternative – is with mother nature's fickleness, we must at any rate take some definite concrete action to protect ourselves.

Reverend Halo: Yes, that is so, but not as in the parable, by building bigger barns! Noah did not escape the deluge by building a stronger house. Yea, he listened to the Lord and built an Ark. As for the others, they scoffed and paid the penalty. Today, let those who can see and hear escape the coming wrath in the Ark of faith! Yea! Let them go into the Ark led by the blood-stained pioneer Lamb!

Treadboards (impatiently): I have not got as far as building my Ark yet. However, our problem, I grant you, is due to human stupidity and mismanagement. Floods are man-made. If you treat the natural environment as merely a meal ticket for convenient quick profits, then what can you expect? But what do governments and their ministers care? As long as the water isn't seeping under their expensive floorboards and ruining their Wilton carpets, it's hardly an issue but merely bad luck on some other poor blighter. Like everything else, it all devolves down to short-term policies of greed with big subsidy payouts to farmers – or rather neo-liberal business consortiums masquerading as farmers while ravaging the land with various forms of intensive farming. Take for instance this land around here at *Lower Wanton End* and its environs. True, we have escaped bad floods here due to there not being any nearby major rivers. But take a look at the hedges which have all been either pulled up or massacred and the trees which are all dead or in the process of dying. So where does the heavy rain go when it comes? Well, it goes into the man-made ditches, that is true, but they only hold so much water. Even in April, out walking around here, anyone with eyes could see how saturated the crop land was as a result of heavy rainfall. Greed, greed, that is all it is. A good system of hedges and healthy, flourishing trees is the obvious, crying-out answer. What you need are the strong roots of trees and ballast of high, luxuriant hedge lines to act as a natural drainage system. Artificially made ditch drains are the pathetically hypocritical answers of farmer vandals who get government grants to destroy our environment in order to create a chemical wasteland. I say, bring back trees, make the countryside full of trees like the parks and decent suburbs of London! There are more birds in the whole of Kensington than there are here in this wretched Cambridgeshire area, which has been degraded into a good for nothing dustbowl desert!

Juniper: Hear, hear, dad. I can see where I get my belligerence from now! You haven't changed an iota! All power and round one to the planet defenders!

Edgy (excited): Oh yes, I couldn't agree more. But why do we go in for this intensive farming? It is not just greed but also population explosion. We should fully appreciate the great example of our Anglo-Saxon ancestors. It was they who created the first proper hedge with their 'dead' hedge composed of hawthorn stakes and hazel tree branches. And such agrarian people acted as a responsible community towards their environment. They did not trash it like us. Their small-sized sheep were grazed in proper enclosures not willy-nilly, free-range over hills, laying waste to all vegetation and saplings, as is often the case today. And consider the vast weald running from Kent to Hampshire and the forestation covering massive areas of England in Anglo-Saxon times and compare this to what meagre little woodlands and tiny so-called forests we have left today! As a result of such high-percentage forestation, our Anglo-Saxon ancestors had superb oxygen quality and good flood protection. Compare this to our car, plane and industrial fumes causing mass pollution. Compare this too to the yearly flooding disasters we're seeing as a result of warming up global temperatures! Yes, and it was the ruthless, money-grubbing, proto-capitalist Normans who paved the way for eventual industrialisation – yes, destroying our once golden age forever!

Having delivered this impassioned speech, Edmund ended with a furtive glance at Juniper beseeching some nod of approval on her part. But the golden haired goddess who would have graced any great Anglo-Saxon king's court was doing her best to suppress a fit of the giggles.

Puff-Up: Golden age! There, you are off again Edmund! There is simply no stopping fanatical idealists when they get going. But your eulogising forgets several obvious things: slavery, famine, war and disease, which to my mind, put all together are far worse than industrial fumes and chopping a few trees and hedges down. For these latter things all actually help to enhance our civilised modern world by making room for such necessities as roads, housing, business parks, nuclear power stations, amongst other things. But concerning your golden age – remember that firstly, Anglo- Saxon society was based just as much as Norman society was on slavery – or any other European society of that medieval era. Contrary to popular romantic belief, peasants, serfs, churls (call them what you like) were the abject pawns of the Thanes who ruled the roost. Secondly, what about famine? If the crops failed due to poor weather, that was it for those at the bottom of the social pile. There was no DHSS, not even a poor law! And thirdly, if it wasn't poor harvests, there was constant warring, raids, rebellions and such like. Moreover, an Anglo-Saxon king's job description was to indulge in warfare against any or all the neighbouring kings bordering his region. Presumably, in between all the endless strife some farming work got done. Certainly, Edmund, there was no time for poetic musings! Fourthly, what about disease? Once you got a few germs you were done for and moreover they must have spread like wild fire. Remember, your golden age didn't even know what the basic organs of the body were and how they were related to each other! Golden age indeed!

Juniper (laughingly): How will you answer all that Mr. Edgy? Miss Puff-Up has really got you there! Get out of that one! I think you and dad are a couple of Don Quixotes, tilting at windmills, whether they have sails or not!

Edmund Edgy somewhat reddened. These words were not exactly conforming to the idealistic script now delicately unravelling in his finely-tuned idealistic noodle. The beautiful streaming haired princess was surely not acting quite like a wonderful Anglo-Saxon reincarnation should. Obviously, she needed some enlightenment (as well as propriety) for her as yet probably untutored brain, in order that the latter could start matching her excellent outward neo-Saxon characteristics. He was just about to enunciate some words in order to effect a worthy Anglo Saxon counter-blast to the extremely cruel siege warfare attack of Melissa Puff-Up when another voice returned to the fray:

Truebore: Getting back to the point about flood protection, the obvious answer is proper and thorough dredging of rivers, canals and water courses. A good dredging is the answer; get rid of all that unwanted build-up of weeds, silt and extraneous wild-life habitat which clog up your rivers and thus cause them to burst their banks after heavy rain fall. A good clean-up, that's what is surely needed. The fault is of nature for being unpredictable, unruly and untidy in the first place, but in the second place, we must do our gardening bit like the proverbial Adam and Eve to keep Eden from getting out of hand.

Dunce: Yes, a good point Mr. Truebore. We must assiduously dredge our rivers. The fault as you say is of an egalitarian basis. That is to say, it is shared equally between rivers and us human Adam and Eve descendents.

Halo (Sternly): Gentlemen I must correct you from overlooking the one important thing: Sin, transmitted ugly sin, dear Sirs, is where the whole fault lies. As the contaminated children of our first parents, the fault lies in the unregenerate. And there are many of them about – even no doubt, some on this very table! *(Here, giving Mr. Dunce a penetrating and frightening look).* On the contrary, the first thing a sinner must do is to dredge their soul in the blood of the spotless Lamb! Yea, then they will rid themselves of much unwanted, defiling weeds and worldly silt which clogs them up! Yea, let us pray that those of us so entangled and clogged up will today be saved by the Lord's irresistible grace.

Treadboards (Ignoring Halo's observation): Dredging, pah! A bit here and there maybe if you must. All the environmentalists I have read, including the one who writes in the *Daily Sentinel* (and obviously knows his stuff), are adamant that intensive dredging is counter-productive and can even aggravate river-bank erosion. No, the expert environmental consensus is that if you dredge the rivers clear, all you are doing is giving potential flood water a nice clear pathway to build up its speed. And then you have got yourself a flood of demonic power; a flood ten times worse in strength when it bursts the banks and comes hurtling over the fields and into your living room! No, rather any day have a clogged up river with plentiful weeds, twists and bends in it to slow the force of the flood current down. Dredging in fact only takes out the natural bottoms of rivers and accelerates silting-up. But tell the damned fool politicians that, when that is exactly what they are allowing to be done with the Somerset levels!

Edgy (eagerly joining the fray again): Of course, they are acting just like Norman vandals, ruining the last vestiges of our once great golden heritage! The Saxons knew also about not building on flood plains. They let the flood meadows do their job efficiently, that is soaking up naturally any heavy flooding. But no, not our crazy Norman-style politicians! Yes, the die was cast for unnatural flooding when the Anglo-Saxons were dispossessed by William the Conqueror, who initiated a vicious era of mega-land-grabbing. This was what set the foundations for feudal-style capitalism; big land holdings, massive ugly castles, fortifications, as well as hideous towered churches which replaced the homely, little Anglo-Saxon buildings. Here we have the origins of land aggrandisement which ultimately leads to today's flood devastation. Yes, Norman greed – which is attested by the *Doomsday Book* – namely, land re-distribution for robber barons!

Puff-Up (ignoring Edgy's petulant contribution): Well, all this may or may not be true Sir Terence; I confess I am no expert. However, I cannot but feel there is generally too much hysteria going on regarding climate change. The "warmists" I am sure, get some macabre kick out of putting the mockers on people. Our British weather has always been known to be unpredictable. What about the ice fairs on the Thames centuries ago? What about vineyards in Cornwall during Roman times? There is, I feel, sometimes a religious-type fanaticism (looking knowingly at Edgy) in those who love to make out that all nature's excesses are man-made. The ball is thus put in our human court, as if we are capable – or should be capable of sorting it all out! What hubris to think that we can sort out the weather which is a result of colossal forces outside even our advanced technological control! We may be able or nearly able to sort most things out today, but surely not the forces which dictate to us the fickle weather! And all this green legislation will achieve is to further deplete our shrinking manufacturing base and cause serious harm to the economy. Why waste money on useless ornaments like those irritating wind farms and state-subsidised solar panels?

Juniper (turning to her father): Well, dad, what do have to say to that? Good on you, Miss Puff-Up! I'm not that sure whose side I'm on regards all this environmental caboodle, but I think you seem to be the winner here in terms of getting the last word in – for look, I think here comes the coffee and cheese. Isn't it a good time now folks to call a truce at least for the present? Let's just say that the environmentalists like you dad and Mr. Edgy (turning to her father and Edmund), can continue to plant olive trees for when things warm up and the rest of us can continue planting our runner beans, potatoes and carrots!

Whether or no Sir Terence, Edmund Edgy, the half-way house and somewhat fence-sitting Mr. Truebore or even the genial Mr. Dunce had anything to say further at this juncture, I will not tax the diligently patient reader beyond his brain saturation limits. Rather, I will re-orientate my authorial zoom lens to focus upon what those at the other end of the main table were saying at around the time parallel to this topical, hot-potato conversation. The flow of life must move on as they say, or rather in our case it must slightly move back to give other guests a fair hearing.

Chapter Nine

LOWER END OF MAIN TABLE

The adjective 'parallel' appearing at the last chapter's curtain-call paragraph tempts one – or in truth, rather *me* as the 'string-puller' – into meditating on what a parallel world this is we live in. At any given moment every active speck or conglomerates of specks in this world is doing something parallel to every other speck or groups of specks within this busy globe. What a world of busy parallels we live in! The whole world is engrossed with its parallel 'doings' from Africa, the Americas, Asia, the Pacific and Europe – the last of which includes tiny *Lower Wanton End* within dear old Albion's south-east reaches. Why is there all this pother of 'doing'? Well, it must surely boil down to either Darwinian or Designer theistic evolution or Adam and Eve special creation. But why should the whole universe be 'on the go' all the time? Is all this ceaseless activity due theologically to sin which pushes man and woman out of the peaceful garden, or is it due to the billions of years of evolution via natural selection?

Thinking theologically, was the Creator's plan A – Adam and Eve in Eden – scrapped after the deadly apple had been digested? (And if we happen to be God-fearing Christians, we accept that the Good Lord had foreknown in His omniscience, this sinful imploding). In that case of failure, the evolutionary process was a punishment, including of course, for all living things, much toil, sickness as well as mortality. And if that is the situation, the gloss is rather taken off evolution as a plan B. A literal Adam and Eve leaves us in the muck of divine punishment via the eating of that wretched, beguiling apple. Darwinian or neo-Darwinian evolution leave us Godless beings with the happy or not so happy results of what started off as primeval sludge. It would seem there must be at least something to be said for a Designer – even a Sovereign Designer, or Potter, if you please – who doesn't mind working over a very long period of time since the latter is only a convenient construct of His. Such a Designer isn't that bothered if species do happen to fortuitously mutate into different species of kind. Can we not still have the atonement in all its theological rigour? For why, I beg to ask, should Adam and Eve not stand for collective and ongoing human evolutionary sin? Surely, the apple is consumed over and over again; day in, day out, over the whole span of our sin-fumbling and sporadically glorious human time. Are we not all primeval Adam and Eves? That is, the fall is rooted in each of our ongoing histories. It is not rooted in just one static moment of history as per Adam and Eve. But I have shot the authorial bolt and am now indulging too far as a trifling and supposedly neutral, puppet-master. Blame it on my neurotransmitters' sudden exuberance of activity! Forthwith such outbursts must be left solely in the capable hands of my dear free-wheeling puppets, particularly the incorrigible experts such as Tadpole, Hollow, Goodbalance and the non-free-wheeling, happily-conditioned, and well-fed, Babble.

And talking of parallels, and returning to our contestants at the lower half of the main table, let us move without further ado to hone in on what conversational parallels are taking place here. Let us ignore the incidental interruptions which are necessitated by the arrival of the first, second and third courses, and gain as omniscient audio spectators, a more-or-less unfettered transcript of conversational proceedings. Here is, for instance, Clara Clouthard testing the political waters with the homely, mind-sheltered Lucinda Halo, who sits facing her. "Well, Mrs Halo, and what is your opinion of the economy and its present recovery?" Lucinda Halo looked like a little field-house that had just encountered the opening jaws of a big tom cat. However, she made bold to answer: "I think it ought to be abolished. As my dear husband, such a wonderful preaching man, always says to me, it is the devil's lackey and does no one any good. So it cannot be good for any of us if it were to recover. Better by far it dies as a thing of mammon and lets us live peaceful, prudent and God-fearing lives". At this well-drilled, sincerely held and innocent remark, even the redoubtable Clara Clouthard was somewhat stopped in her tracks.

Seeing Clouthard's slightly dismaying predicament, Alison Acrylic took the opportunity to enlighten Lucinda Halo with her own views in regard of the economy. "What is the economy but a kind of political catch-all ideology? Everyone uses it nowadays, Liberals, Neo-liberalists, old-fashioned Conservatists, Labour, UKIP and even the Green party." Ashley Dunce, his political ears ever being alert to the opportunity of verbal consensus, piped up: "Of course, and my party the *CDP*, is not to be forgotten either. Our claim is that we can match any other political party in their views.

Indeed, we should feel greatly distressed if people thought we regarded the economy in ever so slightly a different way from it being a catch-all ideology!"

Havalot (entering the fray): I would not personally use such a phrase as Alison and our CDP leader, Mr. Dunce, have just used to describe the economy, which to my mind borders a little on sacrilege. But let's be clear about where we are today. In our post-modern world, as they call it today, we live in an age where the great philosophic systems are no more and political ideologies such as Marxism are largely discredited here in the West. Something, naturally has to be take their place. We can't live on bread alone without some intelligent idea how to produce and distribute the bread. Well, the dynamic economy, engineered and powered by the free market is the ideal, logical and most probably the final progression for our technological and demanding society of today. And let us face it, all *bona fide*, decent and respectable parties in our country respect the economy. It is the starting and finishing point of everything in politics. Get the economy right, that alone is the key to all wellbeing in any intelligently governed country. And for an intelligently governed, market economy government you of course need extremely astute floor managers. Superior brains, the result of superior education are what is obviously required to put everything in proper order. A smooth running country is a smooth running economy, and a smooth running economy obviously needs an intelligent elite to structure and supervise it. Leadership and quality does not spring from ghettos and bed-sits.

Makepiece: No, Geoffrey, there would be no chance of that in the present regressive state of right-wing politics.

Proper order, but whose proper order? These extremely astute floor managers of yours tend to be plutocrats, coming from wealthy homes, schooled at Eton and other elite establishments. What about those at the bottom of the tree, those whose welfare support systems are being cut in the name of the neo-liberal economy? This is Malthusian social, eugenic cleansing, indeed! The game's simple enough; make life so difficult for the deprived and disadvantaged that they wither away along with the withering Welfare State…

Acrylic: A rather interesting capitalist version of Lenin's withering away of the bourgeoisie State! Of course, in the end we are all really just necessary sacrifices to the great abstract God, *Economy.* The economy is a hungry god. It's not the economy who feeds us, it is rather we who feed the economy. That is what in fact my forthcoming exhibition of acrylic tapestries, which are to be hung in *Tate Modern,* laconically celebrate. I do this by painting on these tapestries large scale juxtaposed replicas of various forms of coinage, paper money and monster silhouettes. Of course everything is arranged in various distorted and inverted perspectives. I must admit it's a bit tongue-in-cheek, but my art has always been tinged with a degree of humour. But I have no partisan interest in politics. My *Tapestries* exhibition – a series of designs – is merely a wry commentary concerning the Frankenstein monster which politicians and social commentators have created and which the public are pleased to feed with their money and lives. When I produce satisfying works of vibrant and translucent colours, then the goal of my art is achieved. Just to produce such unique colouration is enough. One does not need to do much with the right colour configuration apart from a little design. The old fashioned bourgeoisie of course and all those who think of art in terms of Raphael, Rembrandt and Constable, etc., still expect that one should *produce* something; that art is making or telling a story. Such elite ideas are of course entirely irrelevant today

Havealot, Clouthard and Dunce (together): Fascinating!

Havealot: Yes, of course we and all contemporary art lovers immensely look forward to this forthcoming major event in the art world. It would be no false modesty on your part, Alison, to acknowledge that most astute art critics regard you as England's answer to Cezanne and Matisse; the creator of a bright, vibrant and luminous world of artistic passion and poetry.

Dunce: (seeing an opportunity for Consensus Diversity): Of course, this is the *CDP* view for our way forward as a nation: passion and poetry! We need a bright, vibrant and luminous approach to economics, politics, culture and in fact everything! Here is the obvious answer to a consensus that is abundantly fair in its diversity.

Clouthard: But I'm sure Alison that your exhibition will be nonetheless making some kind of cryptic, illuminating political statement if your exhibition *is* celebrating the economy. Your art is renowned for being smoothly contemporary through its delightful lurid lime greens, vivid lemon yellows and vivacious purples. If I may say so, you go with the intelligent flow; there is nothing disturbingly carping or depth-plumbing in your work.

Havealot: Certainly not, we are not and do not want to be in the land of Goya, Munch or Picasso's Guernica – heaven forbid! Celebrate, Miss Acrylic, is absolutely the right word. Our great world of the economy and technological achievements ought to be celebrated not nit-picked by those who are just jealous and envious of gifted, industrious entrepreneurs who work so hard to make this a country worth living in.

Acrylic: My secondary aim after the satisfaction of making colours in themselves, does I admit encompass a desire to be an astute commentator in a kind of slippery, off-hand, mildly sceptical way. It is true I don't intend to make major innovative statements. But that's only because art's time for making such statements has passed. Marcel Duchamp realised this way back in the 1920's, when he abandoned painting. Of course critical artist's like myself, accept that fine art's last big movement, and in fact final flowering, was actually as far back as *Impressionism*. A final flowering because, I maintain that so-called fine art died as a result of *Impressionism*. Not that fine art deserved to really live much longer anyway. For at the time of the first major Impressionists, so-called fine-art had become a static and largely meaningless representational medium. *Impressionism* was right in wishing to change all that official, academic conventionality. After all, at that time art only represented a society of frozen class values. But, impressionists did not realise that in doing away with the bourgeoisie art concept, their alternative approach could only lead to the inevitable final self-extinction of art as a serious medium. You see, when you reduce brush marks to blobs, dots, squiggles, etc., then you are already on the road to either expressive abstract art or non-expressive abstract art. Everything – all the various 'isms that followed in the wake of *Impressionism* such as Fauvism, Cubism etc., merely led to further reductive explorations, such as colour field painting, minimalism, pop-art and so on till we arrive at installations and my own work today. But this modern and post-modern reductive basis is, needless to say, far more open, honest and relevant. The alternative is what we see in regressed pseudo-artists, who mistakenly seek to make a name for themselves indulging in technically finished, idealistic work, that is now of course entirely irrelevant in its datedness.

Makepiece: Considering your views concerning "frozen class values," Alison, I personally look forward to seeing your *Tapestries exhibition* as more than just a veiled comment upon our current inhuman, monetary and market-ridden politics. Surely, your coins, bank notes and monsters must represent a searing indictment upon the right-wing financialisation of our culture, which needless to say, is supremely for the benefit of plutocrats and others who worship so-called meritocracy – that is wealthy politicians and their rich banking and business cronies.

Havealot: Oh, Prunella, I think you are being typically politically subversive! Inveterate left-winger as you are, from the *Morning Monocle*, you must, like an alchemist, always drench every thing – from drama to art – in a Marxist perspective!

Clouthard: Exactly! Prunella, you always get hold of the wrong end of the stick, jumping in like a demented left-wing bull in a china shop! You still sadly live in the 1960's socialist mindset, but we've moved on from all that naïve egalitarian rubbish. This is a market-economy, market-forces culture and the end of the old inefficient public sector, whether you like it or not!

Acrylic: I would only go so far to say that art is merely relevant to the economy as being a commentary upon it. Given that the economy in England *is* culture now, then it follows that all the arts must also be within and subject to this current and perhaps final culture. The plastic arts, nor any other of the arts cannot exist in a vacuum or alternative culture. We can never escape from our contemporary time no matter how great an artistic creator we may happen to be. But particularly in post-modernism, the role of an artist can be no longer radical. Those times have finished. Poets are no longer the unacknowledged legislators of the world, though they might possibly have been so in Dante's and Milton's time. Today, in our technological, materialist western world of faceless and unaccountable multinational corporations – namely, the new power barons – artists and poets can only be more or less ambivalent commentators. If we tried to be too serious, we would be laughed at. The time for revolution is finished. In a market-driven consumer society we are all economic units – even artists, and we have to learn to operate within that basis. That is why art has become a laconic form of sport.

Havealot: Of course, nail on the head! Art, like sport is excellent for the economy and prestige of our nation. It also takes people's minds off whinging! Particularly whinging about the State not being a nanny State anymore, merely because sensible politicians decide to take away the benefits of idlers who can't get out of bed to do an honest day's work! I'm afraid, many of your beloved poor, Prunella, are feckless and it's wired into their genes!

Makepiece: I protest at such discriminating statements! The real idlers are those mega-wealthy individuals and the self-made multi-corporation bosses, who are the real supreme tax dodgers, courtesy of the help of their ultra-expensive accountant advisers. Yes, laws and taxes for the small people

– but not for the land-owning plutocrats, the grouse hunters born with the silver spoon of tax-free inheritance. Likewise, no austerity for bankers, multi-corporation directors and our millionaires in Parliament!

Havealot: I also now protest at such a discriminating statement!

Clouthard: And so do I!

The outraged Prunella Makepiece was just about to defend herself with a timely retort when the reticent Mrs Lucinda Halo innocently interjected: "My dear Reverend husband, George, frequently tells me that all modern art comes from Satan's brush and paint sets. And as he also says, sport and big business are the Devil's playthings. 'Listen to George!' That is always my advice". This meekly spoken and matter-of-fact comment appeared to take the wind out of the sails of our heated combatants. And perhaps providentially, at this moment the coffee, tea and cheeseboard arrived at the table, courtesy of Miss Muffin and her ever tireless team.

CHAPTER TEN

REVELRY AND RECITAL

By the time the church clock struck nine, the special birthday meal of Sir Terence Treadboards was concluding. Apart from the teetotallers, the majority of diner contestants were reasonably well lubricated by their ongoing libations of wine. And in presumably affectionate remembrance of Albion' s time-honoured tradition, began to launch out into competing or complimenting songs (whichever way you may care to look at it). This seemed (to the participants) a satisfying, if indecorous way to fill in the half-hour gap between when Julian Morbid would begin his recital on the Bluthner baby-grand, housed in the adjacent drawing room. The esteemed pianist had just asked leave of Boffo and Treadboards to go and inspect the said instrument and try out privately some of the recital pieces. It was a good excuse as any to avoid what Morbid could only regard as the impending frivolity of a drinking song. The strict teetotaller Reverend Halo, also aware of this deteriorating moral situation, sternly rose from the table, saying to his wife: "Come, dear wife, the besotting fumes of wine are not conducive to the Spirit. Let us edify ourselves by discreetly listening to Mr. Morbid's preparations". And the two of them made their exit.

First to strike up in song were those at the joined tables alongside the front windows.

Babble, Tadpole and St.Bland (the latter, presumably out of devilment):

> We'll have no more of your free-will,
> With a heigh-ho, diddle-dum, nonny-no!
> We'll take it in turns pulling strings,
> With a heigh-ho, diddle-dum, nonny-no!
> We're all well behaved genetic dolls,
> With a heigh-ho, diddle-dum, nonny-no!
> Pull the strings and let the wine flow!

Boffo, Hollow, Goodbalance, Microbe and Morbid (prompted by Microbe):

> Without free-will we'll all be barking dogs!
> With a heigh-ho, diddle-dum, nonny-no!
> So we'll not be your evolutionary robots,
> With a heigh-ho, diddle-dum, nonny-no!
> We prefer to live pulling our own strings,
> With a heigh-ho, diddle-dum, nonny-no!
> We'll fill our cups by our own choice!

This assertion and counter-assertion round continued much in the same vein, presumably for lack of free-will creativity. At any rate there is no need to reproduce any further verses. Let us leave them stuck in their didactic dilemma, to slowly dwindle out in either deterministically ordained or non-deterministically ordained repetitions. However, not to be upstaged by the polemical song dialectics produced by their neighbouring side tables, those on the main table soon followed suit, likewise breaking into their own song of social and political dialectics. This song, as if to show the participants' greater ability and fecundity was framed in a more expanded *Round*, with the right-wing brethren starting off with two stanzas and then the left-wing brethren duly replying with two stanzas; Ashley Dunce in his characteristically democratic mode taking part on both sides.

Song
Havealot, Clouthard, Truebore, Puff-up and Dunce.
All who jump up out of their beds,
Early, early in the dark morn,
They are the golden boys and girls,
One and all our good citizens,
And they shall have manna and spice,
Oh la-de-de, la-de-de-la,
Fill the cup with brimming plenty.

All who stay in their cosy beds,
Late, late in the gleaming day light,
They shall forfeit their benefits,
Oh, tra-la-la, oh tra-la-la!
Out with the feckless, wanton lost,
Marxists layabouts the whole lot!
Oh, tra-la-la, oh, tra-la-la!

Sir Treadboards, Acrylic, Makepiece, Edgy, Juniper and Dunce.

Blessed be all the tax payers,
Ever they be so poor, so poor,

For they do not dodge, evade,
Hail true citizens, they pay up!
With a hey-diddle, diddle-de,
Squashed, squeezed, squelched, yet they sing true!
Fill our jars, let them fill again!

Nasty fat cats, out, out with the whole lot!
If they cry, send 'em to bed with an egg!
Tweak hard all expense fiddlers' noses,
Drain their wanton duck ponds dry,
With a hey-diddle, diddle-de,
Close tax havens, make 'em cough up!
And stop their perks, stop their perks!

Havealot, Clouthard, Truebore, Puff-up and Dunce.
Benefit takers, trounce, and cull 'em all,
Let the shirkers get up and get working!
For blessed is low pay however low,
Better than playing ill by far,
Oats and rhubarb for scroungers,
And make them pay the bedroom tax,
While we fill our brimming jars, tra-la-la!

Oh! Our statistics are better day by day,
They're looking good and so are we,
And the State's a-shrinking a-shrinking!
It's all so simple when you take it away,
A nice clean slate, with clean figures,
Oh, the economy, what a job we've done!
So pass and raise the winner's golden goblet!

Sir Treadboards, Acrylic, Makepiece, Edgy, Juniper and Dunce.

No more banker's bonuses, they're not worth it!
Let 'em sulk and cry, then boot them out!
Good riddance, we'll share out their profits,
But we wont stop there, we'll yet go on,
We'll wake 'em them all up in the Lords,
Shake up the Commons millionaire club,
And let Ofsted send them all packing!

No more cream at the top, only skimmed milk,
and put them all on capability!
With a hey-diddle-de, diddle-de,
Your big society is for a tiny few,
big cats who keep putting on weight!
Let people be true and pay their due,
so drink up and health to the Welfare State!

There were some further *rounds* of replies and counter-replies to this last offering. However I shall not bore you with these as their content further deteriorated into the realms of impolite doggerel through no doubt the participants' varying degrees of inebriation and political intoxication. While these right and left wing musical didactics were going on, Julian Morbid was in the drawing room quietly testing Sir Terence's Bluthner. All Mr. Morbid required was a brief refresher of the music manuscripts containing what he had elected to play for the impending recital. In fact they were favourite pieces of his which he could play from memory. He had asked Boffo and Sir Terence if he could have twenty minutes or so practice uninterrupted on his own. Morbid never liked to practise with anyone else in earshot. However, unnoticed by him, the Halo's had quiet as mice crept into a corner of the drawing room to listen in. The recital was scheduled to start at half past nine.

However the twenty private minutes are now up. Boffo and Dr. Microbe had by now wisely extricated themselves from the rapidly imploding vocal soiree. Sir Terence was the next to join them. Let us – the audience of a hidden dimension – also vacate the dining room for the equally goodly-sized drawing room. Needless to say, the Bluthner, as well as being lovingly polished by Miss Muffin, had also been thoroughly tuned in the preceding week. Sir Terence was as he put it himself, merely "an amateur keyboard dabbler", coping just about adequately with Associated Board, grade six pieces. The beloved Bluthner, with its warm, mellow tonal range, had as mentioned previously, been transferred at Sir Terence's insistence from his Kensington home (currently being "let"), along with a few other smaller, esteemed possessions. Morbid, who of course usually played large grands, had inspected the forty-something-year-old, Bluthner model and was quite satisfied that he could get a responsive tonal range out of it.

"And what do you think, Julian, of my dear baby Bluthner?" Sir Terence asked Mr. Morbid. "Yes, it will certainly do the job musically and this drawing room has suitable acoustics", replied the maestro. " Yes, this is not at all a bad instrument; a responsive action, a mellow-rich tone, with an obviously well maintained soundboard, strings and hammers", he added. "I was told by the dealer, whom I acquired this particular model from in Berkeley Square, that both Brahms and Tchaikovsky used and highly cherished their Bluthners", opined Sir Terence, with some feeling of glowing pride. "Ah, yes," chimed in Dr. Microbe, "these Bluthners, many say they are better than Bosendorfers, Bechsteins and Steinways! It is said that Rachmaninov would not fly to America without two things – his wife and his precious Bluthner! Ah, these great composers and virtuoso performers. I'm sure some of them, like our dear Julian, here, even entirely forsake the opposite sex for their beloved instruments!" Julian Morbid smiled rather awkwardly at this last remark.

"And what will you play for us tonight, Julian?", asked the genial Boffo, tactfully changing the subject. Dr. Microbe noted how Morbid's serious beetle-browed face, seemed now at this question, to become somewhat impenetrable. "Yes, you must give us at least a clue, Julian", Sir Terence added. At this moment, the terrible opposing political duellists, Prunella Makepiece and Clara Clouthard, entered the drawing room. Strangely, at this moment, both these fury sisters of the press came forth armed in their minds with a fixed idea that joined them together unknowingly, in an unusual correspondence of purpose. Both our redoubtable ladies had always had a secret, idealistic crush on virtuoso pianists. Prunella Makepiece's previous marriage to a self-made TV executive had ended as a disastrous failure of opposite political tendencies. They in fact split up over the last general election result, after Prunella had called her husband "a greedy, free-market dinosaur" and he having retorted back by calling her "a socialist Giraffe" (on account of her politics and long legs and neck). Miss Makepiece, as she liked to be known now, for some peculiar reason assumed all great artistic people were naturally left-wing and therefore *the right sort of people*, politically speaking. Whatever the case, she had for some chemically-irrational reason, resolved to at least fall in love a little with our unsuspecting master keyboard artist.

Clara Clouthard had been previously married to a banker, who then seeing the errors of his way joined a large Pentecostal church and embarked on evangelism and in the process giving large amounts of money away. After much arguing about Baptism in the Spirit and the proper usage of money, the relationship folded. Since then, Clouthard had embarked on a liaison with a radio four programme producer, until that abruptly terminated when the latter did a moonlight flit with an apparently more nubile pop singer. Miss Clouthard, for her own part had somehow felt she ought to get involved a bit higher up in the culture ladder and even to start looking into the mysteries of radio three music (as she termed it). At least a briefly passionate affair with a concert hall virtuoso, she thought, might help restore her now somewhat damaged *kudos*. By the way, surely, this if anything, could be construed an act of wilful, perverse choice. Or perhaps not so. Maybe it was merely the inevitable result of genes, conditioned and re-enforced cultural day-dreaming?

Getting in first before her rival, Miss Makepiece seductively volunteered the further question: "Perhaps, Mr. Morbid, you will dazzle us with some glittering Chopin nocturnes, preludes, etudes, ballads or polonaises?" Not to be outdone, Miss Clouthard chimed in (without having Makepiece's better comprehension of what exactly comprised Chopin's piano repertoire : "Or why not, Mr. Morbid, enrapture us with some of Chopin's famous waltzes or his celebrated funeral march?" "Oh, no, not those types of Chopin's works; I'm afraid not to my taste. Not really my type of composer, often too chromatically frivolous! I always go for the heavy-weight classics. In fact, I feel at present very much in rapport with Brahms. So much so that I was almost inclined to give the whole recital over to him. But I know that in a recital such as this, that would be too much for some people," the maestro replied. "Oh, Mr. Morbid, or Julian if I may so call you" opined Miss Makepiece, "I'm sure I could listen to Brahms all night, especially if *you* are playing his noble works!" Clara Clouthard was quick to add rather infelicitously: "Yes, a spot – a big spot of Brahms always goes down well with me!" "Of course, noble Brahms and noble melancholic Brahms" further interjected Sir Terence, adding, "but you must give us *some hint* as to what you will pull out of your heavy-weight bag for us tonight!" "Indeed, Julian, we are all suitably in suspense as to what delights you have in store for us!", beamed Boffo.

Microbe, (almost whispering with concern to Morbid): "Julian, I hope it won't be Liszt's *Les Funerailles* or Sonata in B minor, nor Beethoven's *Hammerklavier*. Remember also, Julian, Brahms' *Schumann variations*, which you must know last time in Oxford was not good for your health – what an effect it had on you at that recital last year! It was not good for me either, Julian. Remember, I worry double – for both of us – but such worry as that piece nearly made me myself go cuckoo, as you say in this country! Also remember, dear Julian, here we are not in the Wigmore or Festival Hall – but enjoying how you say – a charming weekend; we should not tax our emotional energies too much. You know what might happen as a result! We must avoid severe psychological strain – no self-flagellation, please!

Boffo: (apparently oblivious to Microbe's furtive warning): Yes, magnificent works such as those Liszt pieces are, and no doubt Brahms' *Schumann variations*, perhaps it would be too much for some of those here not used to plumbing such depths – although, as maestro, we are entirely in your virtuoso hands; whatever you play, it will all be to the glory of our music-loving Creator, who enjoys and commends everything from Bach to Shostakovich! Though I must admit, for myself, I do relish Rachmaninoff's preludes.

Morbid (firmly): Oh, not to worry, I'm not doing the Liszt, *Hammerklavier* or *Schumann variations*. But these pieces *I shall be playing* are particularly favourites of mine. So what *I will do* is to start with another early Brahms variation, one that is unjustly forgotten in concert halls. Then I will do – and how can one not do? – a Beethoven sonata to close the first half of the recital. After the interval, I'll play another favourite piece – a towering Schumann masterpiece to conclude the recital.

Dr. Microbe, (worried): Oh dear, heavy-weight masterpieces, oh dear! Towering works can collapse, or at least start leaning! Now that Schumann work – it is not, not the *Kreisleriana* – *not* that one! That one is far too dangerous, dear Julian! It should come with a mental health warning!

Morbid: Fiddlesticks! It's these type of works which I must play for my musical sanity. Of course *Kresleriana* is dangerous! All great music is. It wouldn't be any good otherwise. I am not here to play trinket music, just as I am not here to play boogie-woogie! Art is either serious or it is ephemeral rubbish. If you are a capable musician, it is dangerous not to play the deepest and most beautifully serious works. I must keep the torch alight! It is my duty to keep the flame of truth alive and burning brightly!

Microbe: Yes, dear Julian, but these flames – torches of

truth – can scorch and burn! I still shudder at the effect of the final sad, slow march of the *Schumann variations* – deep, yes, deep, but too deep, unhealthily deep, Julian!

Morbid (resolute): It is *my duty*, to the sublime composers, all of them – even Chopin sometimes, particularly his last sonata! We owe it to them – I owe it to them to keep the flame alight by keeping their works bristling with life!

Treadboards (warmly): Of course, exactly right! We must plough the furrows and depths of the universe. We can't waste our time in the soap-operas of everyday mundane culture. Life is too short! I was offered enough parts in trivial films and plays in my time. I could have played parts in *James Bond* films and whacky science fiction rubbish or trendy new, short-lived West End plays. All of which might have momentarily enhanced my reputation – but No! Give me any day: *Hamlet, Lear, Macbeth* or *Falstaff, Malvolio* or even *Sir Toby Belch!* Yes, remember the telling words of Keats' great sonnet on *Lear:*

"…for, once again, the fierce dispute

Betwixt damnation and impassioned clay

Must I burn through; once more humbly assay

The bitter-sweet of this Shakespearean fruit"… These lines perfectly recollected from the middle of Keats': *On sitting down to read King Lear once again*, were declaimed with such a spontaneous panache, that Boffo, Morbid and Microbe gave a delighted hurrah and appreciative clap. At this, Clouthard and Makepiece also joined in as did the other guests such as Edgy, who had also now gradually filed into the recital room.

With the time now fast approaching half past nine, Boffo, the genial host, indicated to the gathered guests the variously distributed armchairs, sofa and other hard backed but suitably cushioned chairs, which had been brought in to supplement the seating requirements. Everyone took their seats, which tended to be what was the nearest one available. Here, we have a full house; even Muriel Muffin and her redoubtable helpers had crept in at the back of the room, bringing with them some kitchen stools. And Julian Morbid is now seating himself comfortably and adjusting the piano stool ever so slightly. The recital music manuscripts are shut; the music is well and truly in the pianist's concentrated, frowning head. There is a sudden hush of silence. Now the curtains have been drawn, shutting out the darkened outside world of decapitated windmill, horse chestnut tree and other surrounding foliage and bucolic environs. The odd hoot of an owl might have been heard a few minutes previously. But as Morbid poised his whole being to play, even the owl decided upon a respectful silence.

"Ladies and gentlemen, the first piece which I am about to play is by Johannes Brahms and entitled: *Variations on an original theme*, in D major, op.21, no.1. This was composed in 1856, the year that Robert Schumann tragically died, leaving his equally esteemed wife Clara, widowed with a large young family to support. It was Clara Schumann who first performed this now neglected work in Leipzig,1860. But now without more ado, I will do my best to bring to life once again this wonderful and masterly work of the young Brahms". So spoke Julian Morbid – the significantly different and bolder Julian Morbid of the concert platform. The music then began.

Alas, poor puppeteer that I am! I do not have a real musician's insight to understand the mathematical technicalities, logicalities, rules and subtly broken rules of sublime classical composers! (Classical composition in its broadest umbrella sense, of course). I, a mere plodding, amateur layman, who am no better – or even less competent – that Sir Terence Treadboards at the piano! I, who can at least pull by means of syntax some puppet strings, but have a job making piano strings produce even a few coherent bars of Bach! I, who can only falter and fumble in trying to describe the feelings stirred by sublime passages of phrasing, sweeping arcs of impetuous notes, dynamics and above all, tonality colourings and gently mind-jarring modulations. I, who would love to unlock, even ever so slightly, the secrets of the pantheon of glorious composers! But alas, my place is only in the audience, along with this cast of created puppets, from (in order of appearance, so far) Treadboards to Babble, who are happy merely to listen with reasonably attuned or at least sympathetic ears.

And so the beautiful sound has begun. It has quickly filled the room, its very air and the very minds and hearts of those in the drawing room – even more so the recitalist is filled with the deeply structured and patterned sound, for he is the human instrument of its transmission. And what is this sweetly invading sound? Technically, a *poco Larghetto* in 3/8 time. But in fully fledged reality, a hauntingly, plaintive theme has broken into the perception, the minds, hearts and emotions of all those present. The resulting variations continue evoking a opening, gradually blossoming flower of deep melancholic tonalities and modulations. By variation five, we now find the gentle contemplation is intensifying its expression through the introduction of counterpoint – a canon of imitating voices. Onwards, now the plaintive melancholy is gradually moving up some gears. After the seventh variation, which momentarily quietens again into an ethereal, child-like wonder, comes the most dynamically powerful eighth variation, where a *fortissimo* level of sound sweeps one along, as does the October wind with the falling and fallen leaves. Henceforth, the tonal expressional weight continues its architectural build up. Julian Morbid is in his element now, the music is flowing out of his mind, through to his shoulders, arms and to his hands. And Morbid seemed to bring off successfully the eleventh variation's continuous, demanding trills, that furthered tightened the piece's gathering climatic intensity. Now suddenly the work has reached its final logical, architectural apex, and finishes as it starts, still haunting in its sound texture, but now completed, logically satisfied; a beauty as always still somehow elusive, ungraspable.

Julian Morbid bows; there is appreciative clapping. Dr. Gustaf Microbe breathes an audible sigh of relief. There is no over-heaviness in this work (although there is nothing lightweight in it either). "Yes, a good choice, melancholy modulations, yes, but that *is* Brahms – however not bordering on the high blood-pressure tragic!" murmured the good psychotherapist to himself. And then Morbid was introducing the next work, a Beethoven sonata, number thirteen in E flat, op.27, no.1. Another sigh of relief from Dr. Microbe. The latter, a reasonable amateur Beethoven expert, knew that this shortish work, from roughly the second group of the sonatas, was not a barnstormer; it was not a *Waldstein, Appassionata,* still less the *Hammerklavier* or one of the other late sonatas. Yet of course there was Beethovinic meat enough in it without plunging the uttermost depths.

Yes, there was enough to be going on with in this work; it had moved well away from the Mozartian sonata form into a more concentrated, improvisatory and unpredictable vein, introducing sudden variations of tempo due to alternating sections within movements. Again, Julian Morbid was well up to the task. The sudden *Allegro* in the first movement puncturing the gentle slow controlled dance of the opening *Andante*. Likewise, in the second movement's similar two tier *Molto allegro and Vivace,* the latter trio section, with its impressive military galloping motif was brought off with impeccable buccaneering aplomb by Mr. Morbid. Suffice to say, after the typically expressive *Adagio*, the work concluded in a whirl of seemingly continuous, rapid momentum, capped with a finale of twenty *presto* bars. All this Mr. Morbid brought off with such controlled sureness, that even Schnabel or Solomon might have smiled.

There was now a break for beverages or more wine for those who thought they had not already had quite enough. During the well-earned sterling applause, Dr. Microbe breathed another sigh of relief. One half done and everything seemed to be going well. "And we do not want anything "going over the top" as they commonly say here", the good psychotherapist murmured to himself as he sipped the black coffee Miss Muffin had just handed to him. So far so good. And for the moment Dr. Microbe excluded the impending *Kreisleriana* from his mind.

CHAPTER ELEVEN

SURPRISING VARIATIONS

Our varied character crew are a-buzz, talking with alacrity while sipping their interval refreshment drinks. Makepiece and Clouthard, both seated as close as possible to the piano, are first off the mark, cooing their rapturous admiration over Julian Morbid. Most of the rest of this select audience are also keen to get a personal, appreciative word in as well, particularly the hosts Boffo and Sir Treadboards. Morbid would have preferred to have had the usual recital hall seclusion during the fifteen minute interval, as such continuous conviviality was not at all to his liking. But now being reasonably fortified by his interpretative transmissions of Brahms and Beethoven, our pianist was managing to cope with the next surge of admirers who had managed to now throng around him and the Bluthner. This particular throng comprised Melissa Puff-up, Geoffrey Havealot, Giles Truebore, Dr. Tadpole, Canon Hollow, Father Goodbalance, Alison Acrylic and Ashley Dunce desperately seeking to make his *Consensus Diversity Party* presence felt.

Dr. Tadpole: Glorious stuff – Brahms and Beethoven! Who could want more? Those Brahms variations, delightful theme of limpid beauty – the stuff of all intelligent natural selection!

Morbid: Of course the thing about the finest variations (such as the Brahms, Op.21.no.1) is that they are a constant creative surprise to the attuned listener as well as to the committed performer. Naturally, all great music has the basis of surprise within it, but we are not of course talking about trivial crash-bang dynamics; the surprises we are talking about are actually functional and germane to the whole overall compositional purpose and structure.

Havealot: Yes, who wants bellowing, amplified pop music or even the current post-modernistic, so-called classical compositions, which you hear all too often at the *Proms* nowadays, with all that discordant insanity of sound! No, we can do without those sorts of surprises – let us indeed have the surprises of the great composers such as Beethoven! But then of course, our great composers, as you say, Mr. Morbid, know what they are about! They no doubt came from the right background and that is what always counts for anything of quality!

Dunce, (enthusiastically): The right background, yes! Crash-bang rubbish is what I and the *CDP* totally deplore, because it is clear that no intelligently diverse, voting person could be for it!

Truebore: As an actor, I personally find life an unbalanced mixture of harmony and discordance. I'm sure Sir Terence would probably agree with me there. *(Treadboards, at the back of the room, hearing this, gave a somewhat grudging nod).* Everything, whether beautiful or ugly, seems to have its reason somewhere down the line. My feeling is anyway, we can't turn time's clock back. We live in a fast paced technological age of discordant surprises and we just have to adapt accordingly. The current music scene, whether classical, pop or jazz is just an inevitable cultural expression of our unpredictable, discordant times. My guess is that what we call discordance is only our contemporary development of beauty. The old aesthetic conceptions of beauty are of course wonderful in their own way but no longer directly applicable to the way we live now.

Acrylic: Yes, that is the whole point, particularly in painting and sculpture. Everything, in the previous cultural infrastructures (prior to the early twentieth century), whether it was philosophy, religion, science or aesthetics – in terms of art, poetry, drama or literature – was based more or less on given systems. These systems have been radically challenged, indeed, bypassed and discarded. They have now collapsed (at least in terms of credibility), and we are in a random, fragmented and intensely subjective, psychological age. It is in this respect, compared to previous ages, a disjointed, discordant age. But the key thing particularly for aesthetics is that there is no longer any gap between it and everyday culture.

Canon Hollow: Precisely so, Miss Acrylic. I find myself spellbound, particularly by your brilliant, luminous colour work, enwrapped in its gorgeous, discordant juxtapositions; surely in your own art you are observing accurately the current symbiosis of art and culture. Of course, this does not mean we should not still be delighted by the greatness of the past – such as the glorious music Mr. Morbid has just played to us. But the soundscape that is truly our own one will no doubt be more likely to be that of the anguished discordance of Shostakovich rather than the classical patterning of Mozart.

Dunce (excitedly): Yes, my party favours a political-socio culture of discordance, but naturally within constitutional bounds. We recognise that discord and concord are both vital to a thriving economy and society.

Havealot: I am sure, Julian *(addressing the now rather nonplussed and upstaged maestro)*, that along with me, you probably would prefer on the whole to play Brahms and Beethoven rather than the modern discordant stuff of say, Messiaen or Shostakovich? *(In reply, Morbid nodded his head).*

Puff-up, (knowingly): Discordant music is now hardly much of a surprise. Atonal music has of course been going since Schoenberg in the early twentieth century. But everything has to progress. We couldn't forever stay either in the classical or romantic periods, could we?

Canon Hollow: Naturally not; life moves on. New developments which are then passed on – inherited you might say in an Lamarckian sense – building on the achievements of the previous, great foundational landmarks. That is, I submit, both the law of biology and all culture as well as all advanced Christianity.

Dr. Tadpole (hurriedly): Life moves on because Darwin's march of evolution continues to gain momentum despite all the reactionary cultural forces! But good culture is good evolution at work. And of course evolution is often about sudden surprises! The fact that we are all here now is one of evolutions biggest surprises!

Professor Babble: The brain moves on when the right genetic factors and environmental conditioning occur. As long as we don't get waylaid by the notion of freedom and the inner person, we will progress with surprises beneficial to future human species survival.

Father Goodbalance, (shrewdly): The surprise of beauty, I believe, is the surprise of the Creator, Himself. Do you not, Mr. Morbid, think that some higher, mysterious power of influence was at work in the minds of composers such as Beethoven and Brahms – even if they were insufficiently aware of it?

Morbid, (bemused from the previous battery of comments, but stirred by this last question): Yes, there can be no doubt. But I cannot necessarily name it as God. I have long lost touch with Him. He seemed to disappear when I became a teenager, at least the God I had known as a child. But perhaps he is somewhere round the corner. I don't know. However, it is not untrue to say that the most surprising and intimate friends I now have are the likes of Beethoven and Brahms, as well as Schumann, Liszt and many others. These are the hidden and yet very real powers and influences which come from both outside and inside me. Perhaps this *is* religion in terms of my own experience. (*And to Miss Puff-Up):* I also enjoy my surprises from twentieth century composers such as Debussy, Ravel, Bartok and Prokofiev, whose various piano compositions are by no means unworthy of the previous great masters.

At this point, Dr. Microbe, who was with Boffo and Treadboards, standing further back near the drawing room door, caught Morbid's eye and pointed to the clock on the wall, just above the Bluthner. The fifteen minutes were up; it was time for the second half of the recital to commence. And so the audience shuffled back to their various kinds of seats. It was now twenty past ten. Julian Morbid was again seated at the Bluthner. He paused to bring himself back into the enchantingly beautiful and passionate world of Robert

Schumann. And in pausing, for a moment Julian Morbid thought he could hear the cry of an engagingly excited man – but a cry that seemed to come muffled by a sad cacophony of lost and aimless human souls. This sad inarticulate human sound was in turn dismissed by the sound of a heavy door closing. The pianist gave a start at this sound within his head, but managed to re-settle himself with some deep breaths.

For a moment, Dr. Microbe's careful examining attentiveness was pressing an amber alert switch in his mole-like head. However, the pianist now launched into *Ausserst bewegt*, the opening piece of the eight movements forming Schumann's *Kresleriana*. And here indeed was a volcanic propulsion of movement! However, I will not vainly waste any further precious time attempting to delineate what I can never as a rank musical amateur ever even properly grasp, let alone express! Suffice to say, though, we are on the unpredictable billowing foam of the open sea. One moment there are foaming crested waves rearing up and the listeners are caught in a wild frenzy of ecstatic, rushing and unstoppable joy. The next moment the audience become voyagers on a beautifully becalmed sea, astonishingly poised in its sadly reflective, resigned stillness.

As the *Kresleriana* progressed, Julian Morbid seemed to be swept along with its bi-polar alternations of fury and stasis. Dr. Microbe, who was sitting a little way back from the piano, was starting to get a bit uneasy as his be-spectacled, scrutinizing eyes surveyed the body and facial language of his esteemed patient. Dr. Microbe felt he was picking up some symptoms of distress as Morbid played the fourth movement, *Sehr langsam*, which was exceedingly sad, melancholy and resigned in its mood. The tonalities here were flooded with what seemed to be the aftermath of a bitter disappointment. But the music was in full flow; there was no question that the now extremely uncomfortable psychotherapist could be a kill-joy and stop the proceedings!

The seventh piece, *Sehr rasch*, was a hive of impetuous movement; Morbid was playing like a man possessed. The plaintive voice of Schumann, calling from that wretched asylum, was now more insistent inside Morbid's fevering head. "Yes, I will not fail you, my dear, dear Herr Schumann", the recitalist muttered as his hands played lightning acrobatics on the keyboard. "Oh this is not good, no, this is too much Id – too much libido gone amok, as they say here!", Dr. Microbe was also heard to mutter, wringing his hands helplessly.

At the final, eighth movement, *Schnell und spielend,* Julian Morbid looked visibly drained and seemed to be slightly swaying at the keyboard. But the music had now subsided somewhat to a kind of gently jogging pace and the melodic matter was transformed into that of a pleasurable huntsman's song. "Ah, this is calmer, calmer", muttered Dr. Microbe with palpable relief. But he had forgotten about the impassioned middle section which suddenly burst open like a firework showering its glistening, angry sparks in the previously tranquil night sky. And Morbid, as his body seemed to lurch and fold over the keyboard, was audibly heard saying by those nearest the baby grand: "I will not fail you, I will not let the torch go out, I promise, Herr Schumann, I promise!" The music recovered from its libidinous outburst, returned to the placid jog-trotting tempo. Schumann's work, having attained its consummation, surprisingly faded into a quietness, like the last dying moments of a brilliant sunset. Rapturous applause immediately ensued. However, Julian Morbid had now suddenly lurched forward onto the Bluthner keyboard, producing in the process a discordant apostrophe. There followed, it seemed, a kind of prolonged, transfixed surreal moment. Then inevitably came faint shocked gasps in recognition of Morbid's slumped figure with his chin resting neatly on the middle 'C' keyboard area.

First to reach Julian Morbid were the redoubtable journalists, Prunella Makepiece and Clara Clouthard. Next was Dr. Microbe, crying: "Oh, maestro, maestro! I did not advise the *Kresleriana*! No, I did not. Oh, my poor Julian, oh dear, voices and too much libido; it's too bad a combination!" Makepiece and Clouthard were with difficulty trying to keep Morbid's thick-set body from swaying off the piano stool. But in another moment the golden-haired Juniper was on the scene, followed by Alison Acrylic and Timothy Tadpole. Seeing that the recitalist was in a kind of exhausted faint, Juniper took command of the situation and after a decisive assessment seconded by Dr. Tadpole, organised the other three women to help her transfer Morbid safely onto an armchair, which was swiftly brought into an appropriate position. Then, with the maestro's head supported by a couple of nearby cushions, Juniper announced: "It's alright everyone, there's nothing too serious here; Mr. Morbid must have got a bit too overwrought in that last piece of music. He's just had a minor faint, nothing more. He'll be alright in a moment. His airway, breathing and pulse are okay; we'll just give him a little liquid to drink and he should be alright in a few minutes". Sir Terence, who had in obvious concern moved forwards from the back of the drawing room, could not help but feel parentally proud of his decisive, no-nonsense daughter. "What a chip off the old block" he thought to himself, forgetting how her former defiance in leaving home, had enraged him. But, he further admiringly thought, here was already the second occasion today where Juniper had showed her unhesitating firmness and ability in a time of need!

In a moment, after being given a glass of water, Julian Morbid was reviving to everyone's relief, (particularly that of Dr. Microbe). "Oh, Herr Schumann", said the maestro, addressing his invisible composer, "I have done it – perhaps not as well as Clara or Johannes would have done it, but I have done my best! I will do better next time, better. So do come again…do come again!" And then, opening his eyes fully, Morbid saw several other pairs of concerned eyes staring into his reviving face. "Oh, Oh, where am I, this can't be the Wigmore", he pathetically said in a confused and bleary voice. "Don't worry, Julian", reassured Miss Juniper, "you just had a minor faint. It was a great recital, but you obviously must have over-taxed yourself in that last piece. Everything's okay, in control; you'll just need a few minutes to recover yourself. Just take a few breaths and relax here in this chair for as long as you want." However, as our recitalist was now steadily reviving, he did not feel this to be an ideal situation for relaxing; not with two silly journalist women cooing round him, plus Alison Acrylic with her platinum-dyed, cropped hair, in close attendance and then this rather intimidating, commanding, tall, slim and flowing haired woman, with her face concentrated right in front of his own face! No, this was not an ideal situation at all!

And thus, because of this undesired envelopment by women, Morbid was soon emboldened to fully revive and insist on his need to retire to the quiet of an adjacent room. Naturally, his psychological mentor, Dr. Microbe, also insisted on accompanying Mr. Morbid. But before going, Treadboards, Boffo and the other guests showered him – as discreetly as possible in view of the fainting episode – with their appreciation for a stirring and memorable recital. On exiting the drawing room door and heading into the dining room, Morbid and Microbe bumped into a young woman moving along with purposeful rapidity. This young and shortish person was adorned with neatly braided chestnut hair. "Oh, I'm very sorry, please do excuse me" the young lady apologised. "That is alright, no problem as you say here" said Dr. Microbe as he escorted his wounded hero into the dining room for the purposes of some discreet therapeutic presence, listening and perhaps evaluation. Hardly noticing the fresh, charming, vivacious face, in the momentarily collision, Morbid merely sighed, groaning inwardly: "Another woman – this place is crammed full of them!"

Esther Halo seemed to surprisingly combine clear-cut resolution along with a beguiling poetical attractiveness. Everyone was now standing up and animatedly talking about both the recital and the surprising coda that had perhaps been in lieu of an encore. But here was another surprise for at least three people! "Oh, dear father, mother, I'm here – it's me, Esther, your prodigal Esther!" spoke the alert and sweetly toned voice of the young lady. The Reverend George Halo and his wife, Lucinda were sitting virtually by the door, under the supplementary lighting of a standard lamp and both intoned gasps of recognition. The dear Reverend, in his astonished shock of excitement, elevated himself too quickly, brushing against the standard lamp which promptly swayed and toppled over onto him. In a moment Reverend Halo was on the carpet with the still glowing lampshade enwrapped about his confused head. "Ah, Jairus' little daughter has come back from the mouth of darkness", the distraught cleric was heard to moan in a somewhat delirious voice. "Oh, father, oh dear father – oh you are just the same dear father, always overreacting to everything!", exclaimed Esther, bursting into a practical oxymoronic demonstration of tears and laughter as she, with her mother and nearby Muriel Muffin helped to extricate the unfortunate cleric from lamp shade and stand.

So here (as well as the third human rescue operation of the day), we have this tableaux of the second little family re-union of the day. The Reverend Halo is again seated securely in a more comfortable armchair. He has plenty of attention with Juniper also checking to make sure there is no serious harm done through the lampshade and fall. Possibly another slight bruise or two to complement those gained in the ditch earlier on – but that is fortunately all. The main thing is that Esther – and it is not her ghost – has returned; the prodigal is safely home. There is a further muted buzz of interest around the drawing room. But there is a third, chemically shaken person, namely Mr. Edmund Edgy, who had been sitting on the opposite side of the drawing room door, next to Guy St. Bland and conversing with him. Guy St. Bland watches with ironic interest as he sees how Mr. Edgy almost palpably quivers with transfixed, helpless fascination at the arrival of Miss Esther Halo. Can this fresh, poetically delightful, vital young creature be yet another re-incarnation from that unpolluted, agrarian and halcyon epoch of Anglo-Saxon England? Two in one day! Yet this short, graceful being was so different to the other – to golden locked Juniper – the latter whose manners, artistic deportment and perception admittedly needed some nurturing in terms of refinement. Furthermore, this daughter of the erudite actor, Sir Terence, also needed to be prised away from the obviously unhelpful relationship with that rather conceited, cropped haired, celebrity artist woman.

Whilst Reverend Halo had been on the floor in the throes of being disentangled from the offending lampshade and stand, our poet had wakened from his transfixion and falteringly asked Miss Halo if he could be of any assistance. "Oh no, thank you – that is kind, but everything is okay", was the pleasant yet prompt reply. But her bright brown eyes along with the rest of her neat, small proportioned features, had just for that moment met and focused on the intense, astonished-rabbit features of Mr. Edgy. The poor idealist felt Cupid unleash several shafts of arrows all at once into his hopelessly vulnerable being. He almost swooned, as if he had suddenly reached the very summit of Parnassus and seen Apollo and the muses. St. Bland gently held Mr. Edgy back, whispering to the latter: "Come now, Edmund, I can see just what you're going through here. It will come to no good, I can tell you! As it's mild outside, I suggest before we turn in for the night, we go for a little stroll outside the house. This will help calm you down. I can see all the signs; Eros strikes again, ha, ha1!" Both young men (who had been allocated guest rooms in the windmill), duly said a few goodnights to other nearby guests and departed the drawing room.

The church clock has now long struck eleven. Professor Babble had been the first to retire for bed, after seeing that Julian Morbid had recovered from his fainting collapse. And now the last of the guests were also making their way via the help of Boffo and Miss Muffin to their allocated bedrooms. Muriel Muffin has found with trustworthy alacrity a spare, though slightly shabby attic room and made up a bed in it for Miss Esther Halo. The said young lady has in the meantime gone with her parents into their allotted bedroom to privately continue this surprising and unlooked for reunion. Three people are left in the emptied recital room. Sir Terence is talking with Alison Acrylic and with his returned, beloved daughter, Juniper. The latter has already genuinely commiserated with him over his recent trials and tribulations and even mildly apologizes for her own past wilful mistakes. And as all three of our remaining characters (in this particular scene) say their goodnights, Sir Terence says: "Well, today this has been a double *Winters Tale of* the two Perditas!"

CHAPTER TWELVE

ADVICE AND SURPRISE

Just a yard or so outside the Rectory's reasonably imposing front porch, we find two contrasting figures, namely the gawky Edmund Edgy and the shorter and more robust figure of Guy St. Bland. The temperature is still clement despite it being late evening. Such an accommodating August night provides the further illuminative benefit of a dazzling array of stars on parade. Several lights from various rooms in the house and some also in the adjacent windmill also help to project additional scientifically produced light for the benefit of the two men. There is thus no reason to feel lost and parcelled up in the dark on such a night as this. However, Edmund Edgy does feel lost in a sea of conflicting emotions. He is also not particularly sure about the company of his newly-attaching companion, who seems, as he nonchalantly puffs a cigarette, to be one of today's wretchedly self-assured and bored dilettantes. In fact, Mr. Edgy is at a loss to understand why this cock-sure fellow seeks out his company, given the latter appears to have no interest in that tragically forgotten and fertile age between the fifth and eleventh centuries when England was truly beginning to produce its unique and illustrious identity. "Yes, this fellow is the very zeitgeist flag-waver of contemporary shallowness", thought the troubled poet to himself. As Edmund Edgy inflicts himself with such thoughts, there is an awkward, hesitant silence for a long moment while a gentle swish of wind soothingly animates the nearby horse chestnut's leaves and branches.

St. Bland (Suddenly addressing his reluctant, semi-silhouetted companion): Why do you care so much about things? Poetry, drama, women and Anglo-Saxon culture? These are just relatives, mere stains against the boredom of our consumerist, technological existence. Why not rather introduce yourself to the reality of post-modernism like the rest of us intellectual wanderers? All of us – including myself – once, for a few brief impassioned and naïve moments of our early youth, perhaps thought like you about delusive concepts of absolute beauty, truth, real deepened democracy and egalitarian causes, etc. Wonderful poetic, philosophical, sociological and literary stuff, but I suggest if you read anyone you might read Jacques Derrida. My general philosophy is the remaining one left by default: Postmodernism. Why bother, why care, who knows, what does it matter? You see, dear Edmund, there are no answers and never really were any – at least not permanent ones. From Plato, Aristotle to Descartes, Kant, Hegel, Comte, Marx and so on, the time of systemized answers is over! Yes, Hume, Sartre and particularly that great iconoclast, Nietzsche, are still interesting because they are *not* hawkers of great all-encompassing systems, although I suppose you could almost call existentialism a quasi-system. But even compared to these three anti-systematics, Derrida is today's only valid starting (and paradoxically) finishing point. And that also means the time of intense meaning is over in all the arts including poetry, drama, novels, art and music. Yes, read Shakespeare, Milton, Keats and Shelley; read

171

the great past novels; listen to Bach, Mozart and Beethoven and see the old masters at the various galleries. But their time is not ours; their meaning is not a meaning we can confidently live by anymore. But to get to the particular issue of the moment, dear Edmund: why bother and enwrap yourself with women – at least why be so seriously idealistic about it! Why bother? I've tried wearing several tee-shirts in my time. It's all short-term gratification, I can assure you! Sexual involvement, whatever the gender, is a red herring in terms of any real happiness.

Edgy (sulkily): What then do you see as happiness?

St. Bland: It is not in terms of objective norms. They no longer exist. For me it consists in detached contemplative and ironic observing. Getting emotionally involved with people is where life becomes messy and unpleasant. I don't even much like getting involved with myself! Most messed up lives today are to do with going in and out of intense relationships, whatever their gender. And what does it matter whether it is same sex attraction or opposite sex attraction – it's all a sheer waste of human energy going down the libido drain! Gender is only a category and one should not look into it beyond that. Most misery is caused by misplaced sexual idealism. Be disengaged, Edmund. Discreetly or not so discreetly laugh at this macabre dance of life, as I do. After all, we're all in the end merely advanced animal organisms thrown somehow or other into the world.

Edmund (sulkily and surly): You are a cynic, Guy! Things did not work out for you, that is all. And why? You have probably always been a cynic deep down and a devil's advocate. That's why. Without beauty and beautiful achievements, life is only boredom. "A thing of beauty is a joy

172

for ever". And those classic words apply to Keats' own glorious verse as well as to Chaucer, Shakespeare, Marlow, Milton and all the other great achievers of our cultural heritage. Great art is *always* relevant for *every* generation. Without our Anglo-Saxon background such as Bede, Alfred the Great, Alcuin, Caedmon and the poet who wrote our first English masterpiece, *Beowulf*, where would we be today? Without that foundation there would be no England. The Norman fascist invasion tried to overturn that wonderful halcyon age of cultural birth by pathological annihilation. It is true they ripped apart our emerging organic paradise, but they did not succeed in destroying the culture. Chaucer and Shakespeare are the supreme witnesses amongst others of the Norman's failure to destroy the glory of early England. And who can live properly without Chaucer, Shakespeare or Milton? What is life without idealism, without romance, without beauty and conception of beauty, without the intoxication of certain aspects of the past and its golden achievements?

St. Bland: Golden achievements? There is nothing golden in life or history. There are only words and actions and most of those spring from our selfish genes. Were King Harold and his men at Hastings any better morally than William the Conqueror and his Normans who finally, with perhaps some good luck, butchered their way to victory? All men are butchers in war as well as potential butchers in their minds. Women may not on the whole be butchers, but they are generally good at egging men on to do their 'duty' and kill each other. The blunt fact is that as so-called 'human beings' we're all skewed; even our idealism is tainted with wired-in destructive libido. Whatever epoch, whatever socio-political time we live in, we carry within ourselves Freud's death instinct. We mess up. The only difference now between us and the Anglo-Saxons and Normans is that because of technological advancement we can mess up big-time. And this is exactly what we are doing in our contemporary world. But consign your 'golden-age' mythology to the rubbish bin. There is no golden age comprising better human beings. The only difference nowadays is that most of us who are not pathologically inclined are sensible enough not to be idealists. But what then is left? I will tell you, dear Edmund: Amused tolerance. Yes, that is my attitude and *raison d'etre:* amused tolerance. I harm no one, but I believe no one, or rather I believe everyone. And as to boredom, this is a psychological age *par excellence* of boredom! Post-modernism's creed *is* boredom. There is now nothing left much to say and what has been said has been commentated upon endlessly till the cows come home. We are glutted with the past, Edmund; so much glutted that we have now become mere mindless consumers of it. Art lovers, for instance, queue up at a Cezanne art exhibition in London just as they would queue up at the after-Christmas sales. What you take to be the heritage of great art is now merely adroitly packaged consumerism. The past, like everything else nowadays, comes wrapped in a boxed deluxe edition with its deluxe price tag.

Edgy: You are a life-killing cynic, Guy! You can't package great art! One would think the way you speak that we are all mindless puppets in the hands of Big Brother corporations. True art is counter-culture that fights against everything big conglomerates and right-wing governments stand for. Meaningful art produces something that counteracts the dead hand of authoritarian conformity. That is what I believe in and attempt to do in my own plays and poems.

Shelley was seriously right when he declared: "Poets are the unacknowledged legislators of the world". The real future is not in science and technology, but rather in free, creatively soaring minds. It always has been so. True creative artists give the lie to those who choose to accept like cattle the fodder the State and media feed them with day after day. Few use their minds and free-will constructively in the purposes of truth and beauty. But free-will is our greatest gift, something you evidently don't believe in. Without it we would all be merely ventriloquist dolls manipulated by academics like Professor Babble. However, we *are living human beings*; consequently we need to make a defining choice in order to have a really deep and meaningful experience of life. How can you sit back and watch all things fall apart? How can you not care? As Yeats said, with great agony no doubt: "Things fall apart; the centre cannot hold;" How can you not care about a world going to pot?

St. Bland: But I assure you I *do* care! The reason I distance myself in amused tolerance is self-protection from ending up like you in your idealism of caring too much. Caring too much is fatal for one's well-being. If you carry on caring too much as you do and getting over-excited about beautiful women (mind you, beautiful on the exterior but a mixed-up mess on the inside), great causes and past so-called golden ages, you will end up ill; you will probably have a psychotic breakdown or at least very likely end up like our poor maestro tonight, who proved a sad object lesson in terms of getting too emotionally involved with a composer who himself ended up in an asylum! I prefer to keep out of the deep end, be myself, remain an amused bystander. And that is the only sensible position to take today. Yes, that doesn't preclude listening in, hearing all the ideas that float around; to mildly enjoy them if you can, but not to be in thrall to any one of them. That is the key thing: Be yourself, be amusedly detached! You have quoted an Irish poet, let me in turn quote an Irish playwright, who said something to the effect that: all great art is merely a stain upon the silence. Yes, no doubt at times an intense and possibly colourful stain – but just a stain, nevertheless!

Edgy: You are a thinly disguised nihilist, then. You want to take part in life but only as an observer. For myself, I want to plunge into life but you merely tolerate it!

St. Bland: It is a better way of enjoying life. Toleration does not give way to disappointment. The moment you start plunging into life you fail to evaluate it. Thus, your happy conception of Anglo-Saxon England, your happy, intoxicated conceptions of Juniper and this new arrival Esther, who no doubt appears to you the very motion of poetic grace! But let me open your eyes, dear Edmund. If you got involved with Juniper, she would eat you for breakfast! She is a tomboy, albeit an attractive one. And consider more, Juniper is in a close relationship with that Alison Acrylic woman, who seems to be an art historian, philosopher, Marxist and entrepreneur all conveniently rolled into one! I grant you that your Anglo-Saxon princess, Juniper, is probably not a Lesbian, for she has no doubt had male relationships which did not come up to scratch – did not satisfy her – and now by default is seeking compensatory gratification through a same sex friendship. This type of thing is quite common. But the point is, whatever her gender, Juniper won't be interested in your type. Sorry old fellow to be cold blooded about it but that's how I read the situation. So, for your own sanity, don't waste your time and energy going down that road!

Edgy: Cynic, I say again! Poor Juniper was probably hurt and messed up in some previous male relationship. That is why she is with that pompous, platinum-dyed older woman! It's only those who have ideals, Guy – only those who can repair the damage of life – the damage inflicted by a cynical and harsh neo-Norman-hearted world! And I suppose you have sized up this wonderful, angelic Esther in the same coldly scientific way. Well, I admit there are certain imperfections with Juniper being a bit insensitive and blunt in her manner, but how can you say anything against Esther, whom you know nothing about?

St. Bland (firmly): It is enough to know that her father is a raging, Bible banging fanatic, who appears to also offer a side-show as a slapstick comedian. Would you want him as your father-in-law? And moreover, who knows if this Esther is not a raging fundamentalist, herself…?

At that precise moment further words were interrupted as two suddenly looming female shapes collided into our two debaters. These figures, Alison Acrylic and Juniper Treadboards, had also been outside (though around the back of the Rectory), for a bit of mild late-night August air, and now aiming to go back indoors, bumped into the paths of Edgy and St. Bland. Juniper, in fact bumped almost right into the face of Edgy, unintentionally supplying him with a brusque parody of the kind of aesthetically romantic contact that he had dreamed of when first setting eyes on her earlier on in the evening. Thinking Edgy was some dangerous maniac prowler, Juniper caught him swiftly in some sort of body lock and in a whisk efficiently flipped him over onto the lawn. This quick-as-a-flash self-defence reflex action was accompanied by a most unbecoming gruff snarl on Juniper's part. Alison Acrylic, however, had vaguely recognised St. Bland, though she did not bump into him head-on like Juniper had done with poor Mr. Edgy. The latter's mild, astonished groans, emanating from his grounded, murkily flailing torso and limbs, quickly convinced Miss Acrylic of Mr. Edgy's unique identity.

"Oh, Juniper, you are so impetuous! There you go again – straight into action!" cried Alison Acrylic; "look what you've done to poor Mr. Edgy!" "Dear ladies, I can assure you we come in peace. We are two mere harmless, bored philosophic aesthetes" declared St. Bland in self-possessed laconic tones. "We have done no wrong to the fair sex. In fact, my poor friend here, I am sure extols them above all else in his tender artistic soul", continued St. Bland. "Oh fiddlesticks to the fair sex. We're all the same now; either capable or incapable human beings" answered back Juniper as she checked the fallen Edgy for any damage and then carefully helped him up off the ground. "Sorry about that Edmund", Juniper said, changing to a more congenial tone, as she smoothed his jacket and disarrayed hair, "but it's my reflex of self-protection against macho men from my Australian days. Also as one trained in self-defence, I don't tend to mess about debating pro's and con's. Anyway, I think you'll live! By the way, you're the third different man I've checked for damage today. It's a good job I'm available!" In pronouncing this last sentence, she gave Edgy a half-laughing smile along with her hand to shake, the latter of which he rather bewilderingly took. "Best of pals now, Edmund. No hard feelings, eh?" she added in an airily friendly voice. "Oh no, of course not", the still in-shock Mr Edgy replied.

Juniper was just starting to turn away to the porch, when being conciliatory, Miss Acrylic addressing both men, said: "Why don't you two, if you feel like it, join us on the miniature train ride that's being organised for tomorrow morning by dear old Boffo? As the weather is supposed to continue fine, there is also planned to be a picnic lunch by the back garden pond afterwards. Why don't we make a little *aesthetic* foursome?" "Yes, a capital idea. I'm sure dear Mr. Edgy is bursting to share his profound knowledge of Anglo-Saxon aesthetics with you both, ha, ha!", replied St. Bland with mischievous alacrity. "Well, then, we'll hopefully see you on the train and at the picnic. Goodnight and apologies for our little unintended collision" answered Miss Acrylic. With that the two women opened the porch door (left on latch by Miss Muffin) and went inside. Inside the front door, Juniper said slightly crossly to Acrylic: "Why invite those two to share a picnic? They're both wimps, particularly the one I knocked over!" "Oh, Juniper" retorted Alison, "I admit that St. Bland thinks he's a pocket-sized version of Oscar Wilde, but the other gawky one's rather sweet and harmless. And I'm afraid he's fallen for your irresistible, seductive attractions!" "Hmpff!", Juniper half-laughingly responded and added: "there's two types of men I have no time for: machos and wimps. But I suppose, if these two comedian philosophers *do* turn up, I'll have to humour Mr. Edgy. Wimps bore me rigid, even more so than machos!" "It will be interesting to observe the poor fellow if he is, as I truly think, smitten with you", replied Acrylic, also adding with a wry smile: "I really ought to do a portrait in acrylics of the poor fellow, to put his helpless idealism onto canvas for posterity".

Meanwhile still standing outside, St. Bland, in his typical oblique baiting manner, volunteered the comment: "Well, Edmund it's not everyday you get literally swept off your feet

179

by a golden haired, Anglo-Saxon woman, is it, ha, ha?" But all the still shaken Edmund Edgy could say, as if in a delirious daze, was: "I made contact with her…I made contact with her…she gave me her hand!" With a little uncontrolled burst of laughter, St. Bland gave Edmund mockingly his own hand, saying: "You will find a woman's hand as slippery as an eel's body. Rather, trust a cynic's hand any day, ha, ha!"

As St. Bland led his dazed companion to the front door, an owl, as a coda, gave a couple of hoots. Whether these sounds were merely gentle goodnight imprecations or whether they constituted jeers of derision, one would not like to hazard a guess.

Chapter Thirteen

BREAKFAST ONCE AGAIN

Before proceeding further, we should dutifully recollect that while St. Bland and Edmund were late Friday night engaged in their friendly polarised debate, Miss Esther was relating to her parents, as diplomatically as possible – and yet with no dressed up deceitfulness, the gist of what had happened between her time of absconding and dramatic re-appearance after Julian Morbid's ill-fated recital. Esther gave positive reassurance that her affair with the lead rock guitarist of *The Shrieking Friars* had not gone the whole hog into full-blown sexual relations. But Miss Halo plainly admitted that she had had an unfortunate young woman's chemically-inspired 'crush' on this man, called Robin, who in his mid-thirties was some fourteen years her senior. However, Esther had always been genetically blessed with a strong degree of cool, intelligent self-possession (a saving grace in her particular, precarious situation), which she must have owed to perhaps a grandparent rather than her generally kind but inflammable father and docile mother.

But how had Miss Halo's deliverance occurred? Esther related that when she first met Robin, he was separated from his wife, the latter who had in the meantime become a Christian. Apparently, the wife by name of Hazel, was very keen to get back together with Robin and still maintained some 'phone and email contact with him. By dint of perseverance, Hazel astutely managed to get Robin to give some free guitar tuition to an evangelical young member of the worship band of her local Baptist church in Gridlington. The said young man had got on really well with Robin and persuaded him to go along to a service at the Baptist church. Robin did come along, not surprisingly bumping into Hazel at the service. Cutting a long story short Robin was converted by dint of the wiles and windings of providence and its humble human instruments, seeing the error of his hedonistic, heavy-rock-twanging deviance; consequently he got back together with his estranged wife and handed in his notice to *The Shrieking Friars.*

Naturally, Robin was keen to inform Esther as soon as possible about his sudden change in spiritual circumstances. Esther was then mightily prompted in her on-hold believer's conscience. She was pricked to go to that particular Baptist church in order to meet Hazel and apologize for her relationship with Robin. This she did and suffice to say, all three were happily reconciled; the erstwhile rock guitarist and Hazel re-establishing their former marriage relationship. After that, Esther further related, she too quitted *The Shrieking Friars,* determined to get her life back onto Christian lines. Miss Halo prudently decided to regularly attend a different church. She picked a high-powered, evangelistic Anglican church, St. Edward's in Gridlington, soon getting involved singing with the worship band. Esther also managed, because of her evident winsome and capable personality, to land an administrative job which happened to become vacant in that highly attended and pro-active church. Cheering her parents further, Esther declared that this job would tide her over while looking for suitable openings in work as a junior partner with a solicitors firm.

"All things work for good" as the famous apostle said (speaking of course in the dialect of faith, not of secular coincidence). Esther was back on track; that is if we can accept (which of course some of us St. Bland type cynics may not), that for her, Christian faith was the track which constituted the root meaning and purpose of her life. Lucinda Halo, in between tears, could only say: "Oh, you naughty, disobedient child, Esther, frightening and worrying us both so much! And you with all your law books, should have known better how to be an obedient child! But, oh! You should have listened – paid more attention to George!" Then, though slightly contradicting herself, she immediately added, "but it is only because you listened to George somewhat, that we have you back once again, unharmed out of the furnace. Oh, you good, sensible child, to see the light again!" The Reverend Halo, himself was even cautiously joyous, despite his fixed suspicions about Anglican churches generally being bastions of devilish, poisonous liberalism. Thus the good Reverend alternately glowered and beamed at his daughter, discreetly brushing away some unbidden tears from his elderly grey eyes.

"You must wonder how I came to suddenly burst into the Rectory in the way I did last night", Esther said, seeing that her parents had not yet asked her this obvious question. "Well, I did wonder and still wonder, my dear returned child", said her father, adding: "I cannot believe you have ever been to this place before. Neither have you been in touch with us for several months – naughty, fallen child! I am therefore at a loss to understand how you came here last night. It can only be great providence, praise the Lord!" "Praise the Lord", echoed Mrs Halo. "Of course!" replied Esther with sudden animation. "Perhaps even you will not believe me, dear old father, when I say that it *was* the good Lord's intervention! After getting myself back on track a couple of months or so ago, I just could not face seeing you both again. Yes, I must admit it! I feared you would even dismiss my return, send me away in parental wrath. I feared that possibility and even after praying simply couldn't brace myself to see you again, possibly to be rejected as a daughter who had forever in your eyes blown her Christian credentials!" "Well the Devil most certainly deceived you and for a while was successful in taking you for one of his own, but like the Prodigal you have come back to us" replied her father, adding: "My wrath was that Satan should entrap even my one and only daughter. But God has granted his preserving grace to bring you back into the fold. Let it never be said that George Halo would never, like the Father, Himself, *not* open his arms wide to receive his repentant, returning daughter! Amen, to gracious providence!" "Amen, indeed", echoed Mrs Halo.

"Well now, dear parents", continued Esther, "let me now explain how providence led me to this Rectory! While I was wrestling two nights ago in deep prayer about the very question of how I should make contact with you both again, a vision – yes, a vision came to me! A picture came to me of a large Victorian type house with a strange sail-less windmill standing to one side of it. The vision then took me away from the house and windmill, down a nearby lane. After a while down this lane, I saw a signpost which said: *Lower Wanton End*, three quarters of a mile. The vision faded and I remember a persistent voice in my head saying: *"go there, go there, this Saturday evening"*. You know, father, I was never a charismatic – one for visions or prophetic words. So how can one explain this? However, I checked the maps and found such a place as *Lower Wanton End* existed. And so, in sheer faith, I packed my travelling bag and drove from Gridlington late yesterday afternoon down here in my newly acquired second-hand car. And so here I am by God's grace!" "Yes, grace indeed, that has brought you back to the old pathways!" replied her father. "Yes, you must now, dear Esther, keep to the straight and narrow pathways which dear George has always instructed you to go upon", solemnly added Mrs Halo.

Having cleared up the Esther situation we may now move safely and confidently onto Saturday morning. The weather forecasters appear to have been correct; the freshly minted arriving day shows all the happy symptoms of being sunny, pleasantly warm and dry. And it was particularly important for Boffo that there should be no rain as the miniature petrol powered train, the *Royal Robin,* pulled open rather than enclosed carriages. A railway trip with umbrellas would hardly be much to look forward to either for Boffo, Sir Terence or their guests. But the weather looked by all accounts as though it was going to be user-friendly to all concerned here at *Lower Wanton End*. The circular train excursion was set to depart at half-past eleven and the picnic lunch was to follow at around half-past twelve.

There is no particular need to dwell greatly upon the preliminaries and preparations leading up to the back garden excursion, but as puppet-master, I make bold to convey some breakfast highlights, indicating the general ins and outs and ups and down of the various conversations. Taking firstly the top of the Main Table, we discover Sir Treadboards heatedly denouncing the modern computer age to Mr. Geoffrey Havealot: "Virtual non-reality! I say, get rid of the internet and all its bird-sounding excrescences, then we can *all* get back to *real* reality! This computer 'culture' is nothing more than a perpetual game which takes us away from vital, top-rank culture". "Well, Sir Terence", the MP diplomatically replied, "I fully understand your point of view, given that you are a great knight of the theatre, having plumbed the depths of Shakespeare's sublime works, yet nevertheless I think we must be careful not to throw the baby out with the bath water". "Fiddlesticks, the baby is not human!" retorted Sir Terence. "But, Sir Terence, the very way we live now is via computers. Whatever one may think there can be no going back unless one becomes a Luddite", rejoined Mr. Havelot, and added: "Let us be starkly honest: Without computer knowledge a jobseeker nowadays is virtually unemployable".

"Here, I must certainly agree with Geoffrey" piped in Giles Truebore, seated next to the said MP on the table's left-hand flank. "How could" (Truebore continued, rising in animated eloquence), "for instance, I and my passengers have got to *Lower Wanton End* so remarkably efficiently without satellite navigation? And what would we do without mobile phones, data-bases and the wide world web which is so conveniently at our fingertips? Are we to go back again to index cards, four-drawer filing systems; opening up large unwieldy tomes for information – such as *The Encyclopaedia Britannica*? And are we to go back to painstakingly writing out everything on typewriters and laboriously correcting mistakes by typex? Surely not, one would hope!" "Yes, that would be going backwards, Sir Terence" returned Mr. Havelot, adding:

"And if we must bite the bullet, let us remember the bullet is actually really a golden egg that has, as Giles just indicated, largely liberated us all from much tedious drudgery". "I prefer to be a Luddite. Let us have drudgery in preference to this technological gadget age. The discipline of it will do us all good – particularly those who spend every waking leisure hour in thrall to these confounded gadgets!", retorted Sir Terence, refusing to budge an inch. "Oh, dad! What a Luddite you are", laughingly commented Juniper (sitting next to her father on the table's right-hand flank), and added: "Get real and come and join us all in the twenty-first century! Buy a quality lap-top and start tweeting, twittering and blogging! Carry your books in your pocket with Kindle and sign up to Facebook! And while you're about it, invest in an up-to-date Smartphone and a handy tablet to jot down the theatrical memories you always intended to write!" Sir Terence, thus bombarded, snorted in reply: "I cannot commune with Shakespeare by little hand-held toys!"

Moving just one place down the same table side as Miss Treadboards, we might also notice Edmund Edgy. The poetical playright seemed ever more in a turmoil of decision over Juniper and Esther. But somehow by a quirk of chivalric Arthurian fate, Mr Edgy had been allotted to sit between both the two said contrasting damsels. Miss Muffin had fitted in an extra place so that Esther could sit at the Main table's right flank, by her parents. Although the unexpected forms of contact with Juniper late last night had given Mr. Edgy a new unsettling, ambivalent hope in that direction, when he found himself sitting down crowned on one side with flowing golden hair and on the other with luxuriant braided chestnut brown hair, a tremulous wave swept all over the poor young man. He had unexpectedly reached two promised lands, but knew not what to do in order to enter either of them. Therefore, instead of expounding his favourite golden age gospel, he could for a while, on the one hand, only muster up the following words to Juniper: "Please can you pass me the tea pot?" and on the other hand to Esther, the words: "Please may I have the sugar?" What he might have wished to say, concerning the wickedness of today's ungrateful Norman-based England and the gloriously contrasting Anglo-Saxon era, which amongst its luminaries comprised the likes of Alfred, Alcuin and Caedmon, could unfortunately not find a route for verbal formulation out through his wind-pipe and mouth. Edmund's troubled feelings and thoughts remained vacillating, locked up in un-heroic confusion.

However, in between talking to her mother, Lucinda Halo, who was seated directly to Esther's left and to her father seated at the bottom end of the table (nearest to his wife), the said young lady did very innocently ask Mr. Edgy the question: "And what are your main type of interests, Edmund?" To which he did muster up the reply: "Writing and reading poetry as well as plays, but…my abiding theme is Anglo-Saxon, golden-age culture". "Oh, you are a social historian as well then?" Esther replied, slightly arching innocently her eyebrows, and in so doing further bewitched poor Mr. Edgy. He mustered a further answer, managing to get up a little steam in the process: "Well, er, yes, but it's much more than that. I want…yes I want most profoundly to see a return to the spirit of that wonderful organic age – that age before tall, monstrous Norman castles, ugly square-towered churches, along with all that wretched fascist, Norman Doomsday Book inspired bureaucracy, largely destroyed

England's primal innocence". "Oh, what a strange idea", replied Esther, in her surprised innocence not bothering to add any further verbal reactions to Mr. Edgy's credo of belief and artistic integrity. After this reply of Esther's there followed an awkward, indeed devastating silence, in which Edmund felt crushed to oblivion. The next moment, Miss Muffin had put a plate of scrambled egg on toast in front of Esther (the latter's choice of cooked breakfast), and also put a plate of fried eggs, mushrooms, tomatoes and toast in front of Edmund. All opportunity seemed now forfeited in our doomed poet's mind. Though we should mention that shortly afterwards the other golden haired, rough-diamond damsel addressed Mr. Edgy, thus: "Well, Edmund, no hard feelings still, I hope? Sorry about my defence throw and you landing on the grass, but you've obviously survived. What are a few roughs and tumbles for a healthy, virile, strapping Anglo-Saxon tough guy like yourself!" Esther, suppressed a quiet smile while Miss Puff-up, seated next to Reverend Halo (bottom end of the table), quickly put her hand over her mouth to avoid bursting into a fit of hysterics. Miss Acrylic merely compensated for forbidden laughter by indulging in a choking fit with her coffee which she managed somehow to avoid spurting out across the table at an alarmed Reverend Halo. Our poetic hero awkwardly smiled, wishing for a giant trap-door to open up beneath him. "What have you been doing, Juniper, with young Mr. Edgy?" asked Sir Terence, and turning to the reddened poet: "Well, Mr. Edmund, perhaps you would be better off studying the martial arts rather than writing plays and poetry!"

What of the other guests? Suffice to say they were all happily chattering away reasonably mildly and unpolemically (on this occasion at least), concerning politics, religion, the state of culture and so forth. Dr. Microbe, upon coming downstairs from his guest room, had bumped into Professor Babble, an occurrence quite common to the latter, who as we have previously noted, was usually in search of a suitable door. After due apologies, the psychotherapist carefully guided the eminent behaviourist to the safety of the bottom end of the side-tables where a place had been reserved for the latter personage. Dr. Microbe took a vacant place up the other table end to the left of Boffo. Immediately afterwards, Ashley Dunce sat down opposite the psychotherapist, filling the last available place. (The *CDP* leader was keen as ever to promote the virtues of his party and thus opted to move to a different table in his desire to win new friends and influence). A few minutes later Julian Morbid came down for breakfast and found the side-table places already filled. Just at that moment, the terrible two-some, Clara Clouthard and Prunella Makepiece appeared, insisting that he sit between them, utilising the three vacant places left on the Main Table. Thus, we may also observe another man in a slight predicament.

Mr. Morbid, separated from Dr. Microbe, now found himself trapped between his two eager, "hyena" pursuers. The inevitable further pestering questions arrived after both ladies had ascertained as exactly as possible that the maestro was now recovered from his unfortunate collapse at the Bluthner on the previous night. Thus, Prunella Makepiece to Mr. Morbid: "Oh, you must simply practise *all day long* to reach your level of concert perfection!" Our recitalist dryly replied: "Not at all. Only just three hours a day now. It's quality of practice not quantity of time that I aim for".

Slightly flattened, Prunella Makepiece rejoined: "Oh, I am sure it must be because you are a born natural genius of the keyboard. Others would have to spend hours and hours each day to reach your standard of finesse and interpretative mastery". Mr. Morbid merely wryly smiled. Not to be left out and outdone, Clara Clouthard jumped into verbal action: "And how on earth do you memorise all those trillions of notes? You must have an amazing mind!" The maestro again dryly remarked in his rather gravelled voice: "There are various mental techniques which help – but mainly, it all comes down to sheer involvement, namely, *living* with the music so that it becomes part – an extension of your own mind and feelings". The two redoubtable journalists continued to ply maestro Morbid with further questions, each vying with the other in trying to frame questions which showed up their supposed knowledgeable musical awareness. The besieged pianist thought grimly to himself, "I shall have to keep batting these wretched nuisance women off for a bit longer, but as soon as possible I shall hide myself somewhere and lose them! Goodness me, though, there's the rest of today to go, until Microbe and I get the train back tomorrow morning! Sir Terence – yes, a decent, intelligent music lover – but was it really worth coming here to suffer this plague of silly women?"

Let us pass over to the side-table with Dr. Timothy Tadpole (sitting on the window-side flank, third down), continuing to extol the virtues of Darwinian evolution and scientific insight, in terms of the human race's progress and beneficial prospects. Professor Benjamin Babble, sitting at the bottom end of the table was nodding agreement whilst demolishing a considerable amount of toast in the wake of consumption of a full-scale English breakfast. "Yes, of course", he gravely said: "if properly harnessed, the insights of evolution, coupled with proper behavioural regulation, can save our planet – particularly from starvation. What we must attempt to do is to establish enhanced behavioural patterns which promote increased efficiency in growing and yielding adequate world food supplies". "Yes, we must feed the hungry", opined Boffo, beaming from the top end of the side table. "There is the particularisation of fair distribution to be considered" commented Canon Donald Hollow, cutting up his sausage with neat precision. "Presumably, you don't mean the trickle-down effect, ha, ha!" interjected Guy St. Bland, who was sitting to the right of the good Canon, on the table flank opposite to the window. Across the table, facing St. Bland, Father Goodbalance ventured: "Fair distribution of resources is sadly an anomaly in a world governed by corporate greed", and added: "It is all very well having great schemes to regulate and share resources, but power and greed are corrupting constants in the human condition".

Ashley Dunce, felt it extremely appropriate at this point to say: "We, at the *CDP*, believe wholeheartedly in regulating and sharing power and greed. We, as a Party, fully understand the economic importance and value of power and greed, but as you say, such things must be both controlled and shared. In fact we believe in a vibrant economy and culture where no child, boy or girl, young or old person will ever be excluded from the opportunity of having their share of power and greed. That is, indeed, our blueprint for twenty-first century democracy". To which micro, party-political broadcast, Dr. Microbe complained: "Excuse me, dear young sir, but if what you say should ever become true, I think I shall need to build bigger, in fact gigantic psychotherapy clinics". Undaunted, Dominic Dunce cheerfully replied: "If, Dr. Microbe, it is proved – and indeed I am sure it could well be – that such medical utilities are beneficial to our economic infrastructure and its growth, we at *CDP* would wholeheartedly be behind such an initiative". Lost for further words, the good mental health clinician thought to himself, regarding Mr. Dunce: "Here is a very strange human animal. What a challenge – what a daunting challenge such a man as he would pose for any psychiatrist, psychotherapist or psychoanalyst, or all three of them! No, for myself, I prefer dear, obstinate Julian – at least there is some positive hope there! But this politician fellow should be in the children's nursery, or what they have on those English beaches – yes, the *Punch and Judy* show, as they say!"

And finally, to conclude our brief breakfast survey, at the bottom end of the Main Table, here is Melissa Puff-up innocently asking Reverend Halo (seated beside her to her right): "And what, Reverend Halo, is your response to today's highly technological and scientific age, with all it complicated issues?" "My dear young lady", the Reverend sternly replies, "the Devil is a modernist and always has been. Let us return to the old ways – that is our only safety." "But", says Miss Puff-Up, " we surely cannot go backwards even fifty years, let alone into Edwardian or Victorian times. We are now in an age – a post-modern age, where we have to make our own choices. We cannot go back to what was done in the past. Things are done – and must be done – so differently nowadays!"

Unperturbed, the venerable Halo replies, his eyes and visage darkening: "Yes, indeed, there is much sin abounding nowadays. That is the difference, young lady! The Devil is like a roaring lion, who having been let out of the zoo, saunters down our high streets and into all our living rooms as and when he likes, to do just as he pleases! And as to this do-it-yourself, liberalistic relativistic age" (Halo continues, now getting into his stride), "all it produces is a hedonistic society of boundless iniquity! A dastardly, mendacious society of Satan's eager pupils." Our critic lady bravely replied: "But surely you don't really believe in a literal devil – or lion-like devil – who roams around at large?" "But I certainly do, young lady!" returned Reverend Halo, adding: "For he delights in any liberal company with their new-fangled talk and whacky ideas. As surely as night follows day, I tell you he is even now happily partaking breakfast with some of us here in this very room!"

Melissa Puff-Up, suitably both enlightened and nonplussed was unusually at a loss for words; she ventured nothing further, and concentrated on buttering some more hot toast.

Chapter Fourteen

IRRESISTIBLE MISSION

The Reverend George Halo, though usually wary of 'modern' poets, had at the breakfast table espoused some interest in Edmund Edgy. Perhaps it was that the antique, Puritan eccentricity of the later somehow chimed with the dear Reverend's own revulsion of post-modern society's current 'depravity'. To Reverend Halo's mind, there seemed to be some indefinite magnetic force which drew his interest and curiosity to the tormented young man. For it was clear to any of spiritual discernment that Mr. Edgy *was* in a state of torment. Our good Reverend judged this to be so because the young man was being pulled by irresistible grace to the crisis of decision and so to repentance and regeneration in Christ. He felt that it was his duty now to tackle Mr. Edgy on the subject. There was also no doubt in the Reverend's mind that this young fellow seemed drawn providentially towards his own company. However, our strict Calvinist Baptist was perhaps not aware that Edmund Edgy's irresistible source of attraction was none other than his own daughter, Esther.

"I must make an urgent preliminary visitation on this young man", the venerable minister said to himself, "just a few well chosen introductory remarks before attention is diverted by this rather worldly toy-train excursion of our regrettably too liberal brother Boffo". Such action was needful sooner rather than later. But the opportunity soon beckoned. Just after breakfast, Edmund Edgy strolled out of the Rectory front door, turning to his right by the pink horse chestnut tree, to look round the outside of the adjacent headless windmill. The Reverend conveniently turned sleuth and now carefully watching his man, saw the Lord had provided an ideal opportunity. There was no one else about; it was at once a remarkably suitably convenient moment, where the necessary words could be said out of others' hearing. Mr. Edgy stood looking up at the windmill situated in a little grassy square. In front of the windmill a driveway led out southwards to a wrought iron entrance gate and thence to the access lane. Slightly left of the drive and windmill was a long flowerbed. The somewhat overgrown flowerbed still boasted some cobalt-blue delphiniums, various hued hollyhocks and glowing flecks of golden rod commanding its back borders. The driveway also led inwards past the windmill's right hand side, turning into the Rectory and terminating at the end of the latter's frontage; at which point there were several parking spaces cut into the lawn. Here rested in peaceful limbo the metallic beasts which yesterday had blazingly (at least at times) sped down the M25, M11 and thence to *Lower Wanton End.*

The sun was beaming like an enhanced cosmic version of Boffo's usual affable smile. The crisp air, emanating from the enamelled blue sky was deliciously fresh, yet mild. This Saturday, now already advanced in hours, had still an aura of mysterious, unfathomable newness to it. There appeared to be no one else about in the direct vicinity of the windmill at that precise moment. Now was the time to act, thought the venerable Halo. Now was the time to have a man to man talk with someone hovering on the precipice of inviting election. So he stealthily approached the Anglo-Saxon crusading poet, who was lost in very likely a Hamlet reverie of indecision. In a moment Reverend Halo quietly but pertinently whispered to Mr. Edgy: "Young man, I understand – the Spirit has confirmed to me – the inner strife that is afflicting you. Unburden yourself to me. Remember, the Lord is gracious, is kind, merciful to all who turn to Him, no matter their sins and troubles". Edmund Edgy had turned round with an astonished rabbit look, fearful that the damsel's father had rumbled his now irresistible passion. (For all thoughts now of Juniper were at least eclipsed at this precise juncture).

"I…I…I don't follow you. I can assure you I have nothing but honourable intentions towards…" stammered Edgy, without being able to finish his sentence because the good Reverend quickly cut in, saying: "That is a good sign, a good sign. The heart must be right, young man, for that is what is needful to be able to receive the goodness the Lord intends for you. Yes, young man, the heart must seek honourable intentions in its reaching out to receive the bountiful riches awaiting it." "I did not realise – nor did I wish to cause you any concern…over my feelings which seem to have overtaken, overwhelmed when I first saw… first saw last night…" faltered the poet, but again was interrupted by the now eager Reverend Halo: "Of course the Spirit has at last caught you up; conviction has overturned your life. You are of course naturally in a divine-stirred-up confusion. And you first saw the light last night. Very good! That was a mighty moment of grace for you. Thank God for the blessed convenience of His prevenient grace! Without that where would any of us sinners be?" Edmund Edgy, feeling that the conversation was now going in a different direction from what he had first perceived to be the case, again stammered: "Oh, I…I…think there must be some mistake, I…I…am an agnostic, though a great admirer of those remarkable men such as Bede, Alcuin and many others of our noble Anglo-Saxon heritage…but…" Again, the good Reverend quickly cut in with due authority: "Yes, of course, my dear young man. At present you are outside the Kingdom's gates. One must naturally be without faith to receive it! It matters not to what degree you were an agnostic or atheist before the glorious moment of justification and re-birth. It matters not! But you must not fight the Spirit's fire. If indeed He has marked you out; if indeed He has elected – chosen you, he will naturally come to claim you. You must therefore surrender – surrender the old to receive the new! Do not fear, I am here to help you at this epic point in your troubled life!" "Oh dear, I must go now, I…I feel… rather shaky…" Edmund Edgy said, mustering a desperate reply, which enabled him to beat a hasty, undignified Anglo-Saxon retreat. But our dear Reverend Halo was not perturbed at the retreat, feeling quite satisfied at what had so far been accomplished. "Shaky, no doubt that is another good sign of the Spirit's convicting work. Yes, in my younger days I have even seen some fall to the ground writhing as they helplessly wrestled with the realisation of their sinful ways. Yes, I will follow this through, dear Lord" he whispered with contented ardour. " I will make a point of sitting next to the young man on the miniature train ride. The Lord's visitation on this young man requires my humble yet firm human co-operation. The desire of his Spirit-opening heart will be helped along by my supportive company. Oh Lord, let me be the modest human vehicle of his surprised joy at being snatched out of the consuming flames of wrath!"

CHAPTER FIFTEEN

CIRCULAR EXCURSION (ONE)

W e are now removed from the convivial breakfast proceedings and find ourselves in the grounds beyond the Rectory's back lawn. The lawn, occupied and enhanced by (the previously mentioned) fully grown spreading copper beech, is laurel hedged on both flanks and to its western rear. A tailored gap in this west-facing part of the said hedge has led us and our variegated company to a nearby wooden siding shed which houses *The Royal Robin*. Garden chairs and tables with sun shields have been brought out of a little store shed adjacent to the sidings shed. The tables and chairs facilitate a kind of outdoor railway waiting room. The seven and a quarter inch gauge railway track emanates from the sidings shed and passes within a couple of yards of the tables and chairs. Hereafter, the line moves about a hundred yards westward towards the considerably capacious Rectory pond; the line then snakes its way round the pond's eastern near side. After this the track heads westward again, leaving the pond and heading towards a small spinney of beeches which are close to a hedge bordering the property from neighbouring farmland. The track passes round the south side of the beeches, travelling parallel alongside the perimeter hedge and then looping round to the north side of the said trees. From thence, the track proceeds eastwards back towards the pond and upon reaching it bears left, travelling round its western further-side and then heading back east towards the waiting room (or platform if you so wish) of garden chairs and tables. The track is just under half a mile in length.

It is ten past eleven. The guests have all assembled with their various degrees of expectation. Boffo and Treadboards are to be found in the opened siding shed where *The Royal Robin* is being fuelled, oiled and given a general rudimentary health check. Sir Terence had never up to now shown much interest in Boffos's miniature train hobbyhorse, having previously refused invitations to take a little circular one car outing with his clerical cousin and Miss Muffin. But now Sir Terence, seeing the post-box red, industrial-type design of *The Royal Robin* in its wide wooden dormitory (along with five uncoupled, small open, sit-in carriages), evinced quite some interest and was helping Boffo with fuelling up and other necessary preparatory measures. "Oh, yes," our beaming ex-Bishop was saying, "I know this little train (which came with the house) is petrol rather than steam powered – which is of course a great shame to a steam lover like myself, but it is quite a steady, albeit slow worker; in fact *Royal Robin* is an apt name, for I have found it as robust, healthy and as user-friendly as our beloved little garden bird!" "So it is a mechanical engine job, then", commented Sir Terence and added: "But I suppose that has its conveniences. I imagine a well used steam locomotive – although more impressive to enthusiasts than petrol, diesel or battery – would at intervals need water refilling stops, require time to rebuild pressure and probably re-stoke the fire." "Yes", replied Boffo, his face gleaming with an enthusiast's absorbed joy: "What we have here is a petrol four-stroke engine with an electrically powered vacuum pump acting as a braking system. The gearbox has been utilised from a used car. The maintenance, as you rightly say, is of course easier and I confess that sadly, my love of steam is not complimented with any great knowledge or great abilities in terms of practical know-how."

Sir Terence looked at the five small, two-seater carriage cars, of which two were on a track to the engine's left and three on a track to its right. "Well," he said, "what I should like to know, dear cousin, is how you are going to couple these carriages onto the engine". "Oh, dear Terence, that is not too much of a difficulty", replied the radiantly absorbed Boffo. He explained that once *The Royal Robin* had reversed out of the siding shed, the light carriages could be given a manual push along their tracks out of the shed; from thence, outside the shed, the left and right sets of carriage tracks merged into the mainline track and the five carriages could easily then be coupled to the engine train. The three younger men, Giles, Guy and Edmund Edgy were enlisted to give a hand; Edgy, Boffo and St. Bland pushing the three carriages and Truebore and Sir Terence pushing the other two carriages. Although Juniper, upon seeing Mr. Edgy's rather feeble pushing efforts, boisterously pushed in next to him, gaily remarking: "Come on, Edmund, this is a hearty Norman girl's work! Let me boost you with a bit of added muscle power !" And with the augmented, mighty effort of Juniper's considerable muscular prowess, the three carriages on the right hand track to *The Royal Robin* suddenly with a pronounced jerk, shot out of the siding shed door with a startled Mr. Edgy still holding onto the last car; the further observed consequence being that our rabbit-faced poet tumbled to the ground in the wake of this dynamic emanation from the siding shed. Seeing the three carriages shoot out apparently by their own mysterious volition, followed by Mr. Edgy's sprawling fall onto the grass, occasioned some involuntary laughter from the other waiting ladies passengers, such as Alison Acrylic and Melissa Puff-Up. But although, stifling some unbidden, rogue smiles, Miss Esther and Miss Muffin both helped up our grounded golden-age advocate. Five or ten minutes later the carriages were coupled to *The Red Robin*.

Excluding Boffo, the train driver, there were nineteen passengers including Miss Muffin. Prunella Makepiece and Clara Clouthard looked in vain for their self-designated man-of-the-moment, Julian Morbid, but the latter had given them the slip for the time being, feigning that he needed some recuperation this morning after last night. Dr. Microbe had tactfully tendered the apology to Sir Terence and was loyally staying with Julian, encouraging him to play some therapeutic and not too taxing Handel and Scarletti pieces on the Bluthner. Muriel Muffin, helpful as ever, had left the two men a share of the prepared picnic lunch which they could eat at their own untroubled leisure. Apart from these two absences all the other guests were in readiness for the short circular excursion. Given there were only ten seats in the five carriages, *The Royal Robin* would need to make two passenger excursions. Thus, the first excursion would take ten people and the second would take the remaining nine. The plan was that each outward trip would involve *The Royal Robin* doing a complete track circuit (start back to start) and then doing a further half-circuit to deposit its passengers at the picnic site situated alongside the Rectory pond's far western edge. The one and a half times round the track circuit would, Boffo thought make it more of an excursion experience for his guests. This outward trip, he computed, would take about a sluggish twelve minutes.

The weather was holding good still. A few favourable bird sounds courtesy of some willing hedge sparrows, a robin (perched on the siding shed) and swallows high above in the promisingly cerulean heavens, helped to promote an optimistic mood amongst Boffo and most of the would-be passengers. *The Royal Robin,* which had lately been sleeping in happy oblivion, was now ready for some action. For its first trip, the group of passengers comprised: Sir Terence and Geoffrey Havealot in the first car; Juniper and Acrylic in the next car; Giles Truebore and Melissa Puff-Up in the third car; Lucinda Halo and Muriel Muffin in the fourth car and Clara Clouthard and Prunella Makepiece in the last car. Boffo, of course, was in the covered driver's cab which was just about tall enough for him to stand up in, although there was a little seat he could sit on. And so the first intrepid party are off as *The Royal Robin* pulls away with a rather grinding noise emanating from the gearbox.

Boffo changed up or rather grinded into another gear. "You must not mind the noisy gearbox, Geoffrey" said Boffo, turning behind him to our affably wealthy MP. "You see", Boffo continued, "it originated from a Reliant Robin van". "Oh, those funny little machines – motorbikes on three wheels! One wonders who on earth would have wished to drive around on main roads in such fibre-glass toys" laughed back the Honourable member of Parliament. "Hence, I suppose the name, *The Royal Robin*?" ventured Sir Terence. "Exactly so", replied Boffo, adding: "I know this is just a composite box on wheels compared to a steam loco replica, and rather a slow ride to boot". "Not at all", replied the Honourable Havealot. "At least this little *Royal Robin* of yours is not quite as miniature as some trains I've been on when opening garden fetes. Some of those trains were not much bigger than model Hornby sets! They had no sit-in carriages like these; rather, it was like being astride a two and a half foot high donkey – one's feet virtually dangling along the ground. Most undignified! Who wants to sit *on* a train. Trains are for sitting *in* not for balancing upon! This by comparison is reasonably civilised, although the carriages are perhaps a trifle *too open* for my liking", continued the MP. "Of course, my dear Geoffrey, I plan to update the rolling stock and have some sides put on them for safety, to allay the mishap of people leaning too far one side and falling out" replied Boffo blithely. Just now the train was traversing the eastern side of the pond which was fringed at intervals with several graciously weeping willows. "I see the pond still has a fairly high water level", mordantly observed Sir Terence.

"Poor Juniper! Your devoted, poetical admirer, Mr. Edgy, seems now to have opted for your new deadly rival, Miss Esther Halo. How devastated you must feel at this signal blow of betrayal", dryly remarked Alison Acrylic to Juniper (who, as we have previously noted was seated with the celebrated artist in the car behind Sir Terence and Havealot). "Deadly rival, nothing! So deadly that I feel devastated in sorrow for the poor girl. The least I could have done was to take 'Prince Edric the unready rabbit' on the ride with me and give her a break! You could see after breakfast that he was delirious in his indecision of whether it was me or her! Male wimps are bad enough – but indecisive ones – that takes the biscuit! One moment I thought he was going to get in the car behind us, but then when this Esther innocently just now spoke some nicety to him, you could see the poor fellow flush scarlet. That was it! He became a pathetic mesmerised puppet, thrall to her unwitting hypnotic power. Poor dear Esther will have her work cut out now to avoid his mooning lover's misery. But I suppose she can take refuge with her father, that funny but rather dour, strict looking man." "Oh, Juniper, you must stop counterfeiting" replied Miss Acrylic, adding: "You are really in love with Mr. Golden-Age, and just playing hard to get in the typical Anglo-Saxon princess fashion! We will soon be in a Bermuda triangle and I will be the jilted jealous woman!" This of course merely exasperated the down-to-earth goddess, Juniper. But Miss Alison Acrylic continued her banter as *The Royal Robin* in unrelieved *Adagio* tempo, slowly progressed, decoratively crunching its gears to the designated picnic stop alongside the western side of the pond.

In the carriage behind, Clara Clouthard and Prunella Pringle were blaming each other for the disappointing unavailability of Julian Morbid. (This at least provided an amnesty from the usual political knife-throwing). "My dear Clara, you were simply plaguing the poor man. It's no good trying to impress a man like that with your so-called musical knowledge. He is a sensitive soul who needs sensitive support – not hounding with mere platitudes", said Prunella Makepiece as she admonished her right-wing rival. "Not at all", replied Miss Clouthard, who continued: "I felt bound to rescue him from your belligerent clutches. He does not want to hear clever intellectual praise from an opportunist who only wants to *use him*, rather than give him the social sort of backing he needs. It's *you* who have driven him away by playing your old blue-stocking game! But men like that don't want to be badgered by blue-stocking women. They would rather have a woman who can help organise the media publicity support which will boost their career. That is something I am far better qualified to do than yourself. I don't live in a Socialist ivory tower; I live in the real market world where business people create wealth and happiness through their own self-achieved merits".

"An excellent micro party speech, Clara", replied her rival journalist, who continued thus: "I can agree with you that Julian is a very sensitive and highly tuned man, (rather like a concert grand). But that is all the more reason why he needs thoughtful intellectual handling, not your heavy-handed, *Daily Hobbyhorse* approach! What does a man like Julian Morbid care about market economics, fat bonuses and the mythology of meritocracy? I can offer him something beyond that, but you have no conception of anything other than that all-too-familiar neo-liberal propaganda!"

"And" replied her antagonist, " I suppose your liberal political correctness, handouts and wealth for layabouts isn't propaganda! Mr. Morbid deserves proper recognition, bonuses and economic success – things which you and *The Clarion Echo* are foolishly and jealously opposed to!"

We leave this squabbling and come to the next two carriages containing respectively the twosome of Giles Truebore and Melissa Puff-Up and twosome of Lucinda Halo and Muriel Muffin. Speaking for myself, I might venture with some authorial snobbery that there is little here of further interest for the discerning reader. As puppet-master I am bound to say that fiction writing ineluctably predicates authorial sovereignty, although today there is a general pretence that fictional characters arrive out of nowhere, like babies delivered by an untraceable stork. However, if sovereign authorial control rules, as it does, it ought at times to be wisely tempered by the wilful waywardness of inspiration. At least this ought to apply to any decent puppeteer rather than those of the *Mills and Boon* varieties. So then, who am I to make such cavalier judgements, nonchalantly consigning some of my puppets to their boxes while putting apparently privileged others onto the stage to democratically air their views? Am I not merely a jobbing puppeteer master trying laboriously to write my first novel? Well, that being conceded, let me with suitable magnanimity, allow a little wayward inspiration to disclose some of what Mr. Truebore and Miss Puff-up have to say:

Puff-Up: It's naturally amusing and pleasantly passes the time to ride on these miniature train circuits. But do you not agree, Giles, that this type of thing seems to be more and more of a retrograde nostalgic fad nowadays? It's odd, is it not, how some people want to escape back into an idealised golden-hued past? There does in one sense seem to be a certain absurdity in playing with enlarged toy trains. One cannot but feel that such people as our dear Boffo are actually only underlining the fact of railway travel's inferiority to our modern road and airway systems.

Truebore: Of course, Melissa. The train at its best today is a useful secondary form of transport, particularly useful at transporting people into car-restricted city centres. But the train is really just a residue of a bygone system of society where people were treated as agglomerates, to be herded together in carriages. Thus, the train does not in sheer principle accord with today's advanced entrepreneur age of individuality and corresponding free choice. As you rightly say, Melissa, this miniature train culture with all its generated nostalgic infatuation, seems to attract people of a certain mentality. It obviously appeals greatly to our good cleric friend, Boffo. And why does this old-hat train culture appeal to him? Why, because he would perhaps prefer to go slower in life, avoiding the new – the new way we now live. He and his religion – dare I say it – hark back to a past superseded culture; a slower world, where there was more of an ambling pace and subsequently time for perhaps pleasant meditation. But we don't have that lee-way of time to amble about any more. We are now in a global, digital and internet age where speed and new development is of the essence. There is no time for poetic stragglers of the old Wordsworth type.

Puff-Up: Yes, teach them at school if they must, Wordsworth and others of his ilk as examples of a past culture. But personally, when for instance anyone quotes me W.H. Davies' lines:

"*What is this life if, full of care,*
We have no time to stand and stare?"

I merely reply: "Of course we have "no time to stand and stare". Culture has changed. It's not appropriate nor wise to use our time in such a way any more. We're too busy and *need to be busy* to fit in with the racing demands of our expanding and ever-changing technological culture. After all, Giles, just these last few decades have been particularly responsible for the achievement of so much technological breakthrough and radical transformation of our world. This of course has left a sizeable amount of people behind and some of them have become – (with a sly wink), I'm naming no names here

– modern day Luddites. But my point here is that none of these rapid achievements of particularly the last thirty years or so could have occurred if we had all been contemplating nature's navel, so to speak.

Truebore: I agree, Melissa. Although perhaps you're a bit too forthright in respect of the old-fashioned poetic types. They were, it is true, even lagging behind their own times, but certainly they did not have our colossal technological advantages. Doubtless if cars, motorways, jet aeroplanes and computers had somehow been introduced into their period and been properly explained to them, they could well have radically modified their over-inflated views of the importance of nature…"

Let us leave their conversation at that point. (They are anyway nearing the picnic site and will shortly disembark the train). Let me now be a somewhat judgmental puppeteer: Giles Truebore and Melissa Puff-Up, in their covertly flirtatious friendship, appear at best as merely pleasantly boring re-enforcers of one another. Let them get on with it, I the puppet-master say. Their very behavioural predictability would only please Professor Babble as an example of the non-existence of free-will. He does have some sort of a point. For in a basic sense all characters more or less perform to 'type'. Human leopards don't tend to change their spots; they just slightly re-arrange the size and patterning of them. They always remain the same old rogues.

As for Lucinda and Muriel, they both seem to know their place, although for the one it is a rather subservient background place, whereas for the other it is a place at least of initiative and creative service. And do we have at least a little window on what these two steadfast and reliable ladies are conversing about? Well, they are going in a contrary conversational direction to Miss Puff-Up and Mr. Truebore. The conversation, such as it is, tends to be punctuated with pregnant pauses. But here is the gist of their punctuated talk; Lucinda Halo is saying to Muriel Muffin: "How I wish things could slow down in our day and age. If only everything went so nice and slowly as this dear old train! Why we can't go back to travelling in trains and do without these wretched noisy, fast cars, I will never know". "Oh, I agree", affirmed Miss Muffin, adding: "People are in such a hurry nowadays. Where are they all going to and why is it so important for them to always rush, rush, rush? And what do they do with all the time they supposedly save by all this rushing? No, my motto is do everything slowly and steadily and everything always gets done in time". To which Mrs Halo further replied: "Oh, Muriel, if only people would follow the old ways, the old paths as my dear George says. And if only people would listen to my dear George! He gets such a small congregation on Sundays. And no doubt all these people who won't come to church and listen to him are too busy driving their fast and noisy cars…"

Well, let us stop the above conversation here. And having now conveniently disposed of the last two carriages, we may follow the first party to its destination which it has at last reached – namely, as already mentioned, a suitably bucolic spot alongside two weeping willow trees on the western side of the pond. The ten more or less eager passengers thus alight and accordingly survey their lunch-time country prospect, inspecting in vain the greenish brown pond water for any interesting signs of life.

CHAPTER SIXTEEN

OLD PATHS, DWARFS AND BEARS

Having deposited the first instalment of human freight, *The Royal Robin*, ably shepherded at the helm by that perennially buoyant Universalist, Boffo, now sets off back to collect the remaining nine passengers. The said passengers are basking in the bright beams of an obliging *Phoebus* and a blue sky flecked with filigree fleecy white clouds. The weather prognosis for the day is now proving itself delightfully accurate. Seated at two adjacent garden tables, we find the goodly company of Timothy Tadpole, Guy St. Bland, Canon Hollow, Father Goodbalance and Benjamin Babble. However, let us first pass over to the other four awaiting, would-be passengers. We find them seated around another garden table, an equally interesting combination of Esther Halo, her father, George Halo, Edmund Edgy and fluffy haired Ashley Dunce. The latter had craftily been given the slip by his erstwhile political, travelling companions; all three for once coming to an unusual agreement, in wishing to have a break from his affable but exceedingly unrewarding, inconsequential sound-bites. As we have noted with regard to the first excursion, Geoffrey Havealot had been honoured to accept sharing the front car with Sir Terence, while Clara Clouthard and

Prunella Makepiece had with pleasurable celerity accepted the last available car. The *CDP* leader, who in fairness can hardly be classed as an action man, was therefore left somewhat high and dry. His being shockingly abandoned in this manner was surely on the one hand an exercise of free-will by those fleeing him and on the other hand an engrained behavioural lack of applied free-will on his own part. Finding himself thus momentarily politically excommunicated, Mr. Dunce felt he must make the best of the situation by entering any available general populace territory, which might prove useful for a bit of discreet *CDP* sounding off.

In this group of four, Ashley Dunce had seated himself strategically next to Mr. Edgy and was facing Miss Halo. Esther's father sat next to her facing the uncomfortably shifting body of the presently mute-mouthed, neo-Anglo-Saxon bard. Mr. Dunce proceeded to properly introduce himself to his three table companions.

Dunce: As leader of the exciting new *Consensus Diversity Party* – which you all will no doubt have heard of in the general media – you must forgive me for perhaps taking the opportunity to somewhat impose upon your good selves. I trust you will not think I am stooping to do some sly political canvassing. Not at all! However, like any true politician, I deeply care about and particularly value the educated public's views on current political and media-raised concerns. In terms of manipulating your views, I certainly would not want to try to influence you one way or the other. Far be it! For we at the *CDP* merely wish to discreetly and boldly draw attention to our manifesto – its great worthwhile aims and projected pathways; for I realise that as yet I have to gain a political seat, and so far in five years we, as a party have achieved three seats on local councils. However, we have much to offer in seeking neither to offend anyone nor seeking to merely go with the flow, as it were. We seek to travel a pathway which unites the good hard working citizens of this land, as we also at the same time seek to travel a pathway which allows people the diversity to be either rich, poor, creative, not so creative; to be industrious, to be leisurely, to laugh or to cry and so forth. At *CDP*, as you no doubt can gather, we believe in mixed pathways.

Reverend Halo: Ah, pathways! Do you not know of the old pathways which lead to the one true narrow road? Have you not read the prophet's words: *"Stand at the crossroads and look; ask for the ancient paths, ask where the good way is, and walk in it, and you will find rest for your souls".* Have you, ambitious young man, considered these pathways which lead to the only true universal way to avoid perdition?

Dunce (rather nonplussed): I confess I have not so far come across them. Are they far from here?

Esther (trying to smother a wry smile): They are not far from anyone, Mr. Dunce.

Dunce (again, confidently): Of course, we should never abandon the past, that is, throw out the baby with the bath water. No! We are for safeguarding the baby and all babies! For we at the *CDP* strongly believe in the great traditions and heritage of our esteemed nation. We also strongly believe in choice, so your prophet's metaphor of a crossroads is absolutely spot-on. One must have plenty of choices – plenty of opportunities – and naturally choose which direction one wants to travel in. But of course, as your prophet's words also clearly indicate, one must have expert informed guidance and that is where *we* come in as an enormously and hugely relevant new party. We say: "Yes, look at the crossroads of choice! But we will do more than just that – we will expertly help you to make the right choices for your lives. And not only that, we will make it even easier by supplying you with the *right* choices. We want every man, woman, boy and girl to take the best turning at the crossroads. It goes without saying that to choose our party in the next local or general elections will be making the *right* choice. I cannot perhaps go as far as your prophet by saying there will be rest for your souls, but what I would say is that to vote for *CDP* is a vote which will give rest and peace to your minds, knowing that capable, resolute and pro-active people with leadership qualities, such as myself, will be at the helm seeking to give people both the old established and excitingly new paths which will bring them fulfilment and never-ending wealth and prosperity. And I would, as a balanced politician make no further statement than these carefully qualified and unobtrusive words which I have just spoken.

Reverend Halo (warming to his task): Mr. Dunce, I see that you have not yet been introduced to the one true universal party, the Church, which for all its sins, is the Bride of our blessed Saviour. I see you are another young man on the threshold. If I may say, you are like many ambitious, cunningly misled young men, enamoured of the variety of false, glittering choices on offer in this decadent and corrupt world-market place. I feel now the call – the indeed urgent call, which prompts me to speak to you even in advance of Mr. Edgy, whom I had most earnestly promised to speak to earlier this morning. However, in light of your undoubtedly enthusiastic, but spiritually uniformed talk, I propose, dear Mr. Dunce, that we share this impending short train journey together in the same carriage. There we can speak man to man, for the time is short and the days are evil. My dear daughter, Esther, (*turning to her and looking at Edmund Edgy*), I am sure you will not mind sharing a carriage with this other young man, Mr. Edgy, for he is also, I feel, on the threshold of the Kingdom, and will no doubt benefit from your own recent refining experiences, concerning the wiles of Satan's depraved activities.

Esther nodded compliantly to her father. She certainly did not relish sharing a carriage with Mr. Dunce and felt somewhat drawn in sympathy to the mooning poet. Edmund Edgy breathed a big sigh of relief in being spared the short journey with the inquisitional Reverend; instead being able to share a carriage with his radiant, sharp-eyed and neat pencil-nosed daughter; she of the beguilingly braided chestnut-hair. Ashley Dunce felt rather confused, evidently not understanding the language of the Spirit. But in the *CDP* leader's lack of exact comprehension, he clung to the compensating thought that there might still be a good opportunity to come to some sort of agreement with the good Reverend during the journey, thereby gaining the latter's and daughter's promise of a *CDP* vote in the future.

Let us now turn to the other train-waiting group of five, surveying their latest topic of conversation. The latter was, I am happy to say, fairly un-contentious by the participants' previous standards, centring on whether there might be living beings on other planets. Canon Hollow had been against such an idea. "It has of course been long since proved that the planets of our own solar system are incapable of harbouring any forms of animated life. Years back the only two possible candidates (after ruling out the rock-cratered, waterless

Moon) used to be Mars and Venus. But Mars, although containing frozen water in its polar caps and probably some rock-trapped underground water, has a virtually negligible oxygen concentration and is also characterised by vast fluctuations of temperature. As for Venus, its carbon dioxide concentration doubles that of the Earth's oxygen. It's too close to the Sun for its own good! Moreover, it has no ozone shield to protect it from ultra violet radiation. Therefore, it is a veritable hothouse with a thick atmosphere which is about as useless for life as Mars' thin atmosphere. Our rare Earth has no competitors here!

Dr. Tadpole (bursting in impatiently): Of course! Of course! But we have moved on, my dear Donald! Mars and Venus are mere science fiction today compared to the exoplanets being discovered almost every minute by NASA astronomers! Forget our little solar system! Only the other day there were another handful of new planets discovered in a 'Goldilocks zone' and a couple of them already show the promise of being more similar to Earth than any known exoplanets so far detected.

St. Bland (cynical): Ha, ha! If these are in a 'Goldilocks zone', presumably their inhabitants will solely consist of surly alien bears, whose staple diet is porridge. Perhaps these alien bears all speak in a quasi-Scottish dialect, dance highland reels and toss cabers! Perhaps their planet is a larger version of Scotland? No doubt we must be careful not to send up little golden-haired girl astronauts to visit them. We don't want to end up in a dreadful space war over purloined beds and porridge, ha, ha!

Dr. Tadpole (undaunted by this witticism): Very amusing Guy, but the fact is that satire is out of place here; for it is only a matter of time now till we find a planet which has the right chemical concentrations and is located at the right orbital distance from its host star. And, Guy, we are finding more and more Earth look-a-like exoplanets in the habitable *Goldilocks Zone.* Sooner or later one of these extrasolar planets is going to be the one astronomers have been looking for! But anyone following the latest developments must surely realise by now that the future lies in red dwarf stars! The fact is that they are being detected all over the universe. They make up about seventy-five percent of all the universe's stars and every time a red dwarf is detected you can be sure it will have at least one planet if not several others orbiting it. It's simple logic: The more red dwarfs, the more exoplanets, and the more exoplanets the more chance that some will be within the habitable 'Goldilocks zone'. And the more planets in that zone, the greater the chances that one at least is going to be Earth-sized, having also the right ratio of water and land mass to host some significant form of extra-terrestrial life.

Canon Hollow: Your argument, Timothy. does not follow nor particularise very well. Just because there are apparently loads of these red dwarf stars proves nothing. Indeed, there are a lot of them; so what?

St. Bland: Bravo, Canon, excellent goal! Yes, what if there are thousands of these dwarfs floating about in space with their acolyte planets; but these planets are most probably all just rocky heat furnaces, only good for cooking instant fried eggs!

Dr. Tadpole: You both miss the point. Firstly, conditions for extraterrestrial life depend on the orbital distance of a planet to its host star. If the planet is near enough it will get the energy it requires for life to evolve and further develop. If it's too near its star – e.g. sun – then of course it bakes and any water will evaporate. But those planets at the right and stable orbital distance will be able to maintain any surface water they might have. As well as meeting this criteria, a planet would also need to be roughly Earth-sized; be host to correct chemical ratios and able to hold an adequate amount of atmosphere. It's chances for life would further benefit from having an axial tilt provided by a nearby moon. These are the crucial variables and there's no reason why they cannot all be found on other planets as well as our own Earth! Secondly, these red dwarfs are important not just because they outnumber all other stars, but also because they outlive everything else in the universe! It's calculated red dwarfs exist for possibly as long as trillions or quadrillions of years; they thus offer exactly the massive time-scale required for evolution on a nearby orbiting exoplanet.

Canon Hollow: Once again, Timothy, your neo-Darwinian assumption, namely that as long as you have bags of time – billions upon billions of years – anything, no matter how improbable or illogical can happen! Billions, trillions or quadrillions doesn't cancel out the improbability!

Father Goodbalance: Such number-crunching becomes ultimately meaningless.

Dr. Tadpole (unperturbed): Meaningless perhaps to our limited and as yet untutored comprehensions – but still true! Anyway, it's not all such number-crunching. Take, for instance our Sun, known as a yellow dwarf – although actually it's a white star, constituting the largest mass within our solar system.

St. Bland (interrupting): Excuse me uncle Timothy, if

the Sun is really white why is it a yellow dwarf instead of a white dwarf? Don't tell me astronomers are colour-blind, ha, ha! And how can a dwarf be a massive dwarf? Another remarkable contradiction, ha, ha!

Professor Babble: Young man, you obviously do not know current astronomy basics. Firstly, dwarf stars vary in size and our Sun happens to be at the top end of the size scale. Secondly, if the Sun were a white dwarf it would be already dead! White dwarfs are just cooling remnants of stars that have died.

Dr. Tadpole: (Returning to the fray): Exactly, and one day when our Sun dies, it too will become a white dwarf!

St. Bland: It gets even more mysterious! So the Sun, although white, is called a yellow dwarf, yet it does eventually become a white dwarf when it gives up the ghost. And it appears not all dwarfs are equal, some are massive dwarfs, ha, ha! Bring in Sherlock Holmes to explain this case to me; I'm only a poor Dr. Watson, ha, ha!

Dr. Tadpole (still undaunted): Let's not get side-tracked on issues of terminology. Instead, let's contrast our fast-burning Sun with red dwarf stars. We all know that the Sun is calculated to be currently in its main-sequence, more or less four and a half billion years old; mid-way through its life-span. For a red dwarf, a few billion years is sheer babyhood! The secret of their incredible longevity is that after sowing their wild oats, sending out loads of flares, they stabilise and burn their fuel at a slow rate. However, in only about a mere five billion years time our Sun will have burnt through all its hydrogen content. Then helium will be its primary fuel; the result being that a billion or so years later the Sun will expand into a massive red giant, engulfing the nearest orbiting planets, including Earth, and thence it will shrink into a cooling white dwarf. Ultimately it will end up as a cold and dark black dwarf. But red dwarfs will be still around trillions of years later They're virtually immortal – none of these low-mass stars have ever yet died. That's why the future is in red dwarfs!

St. Bland: Even more weird! Our yellow dwarf, which is actually white, then becomes a red giant, but afterwards reverts to being a dwarf again; a classified white one this time! Astronomers must all read *Grimms' Fairy Tales.* That's where I've slipped up on my reading matter! My apologies, ha, ha!

Canon Hollow (rather severely): Never mind, Guy, the particularity of solar colour schemes. The point I must re-iterate is that an immense time-scale does not in itself validate in any logical sense the probability of life on another planet. It remains an improbability.

Professor Babble: But the fact that we and our planet Earth are here proves that what seems improbable *does* occur! There are actually proper reasons for the improbable happening. You might think extra-terrestrial life is improbable, but all life on Earth is due to the barely comprehensible coalescence of the right circumstances and corresponding factors. These circumstances and factors need a considerable scale of time in which to meld and develop. We can only communicate together here now courtesy of the fact that our Sun has given life on Earth billions of years to develop its evolutionary processes. Surely, it is then not more than possible that a star which lasts for trillions of years is able to supply the time-frame for similarly evolving life that will not only parallel but far outlast the time-span of our own world.

Dr. Tadpole: Exactly, exactly! I say again, red stars are the key to future survival!

Canon Hollow: I grant that red dwarfs may be slow burners for most of their existence and therefore exist far longer. However, as it is well known, once established they exude only a dim light. This of course means that to receive the requisite heat for evolving life, planets need to orbit close to the red dwarf. And here, Timothy I'm afraid one must deflate your boundless optimism regarding red dwarfs. The problem as it is commonly known is that too close an orbit to a red dwarf risks a gravitational pull of which 'tidal locking' results. And this mucks up everything for the planet concerned! Half the respective planet becomes perpetual day and the other half perpetual night. The side that is always day is too hot and so all its liquid resources boil away; the other side which is always night becomes on the contrary too cold and any water there freezes. So, no water, *ergo,* no life! And another problem, Timothy; if your red dwarf happens to be still relatively youthful, it will constantly throw out flares causing the candidate planet to suffer a huge increase in ultra violet radiation. This will accordingly render your planetary surface sterile and may even strip away its atmosphere. So your dim red dwarfs may rather be red herrings in terms of our and the universe's salvation!

St. Bland: Ha, ha! Both a goal and a conversion this time, Canon Donald! Admit defeat, uncle! Who wants the future of the universe to be in the hands of not very bright – dim red dwarfs! Away with all dumb red dwarfs – let them find a gnome, a gnome planet in a suitable galaxy with a garden pond to freeze or dry up!

Father Goodbalance (mischievously): Goldilocks, red

giants and yellow, red and white dwarfs, indeed! One wonders if it is not a coincidence that such names come out of fairy-tale books. And it is usually us, the clergy, who are accused by you, Timothy, of peddling fairy tales!

St. Bland: Ha, ha! Where does Snow White come into all this? You can't have unsupervised, delinquent dimwit dwarfs running amok all over the universe!

Babble: Young man, the term 'Dwarf' astronomically refers to size – in this case low-mass stars; that is to say, stars much smaller in radius than our own sun-star. That means their luminosity is weak. But as Timothy has pointed out, their advantage resides in a longevity of existence which stretches right back to 'the big bang'. That is why they are obviously important for hosting extra-terrestrial life on planets within close proximity. But of course, for all we know there may be some variety of space-type gnomes living on such planets! Nothing is impossible.

Father Goodbalance: If nothing is indeed impossible, I would prefer to believe in a Creator designer than in gnomes or dwarfs! Why waste billions upon billions of money on space exploration when it is our duty to steward this Earth by alleviating poverty and caring for the environmental infrastructure? What is it to us anyway, even if there are other places sustaining life in the universe?

Dr. Tadpole (un-deflected): My dear Father, it matters a lot! We are making new discoveries about things that *exist!* This is *not* science fiction! Any such discoveries must somehow enhance our own existence by increasing human knowledge and awareness of this wonderful and awesome universe within which just one mere galaxy, we are situated. Yes, we may be tiny finite dots in it, but we are now able to make telescopes and space shuttles which are starting to chart the solar systems beyond our own! Where can obstinate belief in a magician God get us today? It's just clinging onto the past. For many it's just a nice sentimental idea, but such belief is like a sponge which soaks up all our desire and energy to make real contact with all the reality we are encased in. And who knows, there may be resources on an exoplanet in a Goldilocks zone, which one day – albeit the distant future – our increased technology may allow us to reap the benefit of.

St. Bland: But suppose these alien bears on an exoplanet in a so-called habitable zone have better brains than us and have invented excellent long-distance spacecraft? Supposing if they came all the way to Earth; they might, as highly intelligent but greedy alien bears, plunder our resources!

Canon Hollow: That is of course a particularised possibility.

Babble: In terms of our planetary security it makes good sense to continue to scrutinise the cosmos. The more we know the better the position we can be in to survive. If for instance our documentation and observation of the universe continues at the present amazing pace, we may be able to avert any such future danger by sending up a space shuttle with high explosives to blow up any invading alien spacecrafts.

Father Goodfellow: Why must we always blow things up?

Babble: If it is for the safety of the human race from terrorist alien attacks, surely self-defence is warranted. Any such self-defence would of course be based upon a very clear indication from all our latest scientific technology that we were under a real alien threat.

Dr. Tadpole: Of course, of course! We naturally hope that

if there was any possible alien life, whether plant, animal or whatever, that it would be beneficial to us and not in any way a threat to our own planet.

St. Bland: Just a minute! How do we know that we are not all aliens anyway? I personally think we are mutations from an exoplanet in a Goldilocks zone. Perhaps we all used to be extra-terrestrial bears with incredible brains, eating extra-terrestrial porridge and speaking in an extra-terrestrial Scottish dialect! But since these ancestors of ours arrived here by spacecraft millions of years ago, our bodies have mutated unfortunately into *homo sapiens*, while our formerly excellent bear brains have sadly atrophied in England – at least. Only the alien bears who migrated to Scotland have managed to keep their brain power, for they find there a conducive environment similar to their own, original planet. That's perhaps the reason why all the best thinkers, philosophers, engineers, etc., are all Scottish, ha, ha!

Babble: My dear young man, I think you are now indulging yourself in a rather scurrilous flight of fancy.

At that moment, further conversation conveniently ended on this interesting topic of discussion, as *The Royal Robin* was now just arriving back to pick up the remaining excursion and picnic passengers.

Chapter Seventeen

CIRCULAR EXCURSION (TWO)

Some minutes later *The Royal Robin* with the ever-beaming Boffo at its helm was engaged in chugging its way (with occasional gear-box grinding) on excursion trip number two. Dr. Tadpole and Guy St. Bland are in the car behind Boffo at the engine; Canon Hollow and Father Goodbalance are in the second car; Professor Babble shares the third car with his capacious self; Esther and Edmund Edgy share the fourth car and lastly, Ashley Dunce and the Reverend Halo fill up the rear carriage. As to the first car, Dr. Tadpole is leaning forward chatting animatedly to Boffo about the fascinating evolution of trains while his nephew also shows a modicum of detached interest in the relevant details which are bandied about. Passing onto the second car, the two theologically contrasting clergymen are exchanging a few observations concerning theistic evolution.

Entering mid-way into their conversation, we hear Canon Hollow saying: "I personally find neo-Darwinism unhelpful precisely because it only focuses on the survival aspect of evolution and therefore concentrates unduly on the latter's ugly and clinical factors such as mutation and natural selection. But my Larmarckian approach is rather to place the emphasis on an evolution based more ultimately on nature's beneficent 'harmony'. This helps us to make some answer to Darwin's own concern about why a Creator should allow our world to develop in such a cruel, messy and indeed mad, random way."

Father Good balance: I can certainly agree that survival of the fittest has had and still has a disastrous knock-on cultural effect sociologically and politically. A non-ethical based-evolution such as Darwinism gives the green-light to a society such as ours today. Smug, self-made and self-satisfied entrepreneur millionaires see themselves as the fittest individuals in society. They more or less believe themselves to have been naturally selected to their 'winning positions' via their 'greater ability' over others. Accordingly, they believe their huge status and financial privileges are thoroughly deserved. Yes, survival of the greediest, a culture we can all do without!

Canon Hollow: From my point of view, an authentic theistic evolution does not invalidate the concept of providence but rather re-defines it. This is achieved to some significant extent by demythologising God and understanding him rather as a supreme technician; a God of the natural sciences, who amongst other things deals in biological processes and the adaptations which may occur as a result of such processes. Process of course is 'becoming', or in Lamarckian terms, adapting and passing on useful acquired evolutionary developmental traits. All this development is done within the existing framework of what happens to be the 'given', not only at the start point of evolution but at all stages within its subsequent progression. Therefore we can no longer talk about separately created species. Nor can we talk about a specially created man and woman in a specially created garden. Neither is it helpful to talk about sin and a fall. Life is as it is 'given'. Suffering and death are part of the package, for nature has no choice other than to be 'red in tooth and claw'. Human beings, of course, are the apex of evolution's achievement in terms of consciousness – the advanced ability to think and reflect. Yet we, also like the lower natural order are subject to suffering and death. But the problem is, Godfrey, that we have – inexcusably – only made things a lot worse.

Father Goodbalance (interjecting): 'Made things a lot worse'! That surely must be *the* understatement *par excellence* concerning *homo sapiens*!

Canon Hollow (continuing unperturbed,): We humans are culpable, each of us by virtue of our ability to make a bad choice with moral repercussions. Even our apparent non-choices are default choices with consequences. But it won't do to see ourselves as a flawed species *per se*; supposedly so because of a single mistake two adults once made in a mythological garden called Eden. Rather, as we have been created through various processes of developmental freedom, it is a matter of intelligent self-responsibility for us all to act like rational beings.

Father Goodbalance: When you talk about suffering and death being just part of the package, I cannot believe this is how things are meant to be. Death is an appalling anomaly in terms of a loving Creator, whom we are told created all things well at the beginning. Our longings for immortality prove, I am absolutely sure, that we were not originally created merely as a more advanced add-on in the evolutionary series, subject like all other living species to death. Scripture tells us that something went badly wrong and continues to go wrong

228

through the result of an initial and significant failure – 'fall' on the part of our first fully thinking ancestors. Our "first" parents, whether they constituted a small tribe or perhaps a single man and woman, and wherever they were situated, must have been a *special, separate creation.* They must have been somehow very deliberately created *outside* evolution's general slow branching pattern of development; perhaps a localised creation in a special, favourable environment, as symbolised by the Eden garden. I believe our good Lord decided to do this because these archetypal humans were to somehow reflect him more closely than any other creatures he had yet made. That is why they must have been created in such a different way so as to make them immortal. Thus sin – the fall – is the real root cause of biological death. Whoever Adam and Eve represent – two people or a group of people – they were uniquely *a special creation.* That means at their point of advent they were not subject to the normal evolutionary laws of decay and death. They were within evolution in one sense and yet in another sense outside it because of their privileged special creation and all that it signified spiritually.

Canon Hollow: No doubt a worthy attempt on your part to retain the historic 'fall'.

However, if God wanted to break into the slow grinding, particularised laws of evolution, it begs the question of why he bothered with evolution in the first place! I think you are trying to have your cake and eat it, Godfrey! Evolution and special creations can't run both together. You either must have one or the other. God is either consistent in his methods or not. Surely it is clear that humans have evolved through a long process and our very bodies, their construction and

229

functions clearly link us to the various animal species which have all played a part, one way or another, in our evolution. We ourselves arrive in a world which is already there. It is a 'given' world, but 'given' by an incredibly complex mixture of slowly emerging factors.

Father Goodbalance: My main concern with an open, 'given' world which is 'just there' is that one can possibly end up looking merely at this 'given-ness' rather than what lies behind it – the Creator. And Donald, I fear that is the danger your *advanced*, post-Lamarckian brand of Christianity lands you in. You stand upon the precipice of this passing short-term world, intently looking down into its complexities, as if *all* knowledge and insight can only exist through human observing and measuring. Whereas, I myself, would rather spend more time looking across the precipice to where the spiritual kingdom – eternity – lies.

Canon Hollow: You over-particularise your point Godfrey. We can only work with what is 'given', what is tangible in terms of careful human scrutiny. The only real lasting revolution of modern times – which of course developed with startling rapidity in the seventeenth century – is the scientific revolution. All that there is *is* what is 'given' to us. There is nothing else to work with. I sometimes wonder, Godfrey, whether you do not secretly crave for the old pre-scientific chain-of-being world view with everything so conveniently fixed in its allotted place!

Father Goodbalance (an ironic twinkle in his shrewd eyes): Now you are *over particularising* against myself. My concern is that it is all so easy nowadays to get mesmerised by the sciences – particularly the natural sciences. You talk of a new re-vitalised Christianity; a faith re-vitalised by evolutionary principles and associated vast time-scales. You talk of the need to radically revise the time-honoured basis of classical Christianity with all its supposedly outdated doctrines. But such wholesale re-evaluations (which I might say have been very fashionable since the sixties), can be dangerous. Remember Nietzsche? Truth became what was subjectively useful to him, merely as a compensation for his physical incapacities. And following on from Nietzsche's existential example, does not truth today serve multiple purposes in our relativistic society? Is it not merely a conveniently adaptable tool? Truth is malleable and consumerist, suiting whatever job is required of it at any particular moment. But what a dangerous game to play! However, I happen to believe God is a 'given' absolute. We cannot see spiritual absolutes, but they are more real and indeed permanent than all the wonderous, measurable things of this world.

Canon Hollow (now in an slightly aggrieved velvety voice): My dear Godfrey, I am hardly an existentialist and assure you I don't follow Nietzsche or Jean Paul Sartre! They were of course atheists. I am on the other hand a progressive Christian Lamarckian evolutionist rather than a neo-existentialist or neo-Darwinian. The latter is an ideology (with apologies to dear Dr. Timothy), and to boot, merely a crude survival doctrine. What I am seeking is to earth our God's complex truth into the new progressive scientific dispensation which in itself engenders a massive re-evaluation. Old truths must be re-assessed in line with the knowledge that is now transforming the way we live. We must, for a start throw out myths like the fall, virgin birth, atonement and physical resurrection.

"In others words throw out the Bible", wryly retorted

Father Goodbalance. "Getting rid of an historic fall *per se*, means there is no inherently lapsed human condition, therefore no need for the Incarnation and Redemption. Getting rid of the Virgin Birth means our Lord was not divine – not God. Getting rid of the atonement means a do-it-yourself salvation of self-betterment; and getting rid of Jesus' bodily resurrection means only believing in the subjective power of resurrected love. So what is there left to preach? Lamarck, modern wonders of science coupled with a dash of other world religions thrown in for good measure?" "Now, now dear Godfrey", retorted the Canon, "you are being facetious – you will indulge in your droll Jesuit sense of humour; but let me explain my position in more detail…"

Well, this is a good moment – or rather excuse – to leave the two clergymen as matters come to a head. Now we move on past the solo occupant of car three, Professor Babble, who has already fallen into a drowsy snooze. We therefore hone in on carriage number four. Let us see how the lie of the land is between dear Mr. Edmund and the sharply-sweet, enchanting Miss Esther. Here is the latter speaking:

Esther: Why do you make so much of the Anglo-Saxons? What was so good about them? Until Christianity came by way of the Celtic missionaries from Iona and Saint Augustine from Rome, what were most of the Saxons like? They were warlike and cruel like many other primitive peoples who, to be fair to them, did not know any better. Only in the limited, restricted way of kindred did they know the word "love" in terms of caring and kindness for others. Whatever good qualities they subsequently attained all came from gospel values – from Christian missionaries! Yes! Christian values alone taught them how to care for others! In fact, all the generations that came after them, including the Normans and us, owe any goodness they had or have to Christian values. In fact, Edmund, there are only two groups of people in all generations including ours today. That is, there are those who see salvation in the world like yourself – although your salvation is in a past world – and others, like myself, who despite all my flaws and failures, have through God's redeeming grace become connected to a higher and better way of life. Salvation by grace, Edmund – not by utopia!

Edgy (rather bitterly): So, Esther, you are the same as all the others! You want only to pour cold water on all my noble ideals; to see only the savage in Anglo-Saxons, not their organic unity with nature; their simple yet practical self-governing organisation and their beautiful, compact and unpretentious arts and crafts culture. You see their only good through Christianization. And like your father, you are only interested in me as a product for conversion!

Esther (spiritedly): You see any disagreement as a violation of your ideals. But ideals need to stand up to some scrutiny or else they become dangerously untouchable. I am merely contrasting my Christian ideals with your ideals and therefore trying to explain my position – where I'm at. Your ideals are in their face-value way very romantic, but are they true? I believe my ideals *are* true. And why are they true? Why, because they have and are being tested in my life. How can you test a bygone historical era more than a thousand years old? You would need to be time-transported back into that era. And would you really find it so wonderful if you did manage to get back there? I should imagine the cruelty, disease, lack of sanitation, hygiene, poor diet, general insecurity from vicious marauders, would make one want to very quickly return to the twenty-first century!

Edgy: (gloomily): Well, I wasn't maintaining that those times were *absolutely perfect.* However, I still maintain that a small, creative and organic community of togetherness, such as in Alcuin's time onwards, constituted almost an idyllic period compared with our own time. Who can really, if they are serious, contest the fact that our planet now stands on the brink of final ecological and nuclear ruin. And to take England as an example – everywhere, in this once noble land, instead of there being creative beauty, there is only greed and insatiable talk of 'the economy' or 'economic growth'. Everything is reduced to the economy; all we get is consumerism – sales talk, celebrities and sport. Just a neurotic obsession with money! Everything has its price tag – including us! No one wants great art, poetry, drama or literature unless it's a please-the-masses money-spinner. Our popular culture is totally mercenary and what's more it's pulled out the plug on *real* beautiful, uplifting culture!

That's why I look backwards to a time when capitalism was not yet invented!

Esther: I don't necessarily disagree with you, but we have to live in the time we are placed in. It's no good, Edmund, trying to live in an antique shop! We are here today in the twenty-first century not the eighth or the ninth! We have to live where we are *now*. It's never going to be a perfect world. But on the other hand it's no good trying to turn your back on it and seeking instead an ideal of something which is past and gone forever. If you do that, Edmund, people will only perhaps end up making fun of you or even shun you. But what is possible and realistic is to try and make this mixed-up modern world of ours a little better. That's why, with my law qualifications, my career aim is to become a barrister. And hopefully, by God's grace if that goal is achieved I will be in a position to do some good, helping my fellow human beings in significantly useful ways. Look Edmund, we can't just retreat, however attractive that might sometimes seem to be. We must act and do what we can do here and now.

Edgy: (rather petulantly): Well, if Christianity *is* so wonderful in improving life, why are we in such a terrible global mess now? Why didn't God stop the Norman invasion? Why didn't he also stop capitalism and its massive corrupting influence on the whole world? Why doesn't he tomorrow abolish all dictators and corrupt politicians who cause endless suffering and misery? And anyway, what conceivable good can being a Christian do in a world saturated in greed and injustice?

Esther: (laughing): Oh, Edmund, you are now asking me the million-dollar questions! How can I even attempt to answer such things? I am not God!

Edmund: (determinedly): Then you admit that your Christian religion has no answers to the world's problems?

Esther: I admit *I* have no answers to such colossal ongoing problems. Christianity, itself, has no ready-made answers concerning evil and suffering. Christians like myself are merely human – just like you and everybody else. We can't know the answer to ultimate questions. Our answer, as far as it can be said to be an answer, lies in a different direction. It lies in obediently serving our God in *this current world*. Our lives, if we are wired into the spiritual dimension of Jesus can be used as forces for good; we can so order our thoughts, behaviour and actions that we in our very modest, humble ways help to tidy things up a bit around us. Yes, I know that does not sound very much at all in terms of the scale of our human mess; but think of it! If everyone so ordered their thoughts, behaviour patterns and actions in conformity with the surpassing example evidenced in Jesus' life, what a total difference it would make to life today! You see, Edmund, hiding in utopias is not going to solve anything. Only inner transformation changes things.

Edmund: (darkly): But isn't all this supposed transformation, pie-in-the-sky in terms of our hard-nosed times? Surely you are yourself a utopian, just a spiritual opium taker as Marx would have said? You say your God – Jesus – just lets you get on with all this sort of advanced moral improvement. That sounds to me too hit-and- miss, too utopian. And the mess seems to be getting worse rather than clearing up!

Esther: Edmund, have you ever read *Pilgrim's Progress*? If you haven't I suggest I lend you my copy. For this allegorical Christian work makes clear that following Jesus is not an utopian picnic! Being a Christian means working for God *within* the world. It's serving Jesus rather than self-service. We believers don't pretend there are any easy answers, but we seek to follow where our Lord leads us. If we are true to Jesus – and I ashamedly confess it's not always easy to be so – he will remain with us through his living Spirit. I won't go into the Holy Spirit now, but what I'm saying is that faith in Jesus brings us the gift of God's spiritual power. And with that we can do things which are impossible in our normal fallen, weak states.

Edmund: (begrudgingly interested): Where is this spiritual power? Why does it have to be invisible? And how can something invisible transform you…or me?

At this point, Esther leaned forward towards Edmund's face with an arch smile, saying: "Look, Edmund, let me make a little bargain with you – but it's not a bribe, mind you!" At this, she pulled out of her handbag a thin, paperback tract edition of *Mark's gospel*. Edmund was hesitant, but then Esther took out a pen and scribbled inside it: *To dear Edmund, best wishes Esther.* "Now, Edmund, if you will try reading this short gospel account of Jesus with an open mind, I promise to keep in touch with you one way or another. But we can also of course meet again tomorrow before we go our separate ways." The fact shone out in neon lights: the lovely creature had put his name and her name in this little book! Well, even if she *was* a Christian and wanted him also to become one, the joy of receiving something from *her*, suddenly suffused his idealistic rabbit-face with delightful red warmth. "Well, yes..alright, thank you Esther...I'll do my best to look at it...for you. I'll have a try to see what it says". Thus came the faltering words of the love abashed and now seemingly ensnared poet. "Good" replied Esther with a shining smile, and decisive barrister's voice. And at that very moment, *The Royal Robin* was just approaching the western edge of the Rectory pond, where the nine passengers join the other excursion party at the picnic spot.

Is it really necessary, dear reader, to mention much about the conversation in carriage number five? Let us just say that the conversation seemed continually to be comprised of unyieldingly contrary subject matter; neither person attempting or indeed able to tune into the other's blithely conflicting wave-length. Such was each contestant intently and thus obliviously absorbed in their own intentions. So I say, let us conveniently leave off relating the mechanics of Mr.

Ashley Dunce's and Reverend George Halo's train journey conversation and proceed to the picnic. Suffice it is to say that there were no mishaps on either the two short train journeys. No one, particularly the Reverend Halo, fell out of his or her open carriages and into the picturesque algae murkiness of the long neglected Rectory pond.

Chapter Eighteen

PICNIC AND RETURN

Both sets of excursion passengers were now deposited at the picnic site situated at the pond's western side. It only remained for Boffo to make another journey on *The Royal Robin* back to the excursion starting point in order to collect the hampers, plastic garden chairs and tables. For this objective's completion, Boffo required two volunteer helpers. Quick as a flash, Alison Acrylic mischievously whispered in Juniper's ear, suggesting that poor dear Esther deserved a break from Edmund's attentions. As a result, Juniper sprang forward to volunteer and also volunteered Edmund Edgy, exclaiming gaily with a sly wink to Acrylic: "Come on, Edmund the Brute Prince, we can handle this together by our excellent teamwork skills!" "Isn't this your lucky day again Edmund!", dryly remarked Melissa Puff-Up, while Alison Acrylic struggled to suppress a smile that was close to producing an avalanche of giggles. The distracted poet was too frozen by such audacious decision-making to volunteer a refusal, but could only baulk inwardly and outwardly at this now apparently dangerously unstoppable, hypo-active Anglo-Saxon princess of the flowing golden tresses. There was no chance of any escape as Juniper grasped Edmund in a bear-like hug and promptly steered the hapless fellow into the first carriage of *The Royal Robin.*

Guy St. Bland, highly and laconically amused, surveyed Edmund's facial and bodily reactions which at that moment faithfully reflected the fearful prospect of a forced work-liaison with this uncompromising, action-packed Medea. St. Bland would have delightedly accompanied them both. However, there would be lack of carriage space for a third passenger, given that four loaded hampers, as well as stacked chairs and tables were to be transported back to the picnic site. As for Esther, there was a slight frown and wry look which momentarily seemed to ruffle her otherwise endearingly composed face as she observed the overwhelmed, helpless Edmund taken captive by the woman of the flowing golden tresses.

Once seated together on the train and in locomotion, Juniper addressed her nervous companion with a hearty: "Well done, Prince Edmund," giving him also at the same time a hearty bear hug. The shock of this sudden endearingly volatile bodily contact almost lurched Edmund off his pond-side carriage seat into the uninviting algae-infested waters. "Oh no you don't" laughed Juniper, catching hold of Edmund as if he were an awkward rogue rugby ball. "You surely aren't trying to give me the slip by jumping overboard? Well, I can't have you cutting out on me, can I? Be brave, think of Henry V or Coriolanus, as my dear dad, Sir Terence, would say!", she gaily continued. Our troubled poet gargled some confused reply or other. And one must here remember that idealistic poets while having long craved their beloved Beatrice, never quite know what to do when they actually make any sort of tangible contact with the latter. Indeed, they, like Mr. Edgy,

240

when the *contact moment arrives* become only more topsy-turvy as well as exceedingly frightened.

Let us however, not go into further unnecessary details concerning Edmund's forced secondment by Juniper; his feeling that the gorgeous Saxon princess has now become too physically close and demanding for him as she laughingly quizzes and exhorts him while *The Royal Robin* ponderously chugs on its way. Let us also pass over Mr. Edgy's inconsolable pining for the more gentler Esther. And let us as well skate over his hard labour directed by Juniper when he assists her in humping and stacking the chairs and tables, along with the heavy hampers onto the carriages. Let us also pass over the return journey to the pond picnic site, with the now fully loaded-up miniature train and Juniper instructing Edmund (seated in carriage three), to keep an eye open to make sure none of the stacked tables and chairs are accidentally in transit jolted off the back three carriages, while she herself, sitting in carriage two, keeps a watchful eye on the hampers carried by carriage one and two. Needless to say, under Juniper's commanding dispensation the whole operation goes smoothly while Boffo, contentedly at the engine helm, hums: "*What a friend we have in Jesus, All our sins and griefs to bear!*" And shortly, that most dear clergyman and his two helpers are returned courtesy of *The Royal Robin* to the picnic site and its would-be participators.

The four large hampers are opened to reveal the necessary plastic plates and cutlery. What else is there? Well, there are crusty French loaves; a choice of fillings such as chicken, ham, corn beef, egg and cheeses of various sorts such as Brie, Stilton, Gruyere and Double-Gloucester. The above are complemented with all the usual salad appendixes: rocket lettuce, cucumber, cherry tomatoes, shredded carrot, pickled onions, olives and mayonnaise. In addition there are savoury and short-bread biscuits along with various cakes: walnut, lemon drizzle coffee and coconut. Needless to say there is also a goodly supply of grapes, strawberries, bananas, apples and tangerines. For the inevitable accompanying lubricating purposes, apart from non-alcoholic liquids and some tins of light beer and lager for those who so wanted them, there is Sir Terence's favourite medium-rich Madeira wine; some Bordeaux red wine and Australian Chardonnay wine. Clearly, Miss Muriel Muffin and Boffo have both done their homework; everything is in place for a satisfyingly substantial outdoor repast.

We will not burden you with any accounts of the ensuing picnic conversations. Suffice to say that the bountiful presence of all the above mentioned consumables in the pleasant outdoor context engendered a reasonable atmosphere of contentment and fraternity. Edmund was seated with St. Bland along with Truebore and Puff-Up, which was better than being caught up with Alison Acrylic and Juniper, the latter two who were seated with Sir Terence and Geoffrey Havealot. Boffo was complemented by a political three-some: Clouthard, Makepiece and Ashley Dunce. Esther, her parents and Muriel Muffin made a four-some, while not unexpectedly, Dr. Tadpole, Canon Hollow, Father Goodbalance and Professor Babble were together engaged in some reasonably un-polemical conversation about the natural world.

And so we have lightly delineated the setting of our pleasantly bucolic and uncontroversial picnic tableaux. An hour or so later, Boffo and *The Red Robin* take the first instalment of passengers back to the starting-off point by the siding shed. These passengers, be it noted, are not now of the same compilation as in the first journey to the picnic site. After a goodly flow of wine mixed for some of the men with a little light beer or lager (Professor Babble and Ashley Dunce), there was evidently less general concern about who went with whom on the train and in what particular order they went. This was more so concerning the first return journey. In our observation regarding this particular journey, we assuredly find *The Royal Robin's* crew in a rather more boisterous mood due to the now pervading sense of replenished contentment. Sir Terence felt particularly ripe through the influence of good wine to burst into a mischievous, Falstaffian inspired song. And as the train passed alongside the pond, Sir Terence began to sing, encouraging anyone who cared to do so to join in. And those who joined in were Juniper, Alison Acrylic, Edmund Edgy, Prunella Makepiece and Ashley Dunce.

> "Oh, the Somerset levels are a-flooding,
> And it's not too promising in Wales either,
> No, not too good by the Severn and Wye,
> Oh, no, it's not good by the swollen rivers,
> But we don't care, we don't care, and for why?
> We don't live there, we don't live there, no thanks!
> So you won't get much help from us in London!
> Only a rubber dingy and a rubber duck!"

Geoffrey Havelot (sitting next to Acrylic) immediately made bold to answer this sung stanza, and was accompanied by Clara Clouthard (sitting next to Juniper), Giles Truebore (sitting next to Prunella Makepiece), Melissa Puff-Up (sitting next to Sir Terence) and Ashley Dunce (sitting next to Edgy).

Mr. Dunce, we may note, as usual felt that he was always providing a proper *CDP* response by discreetly joining in with both sides. Boffo discreetly took no sides, preferring amid the raucous singing to stick to his job, quietly humming *Guide me, O Thou great Jehovah*.

"We know the answer, we know the answer!
Dredge the naughty rivers and make 'em canals.
Away with trees that stop brick's royal march,
Go forth, build, sell-off our village greens!
No more green belts, let us have house belts,
And bless downtrodden big landowners,
Send their excess water downstream, downstream,
To soak all Marxist whingers, hip, hip, hooray!"

Whereupon this stanza of musical retort sung, Sir Terence and his group struck-up again with a repeat rendition of their opening offering. With that, Geoffrey Havelot and his contrary group also again struck up with a repetition of their musical reply. However, after this Geoffrey Havealot decided to now take the initiative, changing somewhat the musical direction, striking-up an entirely new song. And once again he was supported by his willing cohorts:

"Oh, we're having a lovely austerity,
Oh yes we are, enjoying every minute!
And we're all busy baking delicious cake,
For we won't eat any of your rotten porridge!
We don't need to skimp and save like layabouts,
Sanctions don't exist for us boys in clover,
So snap out of it shirker, get a zero-hours job!"

244

In response to this new musical initiative, Sir Terence happily returned to the fray, again willingly supported by his own song team:

"Oh dear, oh dear, what can the matter be?
For palsied Joan's taken a turn for the worse,
Poor crippled Johnny's just had a nasty fall.
Our Susan's had another bi-polar episode,
While big corporations smile and thrive,
And Jack's cracked on losing his benefit:
You did not score bingo, bad luck old chap!"

During the end of this latter song, Ashley Dunce being rather exuberant due to a mixture of red wine and beer within him, stood up in the carriage, waving his arms about and shaking his blond mop of hair, presumably for added musical effect. Unfortunately Mr. Dunce thereupon lost his balance and swayed dangerously towards the eastern edge of the pond, which *The Red Robin* had just nearly traversed. In instinctive panic, Mr, Dunce clung to Edmund Edgy for emergency ballast. However, Mr. Edgy was not much use for that latter purpose and both of their persons described a slow-motion trajectory out of the carriage into the edge of the welcoming pond. Despite the little flourish of a splash, the other passengers were not immediately aware of this sad mishap as Mr. Dunce and Mr. Edgy had been seated in the last carriage. It was only as *The Royal Robin* was close to pulling into the siding shed that the absence of the two unfortunates was noticed. "I must admit I thought I heard a little splash back there, but assumed it to be probably some ducks on the pond", Giles Truebore casually remarked.

The pond was only a few minutes brisk walk from the siding shed area. Action-Saxon princess, Juniper was first upon the scene. Edmund was by then out of the pond through grabbing hold of a conveniently situated and strongish, over-hanging weeping willow branch. As Juniper arrived, Edmund was just holding out an arm for the floundering, rather disorientated and half-submerged Mr. Dunce. "Well done, Prince Edmund" boomed Juniper, adding: "now let me give Ashley a bit of added help". Quickly flicking off her shoes and rolling up her trousers, Juniper came forward and waded a few steps into the pond. In a moment, with her arms round Ashley Dunce, Juniper gave a mighty heave and had him safely out on the bank where he piteously rolled a little like a bewildered beached seal. As Sir Terence and Alison Acrylic came upon the scene followed by the other erstwhile train passengers, Juniper laughingly exclaimed: "Jumping Kangeroos! It's good I happen to be on the scene this weekend – I've got a full-time job here, looking after you lot!"

There was fortunately no harm done to our heroes, Mr. Edgy and Mr. Dunce, apart from the shock of their suddenly being divorced from the train and getting a pond drenching. It was merely the case of making for the bathroom fairly promptly and then changing into some spare clothes. I am happy to report that the second return journey suffered no similar untoward event as that just described. There was a general atmosphere of greater sobriety and no lusty singing within the five carriages. This was probably due to the fact that the ladies, Esther, Lucinda and Muriel had either drunk fruit juice or if they had had wine, drunk it in moderation.

The Reverend Halo, as already noted, was a confirmed teetotaller; while drinking amounts of alcohol merely sent Professor Babble comfortably and obliviously off to sleep. Canon Hollow, and Goodbalance had both imbibed some wine, but only in sensible moderation. Timothy Tadpole was a little flushed with wine and Guy St. Bland was a trifle tiddly. But with the latter the difference of being so merely slightly attenuated his customary laconic attitude.

Chapter Nineteen

THE GREAT DEBATE

For the remainder of that pleasantly warm and sunny August afternoon the guests had time to disperse, whether to their own rooms to have a lie down and make any necessary private mobile calls, or to chat in the drawing room or perhaps go for short exploratory walks down the nearby lane to visit the adjacent village of *West Wanton*. Boffo was for a while still busy inside the siding shed raptly going through further pertinent details concerning *The Royal Robin's* construction. His keenly interested companions were Sir Geoffrey Havealot, Clara Clouthard, Prunella Makepiece, Timothy Tadpole, Canon Hollow and Father Goodbalance. Alison Acrylic and Juniper had gone for a leisurely walk to *West Wanton*. Following them, shortly afterwards, at their own slower pace were Esther and her parents. Ashley Dunce had thought it a good move to try ingratiate himself and his party policies upon Giles Truebore and Melissa Puff-Up. This he proceeded to do through firstly espying them both at the Rectory driveway by Truebore's impressively sleek metallic, four-wheeled vehicle. Mr. Dunce then enthusiastically voiced his admiration for the said vehicle and its no doubt 'ecological' stream-lined features. Accordingly, the *CDP* leader wangled an invitation to join

Giles and Melissa's intended short lightning tour of the local village lanes courtesy of the fast purring, metallic beast. And I must comment in passing that for some, to be seen driving a car anywhere on a Sunday apparently approximates to a vital personal and social status necessity

As for the other guests, Guy St. Bland had gone up the headless windmill tower top to get a view from outside on the safety railed platform and consequently found himself in the company of Edmund Edgy, Dr. Microbe, Julian Morbid and Sir Terence. The latter, with Boffo's approval, had invited anyone who felt energetic enough to join him on the tower top. Only the three above mentioned men had taken up the offer (prior to St. Bland). Morbid in a quite vehement frame of mind suggested to his psychotherapist that the tower top might be a good place to go to get away from the two "journalist blood-hounds" plaguing and pursuing him. (Neither of the latter had shown any inclination to climb up the windmill tower). Edmund Edgy had gone on the tower top, disconsolate that both the Anglo-Saxon damsels were now out of his range, but particularly so, Esther, whom now definitely had the edge over Juniper. After a highly satisfying picnic lunch, Professor Benjamin Babble had had no intention of physically exercising his commodious figure and instead – through no doubt a result of his established operant conditioning and therefore behavioural patterning – fell soundly asleep in his guest room. As for the redoubtable Muriel Muffin, she was taking a well earned nap in the drawing room. Even for such an industrious one as her, a little sleep was sometimes in order. And more so because there was another big dinner to prepare for the evening, when Miss Muriel and her trusty lady helpers would again be in the fray, cooking for the same number of people as the previous night.

We will not dwell upon the conversational details concerning the Saturday evening meal. Suffice it is to say concerning dinner that Miss Muffin and her trusty culinary and table-serving team came up trumps again in terms of a well planned and exemplary evening repast. To follow in the meal's aftermath, at about half-past eight, Dr. Tadpole had devised a deliberately polemical debate entitled: *Is the Judaic- Christian God, if he exists, a control freak?* This grand debate was to take place on the first floor of the windmill. This, in the windmill's original working days would have been known as the Hurst floor, which then housed the mill's various gearings. Such workings, as we noted in the opening chapter, had been dismantled and disposed of many years ago. As a result of Boffo's creative improvement plans, the Hurst floor was now his general library room, where the book shelves followed the curve of the circular walls. For this great debate, Boffo and helpers had laid out the requisite number of stackable chairs forming a horseshoe circle within the room. Inside the horseshoe's gap was a small, raised wooden platform for the speaker leading the debate to stand upon.

There were some absences from the debate. Julian Morbid caring little for such type of discussions, and still seeking seclusion from his lady pursuers, discreetly gave his apologies via Dr. Microbe and retired early to his room. Dr. Microbe, himself, was cautiously intrigued enough to decide to attend the debate. Juniper had no interest in intellectual polemics and she and Alison Acrylic made their way to the Drawing room where they were joined by Truebore and Puff-up, who also were not inclined to finish the day with a polemical debate. The four of them joined together in various card games, interspersed with relatively nonthreatening conversation topics. Muriel Muffin was relaxing in the dining room, having an agreeable chin-wag and hot beverage with her two culinary associates.

In view of the discussion-orientated personages who were among the guests, Boffo, was quite delighted with the idea of such a grand debate to give the weekend a suitable kind of finale. Boffo appreciated that his old incorrigible but nevertheless likeable friend, Dr. Timothy Tadpole, was itching to have some such debate during the weekend. Of course, Timothy as usual had rather "gone over the top" with his debate title. But then that was typical of dear, loveable Timothy! However, Boffo was rather concerned about his brother-in-law, the equally incorrigible George Halo. Boffo, Lucinda Halo and Esther had all tactfully suggested to the Reverend that attending such a debate might not be good for his blood pressure. Would he not rather be better off either reading, listening to music or just having an after-dinner doze in the drawing room? However, the redoubtable George Halo would have none of it; he smelt atheistic satanic trouble brewing and was determined to be present at the proceedings. Lucinda and Esther determined to keep close to him as calming influences. For Esther's part she was highly interested to see, or rather hear, what transpired.

Edmund Edgy still in an emotional quandary, hovered awkwardly and rather despondently in Esther's vicinity. And so now let us forthwith make our way outside the Rectory, just round the corner to *Wanton Windmill,* enter in and climb the staircase to the first floor library debating room. It is not my intention here to exhaustively record all the rather heated discussion but nevertheless, despite my avowed puppeteer's authorial aims, the reader might find quite a copious dosage of what ensued. I find that these so-called puppets of mine don't do badly for free-will and they seem to get more demanding as to their stage rights as this novel proceeds. Anyway, once again, let us give the floor to Dr. Timothy Tadpole to allow him to deliver his wilfully provocative debate starter.

Dr. Tadpole (with radiant visage): Ladies and gentlemen, I do not pretend for an instant to believe a real Judaic-Christian God exists. Therefore, in terms of this debate, any mention of such a God on my part is purely rhetorical. For it is an incontrovertible fact that today, in our vastly advanced technological world, we only accept things as true if they are sufficiently evidenced-based. That is the way we operate in our scientifically organised Western world. It is the *only* proper way people of our modern advanced intelligence can live today in the twenty-first century. Nothing in this complex highly structured Western world of ours happens by blind faith or some kind of *deus machina* revelation. But suppose we grant for argument's sake that there *is* some kind of God akin to the Judaic-Christian understanding of a universal Creator. Our first question would necessarily have to be what kind of a God is this God? And here I will in a nutshell give my view. If this Judaic-Christian God exists, he, by the *Bible* records shows himself to be a sublime *control freak*. In the *Old Testament* accounts, he shows himself to be jealous with a consistently bad temper which often issues in the liquidating of his perceived enemies. I submit that the *Old Testament* is mainly an appalling catalogue of crimes that this highly irascible God commits against people who somehow "get on his wick".

Most of the citizens of *Sodom, Gomorrah* as well as other

communities of ancient peoples such as Canaanites are wiped out savagely, wholesale – indiscriminately, because somehow they have not pleased this – I would say – very hard to please, tyrant God. This ruthless Biblical God is not even that pleasant to his own chosen people. When, for instance, the Israelites are out in the desert dying of thirst, they rightly start to complain. But is this Jehovah or whatever name he goes under, very understanding? No! Because of his control freak attitude which can't tolerate any opposition – no matter how reasonable – in spiteful pique he either kills scores of these Israelites, leaving their blanched bones in the desert sun as evidence of what it is to even dare question his authority!

Even when we come to the quantitatively milder Jesus Christ in the *New Testament*, we get a load of threatening nonsense about hell fires and eternal damnation for those who won't accept his ideas. He talks about love, shows concern and care for people, so why is he so vehemently against those who rightly can't accept that he, as a mere human being, is absurdly "God" come down to earth? His highly toxic friend John the Baptist spouts out a lot of venom against almost everyone he virtually encounters. Even Jesus' disciples are a pretty nasty lot. What about the two – John and James – who want to bring down heavenly fire upon those people who won't accept what this Jesus has to say? And why should they (and we) have to accept all this vague stuff about: "I am the bread of life"; "I am the living water"; "the light of the world", etc., and etc.? I submit also that Jesus at his worst was no better than a control freak, who couldn't cope with anyone who wouldn't believe in his wild claims to being God. Yes, Jesus was, I concede, somewhat more restrained than his *Old*

Testament father, who also went under the name of the one and only God. But I conclude my case that Jesus was in the end just as much a control freak – a deluded authoritarian – in his fanatical belief that he was somehow God incarnate. And consequently, through such a fanatically held belief, Jesus was quite content to relegate anyone who was not on his side to endless torment in the cruellest place – burning hell – that anyone has ever yet been able to imagine. Therefore, even if Jesus and his more jealous and angry father God did exist, they would both be the most appalling tyrant control freak Gods conceivable. But fortunately they do not exist. Darwin and subsequent modern scientific developments proves this to us beyond doubt every day. So why, I ask, do the churches keep up this illusion, this pretence that we need religion and particularly, why we need a God who the *Bible* clearly attests to being a tyrannical despot?

Makepiece: Religions of course are all built upon control freak gods. And naturally this makes all religions fundamentally dangerous. As we all know, religion from at least medieval times onwards has been responsible for wars, crusades, civil strife and contemporary suicide bombings. It is a positive menace to politics and society.

Clouthard: There you go again, Prunella! Yet another sweeping, unqualified statement. Billions of people in the world are all wrong in their beliefs, except of course you and your Marxist-Socialists!

Dr. Microbe: Is not the truth, my friends, that although many of us here can't live with this supreme transcendental ruler, it appears to me, even as atheists or agnostics we can't live without this or any other type of god! That is why no doubt we are having a debate about a Judaic-Christian God whose existence we are sceptical of. But perhaps it would be more honest for us to recognise that Christianity and all religion comes not so much as an imposition from above but rather from out of our own social group and bonding needs. How can I express it – ah, yes! My understanding is that religion comes from *us* not from out of the sky or some hidden dimension or other. In respect that religion *arises out of human needs*, I suggest that it is important – even fundamental in some way for us all. For I think it is necessary – a necessary illusion for the benefit of providing a healthy, psychologically bonding basis for us to safely socially operate in.

Professor Babble: No doubt religion and certainly Christianity has its uses. As you say Dr. Microbe, it is an illusion, but some illusions have a limited life-span and others at best a modified use still. Christianity has no doubt in the past helped in building up useful survival techniques and institutional aids such as hospitals and educational facilities, etc. However, we now need to exploit those past gains and enduring survival aids for a specifically behaviouristic-based way of human organisation. What we now need is to replicate religion's socially useful past achievements, which we may conveniently sum up as helping to facilitate secure bonding techniques. By taking from religion what has been proven useful for establishing positive social structures, we will gain helpful models to aid us in reconstructing our human social basis appropriately in terms of today's Western, non-religious situation.

Dr. Tadpole: Of course, of course! Though obviously my contention here is that Christian religion and all religions do more harm than good. For if the Judaic-Christian God doesn't really exist, those foolish enough to pursue him are pursuing a mere phantasm and therefore totally wasting their time, energy and gifts. And *if* this God of the *Bible does* exist, he has actually caused and *is* causing a lot of trouble – including religious based wars and civil strife, through his tyrannical demand for blind, unthinking worship!

Canon Hollow: (in a soft petulant voice): It seems that God is either a phantasm or a tyrant. Yet if he does exist he appears to have been somewhat of a useful tyrant in the past, doing quite a few socially-constructive things!

Treadboards: Yes, a once active and successful god who now, like an old work-horse, has been made redundant and put out to grass!

Dr. Microbe: Oh, this Judaic-Christian God of yours is now not even a totem god anymore. He does not breathe fire and smoke, but only eats grass and has four legs!

Boffo: Oh that was rather an unkind remark of yours, Terence! Forgive you and bless you! Rather, what the Church – and I – profoundly believe is that God exists because his purpose is solely to love us. Christian civilisation on the whole attests that God is a loving personal Being of infinite joy and peace, who wills everyone to join him eventually in Heaven! Even the most un-loveable and selfish characters will be rehabilitated in the everlasting Kingdom! There is room enough there for everyone!

Tadpole: My dear Boffo, if your God is a God of joy and peace, how do you explain the medieval Christian crusades, inquisitions and all the wars of religion that racked Europe from Medieval till modern times? One answer only – God the murderous control-freak!

Father Goodbalance (quickly interposing): History is not

quite as simple as you would like it to be, Timothy. In the case of the crusades, the main driving force was self-defence against the Turks who were the initial belligerents, seeking to overrun parts of Europe. One must also accept the mind-set of that pre-modern era. We are of course in a different historical context from our ancestors who did not possess our enhanced awareness, knowledge and understanding. Of course, no one condones the atrocities connected with the Crusades – as indeed, we all, whatever our beliefs, look with shame upon the blinkered inquisition's cruelties. But we should also remember that the atrocities of the French and Russian revolutions were *secular* atrocities that occurred under the nebulous designation of 'liberty'. We should also remember that our previous twentieth century hosted two world wars where the scale of destruction pales all other preceding human wars into utter insignificance. And these two world wars with their mind-staggering destruction and casualties, had purely *secular* causations. No one ought dare blame the Christian God for the mass slaughter, serious injury and misery which these wars caused. Remember the holocaust, the atomic bombings of Hiroshima and Nagasaki – these appalling acts of genocide had no religious inspired causation whatsoever. Take God completely away as our caring, safeguarding, Father controller and there is ultimately no limit to the evil which arises from unfettered, cock-sure human beings!

Makepiece: Yes, but what did the "Church" do as a whole to try to stop such terrible conflicts and their corresponding atrocities? Did not, for instance, in the First World War, both the Germans and English pray to the same Christian God for victory in that pointless blood bath?

Clouthard: Excuse me, Prunella, Bismark and his Prussians were the aggressors; they virtually started the war by deliberately invading France through neutral Belgium. Therefore, the Germans could pray as much as they wanted to – but they were in the wrong and a just God was not in any way bound to listen to them!

Microbe (teutonically offended): I find this rather a simplistic and racially unbalanced view of such a complicated conflict. One must look at the predominant nationalistic psychological bases of particularly the British and German peoples (not of course ignoring the basic psychology of the other main combatant countries). Such psychological study is highly essential for understanding the undercurrent of smouldering reasons that propelled this fruitless conflict for over four years.

Treadboards: Why should God, if he exists, listen to anyone, British or German included? Surely if you are a perfect, almighty God, such as the Christian God, the myopic stupidities of warring human beings must be like continuously irritating thorns in a great lion's paw! Why should this God bother, waste his divine time with humanity – which of course is humanity in name only? Why does this God give our vicious human race time of day? Why does he not instead send another great universal flood, like he did once before – but this time wipe out the lot of us for ever?

Esther (strongly): Because God in his unfathomable grace cares about us and all people. He wants none to perish while there is still time to turn to him.

Boffo (beaming): Because God loves us all and wants us all finally to be happy together with him under one infinite roof in his eternal city.

Father Goodbalance: Because God seeks recalcitrant men and women. And because he does not believe that it is a waste of his time seeking to redeem any who are presently outside his Kingdom.

St. Bland: For my part, dear Timothy, I think God, if he exists, is far more likely to be a *laissez-faire* cosmic ruler. He – if assuming that is his gender – is I believe what you might term as a non-interference God. Why should we view him as autocratic or always chasing after those who don't want to join his system or heavenly club? As far as I can see, we humans do – and have always done – exactly what pleases and suits us. And this Judaic-Christian God, wherever he is, allows us to do all sorts of bad as well as good things. He allows, for instance, genocide and other unspeakable human violations to be committed. Such other violations of course include plundering and despoiling the very planet we all live upon. Whether "God" is the *Old Testament* version God or the *New Testament* version, hardly makes any difference. God, if he at all exists, is a wind-up-the-clock, Rousseau type deity; he merely sets the planetary ball rolling, as it were, and then is content to let it all carry on in its merry or not-so-merry way. If he were a control freak, as you assert, Timothy, then quite clearly he would have put a stop to all planetary misbehaviour as soon as the first primeval swamp jellyfish started to get vicious and attack its unsuspecting fellow jellyfish companions. Ha, ha!

Canon Hollow (velvety and severely): Guy, you have merely moved to the polar opposite of Timothy's equally absurd, extreme position. It will not do to say God – the Judaic-Christian God, as we are particularising in this debate – is either a rabid authoritarian or a completely "hands off", negligent God. As one who takes a revisionist theological attitude coupled with a Lamarkian evolutionary stance, I see the Christian God as situated somewhere in the middle of such extreme positions. He is certainly not sovereign in the crude Calvinist sense. He allows people and the natural world itself a high degree of regulating self-autonomy – something which of course is anathema to the fundamentalist Christian's mindset. But we have come a long way since the first gospels and epistles were written. We now understand that God is not a fire-breathing, condemning tyrant, but rather the cosmic "ground of being" who allows human beings freedom to develop, to gradually advance in their understanding and technical abilities. Thus, let me re-iterate that he is so far from being a control freak that we humans possess autonomy in terms of our self-determination. But that is not to say God stands off from us at a far distance like Guy's fallacious deist god!

Father Goodbalance (ironically): In answer to our dear whimsical Guy, we should have to say that Rousseau's old fashioned clock-maker is no longer a good model for deism. Science has itself updated that idea. The protracted process of evolution which most evolutionary theists believe our Creator supposedly inaugurated necessitates that the watchmaker metaphor should now be exchanged for that of genetic programmer. Thus, the god of the deist is no longer a simple craftsman. Now he is an upgraded deist! He starts off biological proceedings of a much more long-term basis. His formerly distant deistic eye now observes the inevitable genetic programmes which He knows will occur and develop within the evolutionary process. Therefore substitute God the technician, the scientist, for the watch-craftsman God!

Professor Babble (Bursting again into life): Of course we are all genetically programmed, but we do not require a god to programme us. That would, even it were remotely possible, be a recipe for tyranny, for ultra control. Where does the stability of civilisation come in? It comes in precisely through genetic programmes which have been built-up in *homo sapiens* as a result of accrued, evolutionary survival strategies. This has nothing to do with any Christian or any other "god" variety. Survival has to be programmed into us as a species, stage by evolutionary stage or we end up extinct like the Dinosaurs. The programming can only be done through our collective experience as a species. But we are now of the intelligence as a species to modify our programming – to make adjustments, to fine tune it, as it were. This is of course a matter of urgency if we are to surmount the many problems facing us as a species.

Treadboards (laconically): Why should we really want our wretched human species to survive at all? All we are doing as far as I can see is liquidating other species as well as killing each other and to boot, plundering the environment. Let's be honest, we're the most dangerous species on earth – that is, dangerous to virtually every other life form on the planet! Maybe we ought to not think so much about our own species survival but rather think about the survival of everything else on our dear planet! Surely we've done enough damage as it is; what we want now, if anything, is human damage limitation strategies!

St. Bland: Ha, ha, ha, ha! Excellently said, Sir Terence. What do you say to that, dear uncle Timothy?

Dr. Tadpole (firmly): There will always necessarily be fallout damage in evolutionary survival. That is of course greatly to be regretted and when it happens it usually happens because of human greed, such as oil companies who want to drill in the Artic and corporations responsible for mass deforestation in regions like the Amazon. These rapacious organisations consist of corrupt individuals who badly need re-programming in their minds.

Professor Babble: Of course, if I could only get those mendacious company directors responsible along with their compliant shareholders to my lectures and seminars! I should then do my utmost to rehabilitate their minds by a course tailored to wake them up to the possibilities of behavioural modification. Re-education is the only option for those whose genetic programming has been corrupted amongst other factors by a faulty transmission of hereditary conditioning and social reinforcing.

Reverend Halo (growling, while Esther and Lucinda with their arms entwined around him, vainly tug at him): Conditioning and reinforcing, bah! The human heart is evil beyond all hope as the prophet wisely says. *(Turning to Edgy):* Yea, fear the Lord, young man and smite the evildoer!"

Edgy (suddenly impassioned): Those with Norman hearts are the destroyers – the evildoers. Yes, we ought to smite those types who have turned our whole present day culture into a moronic buying, selling and consumer market. Business, economics, giant world-wide corporations and remorseless technology; these are the things that now define the hollow-heartedness of our so-called culture. Such an infectious plague has been growing ever since the golden era of Anglo-Saxon culture was brutally smashed. Ever since the lost innocence of the pre-conquest era, we can steadily trace the corruption of evil in the history of our dear island. We could have stayed a peaceable agrarian based and modest, self-sustaining country, but that psychopath – William the Conqueror and his militaristic business associates changed all that! The way was then made open for all big-time developers and greed merchants! Ownership now on a far more massive scale. Everything valued with its requisite price-ticket. Small was beautiful and exquisitely crafted once in the Anglo-Saxon age but after the invasion the path of so-called progress led inevitably to industrialism, technology, today's neo-liberalism and its culture of celebrity vulgarity. And so we have finally kicked out beauty, truth and goodness! If anything now is programmed into us it is capitalism! It's the only political, social and media game left in town. Everything is market-driven capitalism – nothing else matters!

Havealot (the last word acting as a red flag to a bull): We must not resort to bashing capitalism; that is really a typical left-wing way of blame shifting! Where would we be without those who have striven to industrialise our country and give it cutting-edge technology? Do we not all benefit from our modern forms of life? No, you should not blame a proven structure whose only alternative would be the chaos of something like mass bartering. The very obscene thought of abolishing money gives one the shivers! The blame, if there is to be blame for the problems of our planet is down to feckless idlers who don't pull their weight in society. If all the shirkers in our country had no other choice but to do their allotted share of work, the result would be they no longer had time to lark around on benefits.

Canon Hollow (tactfully): I fear we have gone off-course somewhat and headed away from the particularised scope of our debate.

Dr. Tadpole: Yes, to round things off at this point, we all know – to recite the obvious – that human beings cause quite a bit of a mess. However, the way out of messing up is to grow up and growing up means as much as anything else throwing off infantile notions. The notion of some supernatural sky-policeman – Christian deity, is not in any way helpful. Moreover, if we make this god all-powerful – almighty – as he appears to demand of us, there will obviously be extremely dangerous consequences. For one thing, those who uphold such a god will fashion themselves in its own image and become likewise intolerant and autocratic. Only slaves live in a culture of dependence. However, in the twenty-first century, we who have been emancipated in the West by the rationalistic forces emanating from the enlightenment and stunning progress of science, are slaves no longer. We renounce slavery to superstition and outmoded traditions which were forged in medieval times. Despite human stupidity mainly caused by ignorance, things are on the whole getting remarkably better. I submit that potentially each of us has a perhaps small yet nevertheless significant role to play in the further technological development and improvement of our world. That role is of course conditional upon us both as a corporate body and as individuals following the golden pathway of enlightened science in all its spell-binding power of rationality.

St. Bland: Bravo, uncle Timothy, bravo! You are now well and truly back in the driving seat once again! Ha, ha, ha, ha!

Dunce (cowed by the proceedings, nevertheless feeling he should contribute something or other): Yes, bravo, Dr. Tadpole. We cannot live in ignorance any longer. That is a key plank in the *CDP's* political philosophy: Educate the ignorant to make the right choices. Out with superstition, let us have enlightenment, prosperity, as many choices as we want, healthy bonuses, tax reductions and no interference from gods lacking in understanding of wealth creation and economics!

Halo (bristling): Young man, you are talking absolute twaddle! I had high hopes for you, but I fear that here you sup with a long spoon with devilish influences. Such a debate of flippant blasphemy has no doubt addled your already troubled and confused soul! Yea, it has turned your as yet spiritually untutored head! Repent, repent, I say, before it is too late to find the narrow road!

Boffo (winningly): Oh come, come my dear George! Mr. Dunce – Ashley's words were well meant, if a trifle exuberant and confused; I'm sure he means no harm. Ah, let us forgive and enjoy one another's company, for we are all equals in the Creator's eyes!

Canon Hollow: All very well, but we still seem to be off on a tangent…

Father Goodbalance: Let me therefore attempt to return us back to the question opening this debate: I submit that no supposed control freak would bother to create such abundance of living species. Control freaks don't like abundance. Nor do they like creating – giving life. In my book a control freak is an authoritarian. And authoritarians like to live in a world of sharply defined limits and boundaries. Therefore no abundance, no creativity, only restraint. Freud's idea of paternal religion's original roots – still given some credence today – hinges on a tribal, primal father figure who exerts fearful authority – even when dead he still lives posthumously as a powerful totem symbol. This idea, as I say, still sows a lot of mischievous thinking among anthropologists, sociologists and others who find it a useful stick particularly with which to beat Judaic-Christianity. Such a father figure, totem god represents a dead authority. And yet this dead totem god still exerts an fearful domination over those who are drawn to it. "Thou shalt not!" Prohibition – that is all there is to this negative totem god conceived by infantile minds. In total contrast, the Christian God is a cosmic personality of love not fear. Yet He is also power. For surely it is obvious that there can be no proper love without some sort of backing, sustaining power. You can't have love in a vacuum. Nor can you govern anything, let alone a universe without a good degree of power! But God's spiritual power is a vastly different proposition from human forms of power.

Halo (now getting into top gear): Of course! God is sovereign. He is higher in his thoughts and power than we are! Intrinsically he is almighty and he will use his power whenever he wants to chastise those who are consistently and indeed unashamedly rebellious! Yea, he will use floods, earthquakes, whirlwinds and any other means which he deems fit to punish those who would go blithely their way to perdition. Yea! He is the great controller, but not a purposeless freak – rather the supreme King of Kings, absolute monarch over the entire universe! Such a supreme Ruler has a glorious purpose and plan which nothing on earth or Heaven can possibly thwart. *(And then addressing Dr. Tadpole with a firm, resolute look, the Reverend continued):* My dear Doctor Tadpole, let me say categorically that there is no "if" attached to God's existence at all. He exists. Moreover, the earth is the Lords and also all that within it is His. I dare to refute your God-insulting natural science ideals and their abysmal lack

266

of Biblical ethics. The good Lord made all the species on this planet, one by one in His own divine time. Evolution is scientific hokery-pokery! Neither plants, animals or indeed human beings turn from one thing to another thing. They are and remain what they are. They are, in short, what the Sovereign Lord made them and intended them to be in the first place! Things that the Sovereign Lord makes, do not change willy-nilly just because your dear Charles Darwin thought up a magical idea in his head called natural selection – a rather grand phrase for chance or good luck! You may well point to different breeds of dogs, cats – and even variations in bird species which may exhibit some slight colouring or singing alterations; but such varieties are merely akin to the varieties of different coloured human beings with their differing languages found in the contrasting climates of our world. But do not tell me that an ape is not always an ape and a human being is not always a human being! There are no half and halves. Apes do not suddenly learn how to form an alphabetical language! And your dear fossil evidence only gives us *what there is* and therefore only attests that creatures and human beings were created, fixed as one kind and did not change into other kinds. I don't deny there were some little developments here and there. But species changing into other species – no!

Dr. Tadpole (showing some frustration): So dear Reverend, Adam and Eve in a sudden flash were just popped into position on this earth by a divine stork. The first humans thus arrived – as your literalistic Biblical story would have it – fully fledged, without having to worry about starting off as babies, then going through childhood and the trials connected with puberty! An extremely convenient short-cut for them both!

And prior to that all other life: fish, reptiles, insects, birds and mammals all appeared one after the other out of your magician god's hat. That is of course a very convenient not to say highly compact way of explaining everything without an iota of science. However, such a naïve fairy-story explanation is now ludicrously pre-Darwinian and deservedly obsolete!

Boffo: (trying to smooth things over): Ah, yes, we will always have our differences of beliefs and opinions. That is part of our freedom and rights as humans. Our loving Father wants us all to have free expression. But we must show our gratitude for such freedom by bearing with one another. The gracious Lord will gather us all up in the end, even if we struggle against him in the act of being gathered up! Some hardened hearts will have no doubt longer in the reforming purgatorial workshop than others. But God is patient and wants us *all* to live with him eternally as one ultimately big cosmic happy family! Surely this is what we must always remember, even when we have our little disagreements and indeed, sometimes not so little disagreements.

Makepiece: Excuse me, but what evidence is there that such a God of love exists? You are surely only talking about your subjective feelings. My subjective feelings are different from yours in this respect. My dear Boffo, you need to be able to rationally demonstrate that your God exists and is what you say he is in terms of love. How do *you* know for instance, that this Christian God is not a control freak?

Clouthard: Excuse me, Prunella, there you go again. Fifteen centuries or so of Christian culture in this land of ours counts for nothing with you. I bet you never open the *Bible*! I take mine off the shelve quite often. God is a God of love, but he will not tolerate scoffers. Those are the ones who will find themselves cast off on Judgement Day! Who will be given the divine elbow? You can be sure it will be mainly socialists, Marxists and good-for-nothing work-shy types!

Havealot: Of course, Clara; God, if he exists, most definitely wears a blue jacket and tie! His sort of self-education in Heaven, although on a vastly higher scale, would nevertheless relatively accord with the educative principles of Eton and Harrow. Miscreants and wastrels are punished by their own class idleness, but those who actively conform and follow the right educative policies will more likely be rewarded and land up in the promised land of success and fulfilment...

Treadboards (darkly): If there are no artists, playwrights, poets, musicians, writers, actors and actresses in Heaven, it will be a mighty dull place. I don't personally envisage Heaven as structured on the same lines as a prestigious Public School. No doubt in such a type of Heaven, everyone would be talking about the economy...

Canon Hollow (his silky voice rather peeved): I fear we have strayed once again into some by-waters in terms of the assertion which opened this debate...

There is a short silence. Then Esther speaks with a tremulous yet controlled voice: "Dr. Tadpole, you are clearly an atheist, are you not? *(He nods gravely).* Esther continues: "Yet despite that, you seem to think you have the right idea concerning God's characteristics – that is, if he exists. But your founding premise is that God doesn't exist. That being so, you have nevertheless talked confidently about God being a control freak. You talk of God's character hypothetically, because you are virtually positive in your mind that of course God does not exist. So I ask what then is your point of characterising someone or something (perhaps a cosmic force), that does not exist? Why waste any time over a non-existent transcendent being? What can be the point of making idle speculations about the characteristics of a God you have already decided does not exist? Or is it that deep down you are not really so sure after all of your atheism? Does not the idea of giving God a possibility of existence perhaps secretly appeal to you? But why might this God secretly appeal to you? Perhaps you require this God to be someone you can put in the dock; a transcendental someone whom you can stick the blame onto for all that you see as unjust and rotten in the world? God is still useful for carrying the "can", so to speak! And clearly, Dr. Tadpole, and you too, Professor Babble *(casting a bold look in his direction)*, obviously desire that science and its purveyors are absolved from all blame for our world's many troubling problems and issues. So, God is useful even in a hypothetical existence, in order to receive the blame for all that goes wrong in human history! And here, unwittingly, you have hit halfway onto an actual Christian truth! Yes, indeed God in Christ has taken upon himself at Calvary the judgement, the blame, the guilt which should rightly be our judgement, our blame and our guilt for the mess we make of this world and ourselves by our self-centred thoughts, words and actions".

Esther paused for a moment, then continued: "The real question which ought to have been raised in this debate is this: *Is it us or God who is to blame for the crises we face in our world today?* Clearly, for you, Dr. Tadpole, God does not exist. Therefore he cannot be to blame for the world as it is today. I submit then, that the blame can only reside in human beings. And that includes us all – each one of us, me, you and everyone in this room are part of the problem. We are all responsible. We are where we are today – in a global mess – because all humans to greater or lesser degrees are latent control freaks. At bottom we all tend to pursue a self-centred power agenda which ultimately sets us against each other and He who made us. And I would go so far as to say, the only way out of this dilemma is for each of us to oppose boldly and intelligently all control freaks, whether in government, big business, local business, or in our educative systems, local government, Parish councils, Rotary clubs, or even in our neighbourhoods and own families. But I would go finally even further than this and say that the very first thing of all we must do is to fight against and abolish as much as possible the control freak in each of us. And the only way we can do this is to seek Jesus Christ and be radically renewed in his transforming image: Jesus Christ, who is God, one with the Father and the Holy Spirit."

There was after this a great hush within the circle of debaters. Some people had open mouths of astonishment in respect of Esther's speech, as if she were some re-incarnated version of Joan of Arc. Canon Hollow could only be heard to silkily mutter: "What extraordinary particularity this young lady has exhibited!" Father Goodbalance's eyes twinkled with ironic pleasure. As for Guy St. Bland, he wickedly smiled at the strangely immobilised Timothy Tadpole, saying: "Well, uncle Timothy, well! You have now met your match at last! You must now be suitably gracious in defeat!" Not even Timothy Tadpole could speak, surprisingly seeming to have been put out of kilter by the sudden measured eruption of Esther's volcanic utterance. As for the Reverend Halo, he was dumbfounded with shocked admiration for his daughter's speech. What of Edmund Edgy? He too had admiration; there was indeed something more to Esther, a hidden powerful energy which seemed to further bewitch his mind and hold his confused emotions in thrall to her.

As the time was now getting on, Boffo felt this silence heralded a particularly appropriate moment in which to draw the debate to what he imagined as a reasonably happy and satisfactory conclusion. And this our dear Boffo did, thanking everyone for their valued participation in the proceedings. A proceedings which Boffo cheerfully acknowledged in his rounding-up speech that "would never leave everyone as one agreed, unified, contented and happy unit of people". "Although" he added, beaming, "we must remember that all such differences will dissolve in Heaven, when the lion will lie down with the lamb and vice versa; when we shall all indeed be one big, happy, extended and reconciled human family, as I firmly believe our good God has ever planned it to be so".

CHAPTER TWENTY

TO THE TOWER

Sunday morning arrived at *Lower Wanton End* and with it a sprightly westerly breeze, along with an overcast sky. The early August fields had now lost any remaining gold sheen from their ' summer souvenir' residue of stubble. The cloudy sky transformed the landscape below it into a darker hue. There was talk of possible light drizzle entering the equation during late afternoon. Already there was a scattering of worn out sun-weathered leaves under the chestnut tree by the windmill. Despite the breeze and loss of sunlight the temperature was relatively warm. Julian Morbid was keen to get away with Dr. Microbe as soon as possible in the pre-booked taxi which would enable them to catch a lunch-time train from Cambridge to London. The pianist was still furiously trying to avoid Prunella Makepiece and Clara Clouthard. This he did by making some excuse straight after breakfast and shooting forthwith up to his room; thence he hid under the bed. However by and by, a letter was quietly slid under the door of his guest room and shortly afterwards another letter appeared in the same fashion.

Esther had left the Rectory after breakfast in her modest sized car. She had said a few brief encouraging words to Edmund just after breakfast by the windmill. There was an intimation on Esther's part that she would keep up a contact of sorts which gave the love-lorn poet some faint grounds for hope. Esther had taken Edmund's telephone number and address and left it that she would contact him. This stipulation seemed rather suspiciously like evasion from Mr. Edgy's point of view. In mitigation it should be pointed out Esther had said that she was in process of looking for new lodgings – possibly sharing with a female friend of hers, and so her present address and landline would shortly be out of date. On the other hand, Edgy mordantly noted that Esther had not mentioned giving him her mobile number. Edmund feared the reality was that he would never see the un-replicable poetic animation of her face and figure again.

As for Juniper, she and Alison Acrylic had soon after breakfast made an early get-a-way on their power-crazed four-stroke, two-wheeled machine. Sir Terence had had his last goodbye for now with Juniper; the latter blithely promising to soon get back in contact with her father. Sir Treadboards was left nevertheless feeling empty. Knowing his daughter, it might be a while till she made contact again. He felt the 'black dog' depression looming within him. But as for Edmund Edgy, there was a gaping empty void after his having seen Esther drive off and then Juniper and Acrylic also take their leave. So that was it, he thought. Both these two spell-bindingly beautiful women, with faces and figures which would have graced the court of King Arthur, were now gone; gone out of his life probably forever. This seemed to be the conclusive thought of our desultory poet cum playwright. The time was now half-past ten. Mr. Edgy was due to go back to London with Giles Truebore and Melissa Puff-Up just after a mid-day snack at the Rectory. But Edmund had no inclination in his heart to be a passenger in Truebore's grand metallic beast, listening to these two self-satisfied acquaintances of his who were on a different planet to him. And now these two acquaintances seemed in his darkening thoughts to be your typical celebrity, chitter-chattering media folk; to be avoided like the plague. There would be no sympathy from such neo-Normans he bitterly thought.

Thus a forsaken and forlorn Edmund now stood alone by the flowerbed situated left of *Wanton Windmill's* entrance door. This was where Esther had taken leave of him about three quarters of an hour ago. Half an hour after Esther had left, St. Bland had popped by, but the poet was in no mood for much talk, apart from a few words delivered as dark and obtuse mumblings. St. Bland tried his normal languidly joking style: "Now Edmund, the jolly old world is still spinning round, you know! Life is still worth living even without your two now departed Anglo-Saxon princesses!" The only response was: "It's too late now Guy. I have been born in the wrong epoch. I am, as Keats said, in need of having the fine tip cut off my soul! But that will do no good! No, I know that I am a mere blot upon this mindless neo-Norman world! It's best you just leave me to my destined fate." "Oh let's not be too tragic, Edmund" St. Bland remonstrated. But being unable to elicit a further response, he shrugged, turned on his heels and sauntered off.

And so it was, quarter of an hour after St. Bland's dismissal, Edmund decided to make his way up the windmill. "I will go out of the trap door at the top, and there I will at least get some fresh air. And then? What is there to lose if I…if I suddenly floated off over the railings and… Well, Chatterton, Keats, Shelley, Owen; they all seemed to have a knowing hand in snuffing out the great promise of their young lives... Chatterton: poison; Keats nursing his brother and catching a fatal illness thereby; Shelley going out on the lake in a light sailing boat – and refusing to ever learn to swim! And then Owen did not have to go back to the Western front – but he did and that was tantamount to suicide, returning there! Why not add myself to this list? Poor Edmund Edgy, whom no-one will ever take seriously! Edmund Edgy, who has it in him to forge a reformation in poetry and drama, and yet people only want celebrity poets and celebrity dramatists who write money-spinning musicals!"

Such thoughts were traversing through the displaced poet's brain as he climbed the connecting stairway. He duly arrived at the fifth floor, entered Sir Treadboard's small study/ bedroom area and then mounting a couple of steps, opened the trapdoor just above him in order to go outside on the windmill top. Edmund clambered out expecting no company apart from the westerly wind and a flapping flag. However, he was met by the hunched figure of Julian Morbid holding onto the safety railing, gazing westwards into the boisterous wind. Upon seeing Mr. Edgy, the pianist merely turned round to face the latter and pulled out two letters from his jacket. Then waving the said letters in the air, he exclaimed: "Look at this! And look at this! Not one but two letters – one each from those crazed journalist women!" Mr. Edgy, grabbing hold of the nearest railing was, as it were, frozen in mid-step on discovering such unexpected company at such a crucial moment. Thus taken aback he could only evince his trade-mark rabbit look of astonishment. Unperturbed by Mr. Edgy's sudden visitation, Julian Morbid continued: "Look at these letters! Do you know what's in them? Ha! They are both letters containing marriage proposals! Yes, these madwomen have both written to me – saying…how much they admire me…and…they inform me…that they are in…love…with me!" Mr. Morbid's indignation rose higher: "I would willingly believe these are malevolent jokes in extremely poor taste – but no, I do believe they *are* both madwomen, crazed out of their tiny skulls!"

Mr. Edgy's rabbit astonishment still precluded him from engaging in any sort of verbal reaction. But Julian Morbid continued in his compensatory rage: "They each talk in their letters about being able to give me encouragement, help, security and artistic tranquillity! Tranquillity – I would get about as much tranquillity from those pair as from a couple of wild hyenas! I thought I had escaped them both yesterday by avoiding the train excursion, picnic and library room debate. But no! Just when I thought it was safely all over this morning, with only a hour or so before the taxi picks Microbe and myself up for the station – then these twin Medea furies strike by letters!" Edmund Edgy was still transfixed. Unbothered by the lack of verbal response but also perhaps inwardly pleased he had someone to sound off at, Julian Morbid carried on: "Well, this was the trigger – yes the trigger! Yes, I suppose I am vulnerable. I am an artist – a musician – not a mere crowd-pleasing juggler. I am of course over sensitive to this vulgar world – yet I will not be dragged down by opportunist media women; they will not collect me as their cheap trophy! No! My time has now come. Perhaps I was a fool to think I could go on living on the edge of it all – hearing voices, even if they were real – my great composer friends! The props that have previously held me together cannot suffice now. Beethoven and Brahms will surely be there to greet me when I come to meet them – when I…jump…." Then suddenly as if in an after-thought, the distraught concert pianist focused more sharply upon Mr. Edgy: "Are you here just for the view…or are you too pursued by mad hyena women and here to jump?"

The sudden appearance of the verb: "jump", now made Mr. Edgy's own heart jump. "Jump?", he gasped, as if that had never crossed his whirling mind. "No, no, you must not do it – you are a great artist, a real man of the true forgotten England!" "Ha!" snorted Julian Morbid and turned again to face the full force of the westerly wind. But just at that crucial moment the trap-door sprung open again and Sir Terence Treadboard's apparition emerged. "Good lord!" the latter cried upon seeing the other two men. Edmund Edgy was rendered once more speechless and immobile. However, Julian Morbid seemingly unperturbed addressed the new arrival: "Ha, good morning once again, Sir Terence. We meet now in sadly different circumstances, I do believe!" The latter, seeming greatly peeved to find he had entered upon company, merely cooly retorted: "No doubt I should ask the proverbial question: "Do you come here often?" He then immediately added rather belligerently: "Well, in my case *I do!*" Sir Terence continued in the same irritated tone as if in an aside to himself: "One cannot even finally discharge oneself in peaceful privacy! It has come to this, even at the crucial moment – a wanton over-crowded world! I came up here for a discreetly tragic finale and instead am confronted with a veritable departure lounge!" His two companions were now both suddenly gripped with an embarrassed uncertainty of resolve. The theatrical Knight somewhat cantankerously broke the awkward silence: "I see, my good friends there is a queue for ending it all! Very well, but I believe in seniority and in terms of being a Shakespearean thespian, I crave gentlemen your patience in order for myself to take priority in the matter of leave taking! I have here no Cleopatra to hear my final lines: "I am dying Egypt, dying!" But I shall instead deliver to you a prior speech of the noble Roman – before I go over the railing. For like Antony my time has come, yes, for it is now beyond doubt that: "The shirt of Nessus is upon me!"

With that Sir Terence suddenly rushed with Hamlet-like elan past the other two immobilised men and clung against the south facing railing. His body turned southwards and he stared resolutely into the considerably animated, overcast sky. The top of the out-of-blossom pink horse chestnut tree was more or less just below him. Sir Terence then turned back towards his tower companions: "So good friends I grant that you would listen with some appreciable consideration to my Shakespearean swansong before taking this final departure for the great unknown! I crave only of you dear friends, not to be too critical if I should miss out a word or line here and there! Remember I have now turned three score and ten!" And thus he began fixing his eyes particularly on Mr. Edgy:

"Unarm, Eros, the long day's task is done,

And we must sleep." (Then looking at Mr. Morbid and waving him away): "That thou depart'st hence safe

Does pay thy labour richly; go." (Then reverting his gaze to Mr. Edgy): "Off, pluck off,

The seven-fold shield of Ajax cannot keep

The battery from my heart, O, cleave, my sides!

Heart, once be stronger than thy continent,

279

Crack thy frail case! Apace, Eros, apace!"…
No more a soldier: bruised pieces, go,
You have been nobly borne. From me awhile.
I will o'ertake thee, Cleopatra, and…"

Sir Terence was stopped in his iambic flow as the trap-door opened once again. There emerged the banana-shaped face of Boffo followed by his medium-sized figure. After him quickly followed the Reverend Halo with his abundant mass of frizzled grey hair. And again, immediately after the latter yet another new arrival: Guy St. Bland. Upon seeing Sir Terence with his back against the south railing, Boffo with aclarity brushed past Edgy and Morbid towards his cousin, frenetically seizing hold of the latter's gesticulating arms: "My dear Terence, my dear Terence…as an angelic voice in my head warned me…you are here…but I must gently restrain you from your unhappy, impulsive mind!" In swift replication, Reverend Halo also rushed to Julian Morbid, hardly aware of the other men on the platform: " Ah, my sad, sorry fellow brother, I have come by the Spirit's insistence to pluck you from the dark abyss' brink! Turn away from this dread act, I say, for the everlasting wings of safety are near!"

What though had urged St. Bland now to the tower top? Shortly after having tried unsuccessfully to engage Edmund in conversation by the windmill, St. Bland had experienced an uncharacteristic premonition which led him back to check up on the doom and gloom poet. Glancing up at the tower top, St. Bland could detect what appeared to be a moving figure. That was enough for him. "The silly blighter is going to top himself! Typical crazed idealist! Poor old Eddy the unready! Well, inconvenient as it is, I can't just stand here and let him be a complete idiot – I must do the good Samaritan thing and save him!" And off into the windmill and up the tower Guy went, forgetting now his customary lazy paced locomotion. But once up on the tower top and despite a bit of puffing and nervousness, St. Bland regained at least his outward languid approach. Moving towards Edmund, he said in his usual nonchalant tone of voice:

"My dear, daft Edmund, observation and intuition have obliged me to come to talk you out of doing anything incredibly stupid for the sake of two here-today, gone-tomorrow women!"

Meanwhile a small anxious and perplexed group had gathered below the windmill. This group comprised Dr. Gustav Microbe, Lucinda Halo, Dr. Tadpole, Canon Hollow, Father Goodbalance, Giles Truebore, Melissa Puff-up and Muriel Muffin. It should be mentioned that the latter lady had given the alarm to Boffo concerning Sir Terence. After Juniper's leave-taking, Muriel Muffin had over-heard the thespian saying: "Well, this is it. Will Perdita come back twice? I doubt it. Troilus would have more chance of seeing his lost Cressida again! No, I am bereft of both wife and daughter again. I will up to the tower…to the tower, I will go!"

As to Dr. Microbe, he had seen signs of nervousness in Julian Morbid, who was, as we noted, extremely anxious to leave the Rectory and finally elude his female pursuers. After breakfast, Mr. Morbid had disappeared from view and no one seemed to know where he was until Melissa Puff-up said she had seen the pianist furtively making in the direction of the windmill. Red lights then started flashing inside the psychotherapist's mole-like cranium and he feared the worst. However, as a sufferer from vertigo, Dr. Microbe asked Reverend Halo (who was nearby at that moment) if there was anyone able to look on the tower top for his unhappy patient. "I will do it myself! There is clearly no time to waste. The deadly lion seeks its prey even as we speak. I will make haste!", replied the cleric. Without further ado he determinedly sped towards the windmill.

Returning back to the crisis scene up above on the tower platform railing, we see Sir Terence struggling with his clerical cousin and angrily exclaiming to the latter: "Et tu, Brute? Then fall, Caesar!" But in fact great "Caesar" did not fall anymore than did the other great Roman, Antony. For in trying to pull Sir Terence away from the south railing, Boffo was himself in a rather precarious position. In a moment certainly not ordained by his kindly Universalist God, poor Boffo had somehow flipped backwards over the railings and proceeded to travel aerially downwardly towards the gracious spread of the adjacent horse chestnut tree; his long thin limbs and well trimmed, wavy-shaped beard fluttering incongruously in the wind. On the west railing, Reverend Halo was also wrestling Jacob-like with Julian Morbid, who angrily exclaimed: "I will not be interfered with – the twin furies shall be denied…they shall be denied…I shall escape them!" The robust cleric was up against the railing trying desperately to pull Morbid away. Suddenly the latter managed to give his opponent a sharp push away from himself. This apparently innocent and unpremeditated action unfortunately precipitated Reverend Halo's square, compact body into an aerial manoeuvre over the railing and thereafter downwards below the windmill's western side. Here, the audience with the better viewpoint comprised some bemused piebald cows who were minding their own business in the farmer's field just behind a dividing hedge.

Guy St. Bland had been talking to Edmund Edgy in his usual amused laconic manner, rather than rushing forward to interpose himself between the railing and the self-sacrificial victim. Edmund Edgy had already felt deflected from his spur-of-the-moment purpose as a result of both Julian Morbid's and Sir Terence's similar intentions; and both of these latter persons' intentions had in their apparent resoluteness rather put his own tenuous decision in the shade. What, for Edmund, further decisively drove out all thoughts of choosing to attempt flying unaided, was the sudden awareness of first Boffo then Reverend Halo disappearing over the railings, accompanied by their astonished cries. The focus was thus conclusively shifted and Edgy, St. Bland, along with Morbid and Sir Terence were now all united in following the dual gravitational mishaps of both Boffo and the venerable Halo.

As for Boffo, during his rapid descent he had managed to stretch out and grab a conveniently near sturdy branch which was strategically placed by providence half-way down the horse chestnut. As for Reverend Halo's fate, Providence smiled again, for the cleric's downward spiral of flight issued in him landing within the Rectory garden, amid a giant compost stack comprised of copious grass cuttings, faded flowers, straw and weeds. This grand and healthy mixture thankfully ensured a relatively soft landing. There was merely the inconvenience of our dear Calvinist parson being embedded in a rather fresh smelling cocktail of organic compounds.

Sir Terence, Julian, Edmund and Guy all made their back via the trap-door and were soon down and out of the windmill. Dr. Tadpole was quickly in attendance at the scene of the compost-immersed Reverend Halo. After the latter's gentle extrication from the compost heap, Dr. Tadpole was able to pronounce that there appeared no obvious damage done to the Reverend apart from the considerably disorientating shock of this sudden fall. In fact the cleric was mainly heard to jabber: "I have saved him, yea, I have saved him, but in doing so I have gone into the very depths of Pandemonium – Lucifer's dark and rank-smelling abode!" Miss Muffin was soon at hand with the classic calming remedy of a cup of strong tea and a plate of custard cream biscuits. As for Boffo, he was still precariously perched on the branch that he had managed to grab hold of, having consequently slowly worked his way along to a safer position nearer the horse chestnut's main trunk. The question was how to get Boffo down to *terra firma*. Miss Muffin, redoubtable as ever in her common-sense helpfulness, led Giles Truebore and Guy St. Bland to where a long ladder was stored in the little shed near the sidings shed. Then the two men between them conveyed the rescue device to the said tree.

Once the ladder was by the chestnut tree in a safe position with Giles Truebore keeping it secure, Guy St. Bland duly climbed the ladder and was able to check on Boffo's condition. The latter was naturally shocked by his sudden dislocation from the windmill platform and was somewhat burbling: "Oh, Terence, oh, where is the poor man? I have been most untimely wrenched from my dear troubled cousin – oh, dear Terence!" But bit by bit St. Bland managed to guide Boffo safely to the ladder's top rung and thence slowly and safely down the remaining seven feet or so from the cleric's sylvan perch to the ground. Once down, the disorientated cleric was given a good check-over by Dr. Tadpole, who again could detect no obvious physical damage. Muriel Muffin was at hand again to strongly encourage Boffo to partake of a strong cup of tea along with the custard creams. In fact everyone was encouraged to regale their taxed spirits with tea and biscuits, although Miss Muffin's one special exception was to discreetly bring out to Sir Terence a glass of his favourite brandy.

"Well, Edmund", Guy St. Bland dryly commented, "we have just witnessed not one but two flying parsons!" "If not for those two parsons and yourself there might have instead been a flying poet, actor and pianist", Mr. Edgy darkly retorted. "I have been into the inferno and yet the sovereign Lord has even thus delivered me", solemnly declared the Reverend Halo. "Amen to that" echoed Lucinda Halo. "A smiling Father God holds out his very own everlasting hands to protect us all" said Boffo, feeling now somewhat revived. "I for one will hardly forget the extraordinary particularity of such as these events", murmured Canon Hollow in his trademark velvet delivery. "We have much at all times to give thanks for", opined Father Goodbalance in his quiet, measured voice. "I have enough case material here for a giant symposium; enough material to occupy me for ever, I think!" uttered a bemused Dr. Microbe. "I should like to go home away from all this fuss", wearily muttered Julian Morbid. Timothy Tadpole remarked: "Well, thank goodness, our dear Boffo and Halo have got away with it lightly! No obvious breakages or damage that I can see. Though if there is any doubt, a check-up at A & E would be sensible. But thankfully there were not more falls from the tower!" "This and not last night's debate appears to be the true finale of your birthday weekend, Sir Terence", Melissa Puff-Up ventured to the by now slightly more brandy-composed thespian. "Yes", opined Giles Truebore, "while debates are interesting enough, this, despite its frightfulness is the drama of real life; what I suppose, Sir Terence, no other dramatist can convey as closely as Shakespeare does". Sir Terence nodded and shrugged his shoulders: "As the Bard has it: "All's well that ends well"."

Epilogue

About six weeks later, near September's close, if we should happen to be within the enormous entrails of a certain vast and monstrous sized hospital, who should we meet but three of our former contestants sitting together in the fracture clinic waiting room. Here we encounter Boffo with his right arm in a V shape, emblazoned by plaster. Two chairs from him is George Halo, his left arm also in a V shape fortified by plaster. Sir Terence Treadboards is sat regally between the two of them, plaster-less. At this precise moment, with some lines of *King Richard III* for an unknown reason spinning in his brain, Sir Terence was feeling like a bored, glowering and redundant Gloucester, without a theatre to shine in. He thought amusedly to himself, "well, cousin Boffo could make a gullible enough if rather too comic Duke of Clarence, but methinks friend Halo might make a reasonably passable Duke of Buckingham!"

The theatrical Knight, since his birthday weekend, had after some cajoling from Boffo and Miss Muffin, begrudgingly paid a check-up visit to Dr. Microbe's psychotherapy clinic. At any rate, Sir Terence felt at present more equable and confident in mind and was even pondering a recent enticing offer of playing Sir John Brute, in a radio adaptation of Vanbrugh's play: *The Provoked Wife*. Sir Terence's mental well-being had also been boosted by the pleasure of a surprise return visit from Juniper a few weeks ago, and it is likely that this had been more beneficial than Dr. Microbe's supposed wealth of psychoanalytical acumen. Juniper was after all a good, caring Perdita! Perhaps not a Cordelia, (how could Juniper ever be a Cordelia?), but she was showing at last some filial concern for her dear old theatrical king of Sicilia, Leontes. Moreover, concerning early October, Juniper had invited her "dad" up to a private preview of Alison Acrylic's latest exhibition at the *Tate Modern*. Sir Terence would spend the weekend with his daughter and Acrylic in London. There was also talk of all three of them going to hear a sufficiently stabilised Julian Morbid play Beethoven's fourth piano concerto at the Barbican. (However, Dr. Microbe had evinced some concern that the pianist was lately becoming more reclusive, particularly possessed by a fear of "hyena" journalist women with marriage intentions).

"Well," said the theatrical knight, addressing aloud both his companions, "they will call you both in a minute to get rid of all that clobber adorning your arms." Turning specifically to George Halo, Sir Terence added: "And you, my good fellow, were told last month you probably had neither break nor fracture, the plaster being merely a precautionary measure. Let us hope that is so." "Yes, Sir Terence, that is correct. The sovereign Lord has seen fit to be merciful. Yea, I believe he ordained it even so before the foundation of the world" replied the Reverend in a measured, predestined tone. Sir Terence turned to cousin Boffo: "And you cousin, a minor fracture without any complication?" "Ah, yes, indeed all's well that ends well" Boffo replied, smiling through his long and bright-eyed face which also trailed with it his trademark finely tapered black beard. The beaming cleric continued: "Yes, just a simple wrist fracture, nothing beyond that. The gracious Lord's angels made that dear horse chestnut branch my blessed haven – the everlasting arms are always there. We must be thankful that our loving Father always knows our needs!" "Yes", retorted Sir Terence, "even when we are spiralling downwards through the air apparently to our doom!" "Ah, my dear Terence, you forget the Apostle's great rhetorical words: "Who shall separate us from God…neither height nor depth", the former Boffosbury Bishop, cheerfully replied. "That is true, providing one has one's name written down in the Lamb's Book of Life", added Reverend Halo with due gravity. "The only book of life I know is that which comprises the Bard's incomparable works", asserted Sir Treadboards with definitive emphasis. And then most mischievously declaimed (with discreet gusto), Sir Toby Belch's infamous lines: *"Dost thou think because thou art virtuous, there shall be no more cakes and ale?"*

After that apparently unanswerable remark the three of them were silent for a while. Every so often a man or woman scuttled into the clinic and then quickly out again trundling a trolley loaded to the brim with patient case notes. Other staff members shuttled back and forth on various modes of business. Once or twice a porter wheel-chaired a patient into the clinic. Another time a porter was seen going towards a store room in the clinic, his octopus-like arms managing to carry about six pairs of elbow crutches, plus a zimmer frame somehow wrapped round his head, shoulders and chest. By the by, Boffo opined: "Hospitals, wonderful example of what Heaven will be like, everything happening like clockwork; everyone working happily together and conscientiously caring for one another". "In theory", retorted Sir Treadboards. The latter falling no doubt into one of his compensatory critical modes, added: "There is much apparent wastage here; endless long corridors which waste the time of both staff, patients and visitors. Those people pushing trolleys back and forth – they probably waste hours walking miles from A to B in this labyrinthine den. Even Theseus using Ariadne's thread would be hard put to find his way around here! All this waste of one's energy and time in the name of centralisation! This infernal mania for having one vast and ever spreading place covering a massive catchment area. Yet this gargantuan site is only centralised for those who live within its vicinity. For most other people on Cambridgeshire's borders and those beyond, it must involve almost a day's hike! Go back, I say, to reasonable sized hospitals, as in the past. And build more of them. Let each little town have one. They can still be reasonably specialist up to a point. One thing is certain – they will be more human. Here, you only need to take one wrong turning and you might end up meeting the Minotaur!"

Reverend Halo (to Treadboards): Our dear brother Boffo as usual paints too sanguine a picture of a world infected by our original parents in Eden, who succumbed to the snake's cunning venom. As you rightly say, Sir Terence, we are in an infernal place of dark corridors where the devil stalks around to his heart's content, like a roaring lion!

Boffo: My dear George I do believe you would see a roaring lion even in a kindergarten. *(Becoming uncharacteristically serious):* "There is no fear in love, But perfect love drives out fear..." I have always feared that your "correct" reformed theological rules only lead to fear and punishment. If instead you were to concentrate on the one and only law of our Lord, which is of course Love, you might enjoy more the delight and cheerfulness that all Christians should enjoy.

Reverend Halo (slightly taken aback): I do not deny love, what I deny is the devil's liberalised grace. The road is narrow but *you* would have it as something akin to the M25, where Christian back-sliders, hard-grained sceptics and confirmed reprobates all can make their easy passage into the Kingdom. That cannot be. Our Lord would then have died for nothing. For those who besmirch the faith: daily taking the Lord's name in vain and who are habitually glutted and debased by evil excesses, if I say, such as these can at the last stroll into the Kingdom and get off with merely a stern caution, a slapped wrist or writing a thousand or so lines, the righteous might as well go and join them! No! Our Lord did not go through with the atonement just for confirmed evildoers to get a free heavenly meal-ticket on Judgement Day.

Just then this tricky and somewhat prickily developing conversation was interrupted by a nurse calling out the name of Percival Evergreen (the name we mentioned very earlier on in our story, but which usually is supplanted by the user-friendly nickname: *Boffo*). The latter rose from his chair, patted his warring clerical brother on the shoulder, saying: "*Shalom,* my dear friend", and went off in the direction of the nurse. "Ha, my good fellow", said Sir Terence to the remaining cleric: "Was it not your divine providence that intervened most appositely at this moment of keen dissention? But let us now instead, like Falstaff "babble of green fields", of less contentious, happier things. You, like myself, have a beautiful if somewhat naughty daughter returned intact, still a rose in bloom, though we must hope one that is now somewhat wiser and mature. All in all we must therefore be thankful for such unexpected deliverances of our prodigal daughters!" *(Halo gravely nodded his assent).* "Well, then," continued Sir

Terence, now developing a more affable mood, "and how is your dear Esther doing? Does she still have, I might discreetly ask, any contact with that Anglo-Saxon crazed poet, Mr. Edmund Edgy? I had noticed at the birthday weekend, that he at one stage seemed partial both to Juniper and to Esther. But Juniper would have been too rough by half for the poor fellow. And she seems to have gone off men at present. She never liked poetry or drama anyway. Always a visual girl and wanting to get amongst the action. A job to control her from the word go! Like her mother, a wanton uncontrollable female! No doubt the poor fellow was up on the windmill tower, his poetical "*eye, in a fine frenzy rolling*", feeling like the proverbial spurned poet, when both our Siren daughters abandoned him Sunday morning!"

Reverend Halo: Yes, these demented poets are indeed strange animals. They live in a world of their own. But there may be hope for young Mr. Edgy yet. As to my dear and only child, I am gratified the Lord has retrieved her out of the fiery furnace of unwary youth's temptations. She is now set on becoming a Barrister and seems to be diligent in her pathway to that end. I do believe Esther is still in contact with Mr. Edgy. In his case, we must pray the Lord's seed has fallen on fertile ground. For the anchorless young man is as you say a rabid enthusiast; his head full of incredible fantasies which render his soul like a helpless bubble that unwittingly floats about in peculiar and unprofitable byways. Whether Esther would find the time to fully reform such a quirky – yet somehow likeable fellow, I do not know. Esther may be unlike your daughter, Sir Terence, but she has always had a clear-cut mind full of resolute purpose – unhappily at times with too wilful a purpose. Yea, it is doubtable whether Mr.

Edgy is too contrary, too fantastical in nature to at all suit my dear daughter.

Sir Terence (agreeing): Mr. Edmund Edgy is indeed a quirky fellow. One wonders if *any* woman would ever take him on and manage to cope with such antiquated idealistic views. (*Then somewhat wistfully adding):* However, I sometimes think we are all rather quirky mortals; perhaps at bottom disorderly puppets, having somehow escaped the control of a cosmic puppet master who now and again indulgently for his amusement, lets us have a little taste of free-will. Perhaps I am in danger of becoming a religious behaviourist! *(Sighing):* Ah, well, whatever, a wanton, madcap world, my masters!

Shortly afterwards, Percival Evergreen – Boffo – emerged from out of a bend in the clinic's inner corridor, his arm now un-plastered. Beaming at George Halo, he said: "Your turn next! And afterwards we three can return to the Rectory, where I dare say dear Miss Muffin will provide us all with a lovely salmon salad lunch along with a most welcome pot of hot tea!"